LEARNING TO USE

EXCEL

FOR WINDOWS '95

GABRIELLE LAGAN

Heinemann Educational Publishers,
Halley Court, Jordan Hill, Oxford OX2 8EJ
a division of Reed Educational & Professional Publishing Ltd
Heinemann is a registered trademark of Reed Educational & Professional
Publishing Limited

OXFORD FLORENCE PRAGUE MADRID ATHENS
MELBOURNE AUCKLAND KUALA LUMPUR SINGAPORE TOKYO
IBADAN NAIROBI KAMPALA JOHANNESBURG GABORONE
PORTSMOUTH NH (USA) CHICAGO MEXICO CITY SAO PAULO

First published 1997
2001 2000 99 98
10 9 8 7 6 5 4 3 2 1

A catalogue record for this book is available from the British Library on request.

ISBN 0 435 45475 7

Pages designed by Moondisks Limited

Typeset by TechType, Abingdon, Oxon

Printed and bound in Great Britain by The Bath Press, Bath

Screen shots reprinted with permission from Microsoft Corporation

contents

how to use this book

This book is designed for anyone who wishes to take a simple step-by-step approach to using MS Excel, from the basic skills of spreadsheet applications to the more advanced features of the program. It assumes no prior experience of Windows or spreadsheets. The book has been written for MS Excel 97. It can also be used for MS Excel for Windows 95 v 7.0 but the position of certain buttons, i.e. *OK* and *Cancel* in the dialog boxes are to the top right instead of the bottom right (as shown on all screen dumps).

The 'Introduction' to this book explains how to use Windows 95 and the techniques required for using Microsoft Excel. It is assumed that Windows 95 and Excel 97 have been installed using the default settings. If your screen looks different from that in the book, then you will need to check that the defaults have not been changed.

Section A is designed for complete beginners who wish to learn fundamental spreadsheet application skills and is suitable preparation for basic examinations such as RSA CLAIT Stage I.

Section B is designed for those who wish to extend their knowledge and spreadsheet application skills and is suitable preparation for examinations such as RSA Integrated Business Technology Stage II and RSA Spreadsheets Stage II.

Each unit is preceded by objectives, which set out what you should be able to do by the end of it. Information is given on how to carry out key functions and this is then followed by practical tasks with step-by-step instructions to ensure that you have fully understood the concepts and are able to apply the skills.

At the end of each unit there is extra practice for those who feel they would like to do additional tasks to reinforce what they have learned. The extra practice tasks are followed by the YOYO tasks (You're On Your Own). These tasks are designed to set you off on your own, carrying out each task without the guided instructions. However, the step numbers in each YOYO task correlate exactly with the step numbers in the extra practice tasks, so if you do get stuck, you can simply refer back to the appropriate step number in the extra practice. At the end of each section, the examination guidelines are given and there are mock examination assignments to test your knowledge and skills. The numbers which appear in the left-hand column of all the assignment objectives refer to the assessment objectives laid down by RSA Examinations board in the scheme guidelines. These guidelines are available directly from RSA.

A 'Databank' provides a quick reference to common commands required for each examination in the form of exam *memory joggers*. When you need reminding about how to carry out a command you can use these, rather than having to leaf through the book.

A Record of Progress sheet is also provided for you to make a note of your progress, as well as keys to the tasks, for you to check the accuracy of your work.

Guidelines

- Read and follow the instructions very carefully. Each unit builds on the objectives of the previous one, so it is important that you have fully understood one unit before moving on to the next.

- Check your work with the keys after you finish each task and make sure that your work is accurate before continuing.

- Remember to key in your name (or initials) and the filename at the bottom of each spreadsheet. This is good file management practice and ensures that you will easily be able to retrieve your files.

- Save all the files – you will be asked to recall saved files from previous units and to amend them in later units. To keep things simple, instructions have been given for all files to be saved to a floppy disk in Drive A.

- At the end of the working session, make a note of your progress on the record sheet. This will also let you see where you left off when you next come to continue your work.

Read and go

 In each unit, the steps for carrying out key functions are given twice. First, the steps are described, and are preceded by the symbol for 'read' the instructions (in the margin). You must read through the instructions carefully – the information will inform you of *how* to carry out a particular objective or function. Do not use the keyboard or the mouse at this stage.

Next, the same steps are given as numbered instructions in a series of tasks. You can, at this stage, go ahead and carry out the functions indicated. The tasks provide you with the most appropriate method of carrying out instructions. Sometimes you will be instructed to select from the Menu Bar or the Tool Bar whilst at other times you will be instructed to use the keyboard shortcuts.

Your choice ...

In each unit, the steps for carrying out instructions are shown by a number of different methods. For all instructions you can choose one of the following methods, although there is not always a keyboard shortcut option.

Selecting from the Menu Bar
You can do this using either the *mouse* or the *keyboard*:

Using the mouse:
- Position the mouse over the required menu option, e.g. **File**.
- Click once to display a list of menu commands.
- Click once on the required command, e.g. **New**.

Using the keyboard:
- Press the **Alt** key to access the Menu Bar.
- Press the *underlined* letter of the required menu option, e.g. **F** for **File**.
- Press the *underlined* letter of the required command, e.g. **N** for **New**.

To leave the Menu Bar, click once outside the menu area, or press **Alt**.

Selecting from the Tool Bar
Position the mouse over the icon, e.g. the ▯ **New** workbook icon. Click once to select.

Selecting a keyboard shortcut
Press and hold down a combination of keys at the same time, e.g. **Ctrl + N** means you should hold down the Control key while you press the N key.

---

introduction

Windows basics

Hardware

The physical part of the computer, all that you can see and touch, such as the screen, the processing unit, the keyboard, the mouse and the printer, is known as the *hardware*.

Throughout this book you will be shown how to use the mouse to select from the menu or Tool Bars. Sometimes the keyboard can be used as a shortcut, and this is also shown.

Software

The hardware needs instructions to make it work. These instructions are the *software*. When running Excel, two main kinds of software will be used:

- The software written to perform basic routine tasks is called *operating systems software*, as it is concerned with running the system, or making it work. When the computer is turned on, special systems files on the hard disk are automatically loaded into the computer's memory. These continue to operate in the background, loading and running software, whilst managing and backing up your files. Until August 1995 the most common operating system for PCs (personal computers) was MS-DOS – Microsoft Disk Operating System. Since then, Windows 95 – which is a major upgrade of all the earlier operating systems – has fast become the standard and all new computers have this pre-installed. Windows 95 is the software which acts as an interface between you and the hardware, to enable you to use the software applications. It gives you a user-friendly screen, with graphical and easily understood ways of performing tasks.
- The software which will enable you to create and develop spreadsheets is Microsoft Excel 97. This is a software application that runs from within Windows 95. It belongs to a category of programs known as the MS Office Suite which are designed to complement each other. This is known as integrated software and allows you to easily transfer and copy information from one application to another. A particularly useful aspect of this is that once you have learned commands and techniques in one program, you can use them in other programs (e.g. once you have learned to adjust the column width in Excel, you can use the same technique to do this in Access).

The desktop

When you first start Windows 95, the screen – known as the windows desktop – displays a number of *icons*, or small pictures which represent the basic components of your computer. When you select one, such as My Computer, it runs in its own rectangular area on the screen, known as a window. Think of your screen as a *desktop* on which a variety of documents and objects can be placed, each being displayed in its own window. These can be placed side by side or on top of one another. You can work on several projects or programs at the same time, transfer information between them, bring new ones on to the desktop and remove those you don't need. The ability to switch between applications or documents is known as multi-tasking. You can also reduce an application window back to a *task button* to free space on the screen and this will be placed on the **Task Bar** at the bottom of the screen. These task buttons indicate the names of programs that are currently running. The *start button* and the *clock* are also displayed on the Task Bar.

Use the mouse

A mouse is a hardware device that lets you select options from the screen and is the easiest way to work with windows. As you move the mouse across your desk, an arrow-shaped *mouse pointer* ( ) moves across the screen.

The mouse has two buttons, the left one being the *mouse select* button. The right button gives you quick access to editing and formatting commands, which vary depending on the cells you have selected. Common actions to select from the Menu Bar or Tool Bar options using the left mouse button are as follows:

- **Point** – position the mouse over the object, text or area on screen.
- **Click** – point at the object and click on it once (i.e. press and release the *left* button).
- **Double-click** – point at the object and click on it twice (i.e. in quick succession, press and release the *left*

button twice). If this does not seem to work, try again, this time clicking a little faster. Make sure that the mouse itself does not move whilst you are clicking. Double-clicking allows you to perform an action more quickly. The mouse pointer will change to an *egg-timer* (⏳) symbol, indicating to you that you must wait patiently whilst the action is being carried out.

- **Drag** – point at the object and press and hold down the mouse select button, whilst slowly moving the mouse. Release the mouse select button when the object is in the appropriate position.

Use the keyboard

A standard keyboard has letters arranged in the *qwerty* layout, with numbers along the top and the ↵ (**Enter**) key to the right. Above this are the *function keys*, which perform different functions in different software applications.

The keys on the right contain *cursor movement keys*, i.e. **Page Up**, **Page Down**, etc., and *cursor arrow keys*, i.e. ↑ (up), ↓ (down), ← (left), → (right).

To the extreme right is the *numeric keypad*. Ensure the Num Lock key is on, usually indicated by a green light. When working with spreadsheets, you should try to use this keypad to key in numbers and calculation signs, i.e. divide (/), multiply (*), subtract (-) and add (+). This keypad has been designed for numeric work and also has its own decimal point sign (.) and its own Enter key (Enter).

Start Windows 95

Now we are ready to start Windows 95. Depending on how your computer has been set up you may be asked to enter a password when you first switch on – if you click **OK** without typing one in when this is first displayed, the instruction will not appear again. A welcome window may also be displayed. This is useful when you are a beginner and you can click on the **Windows Tour** button to explore this useful information about using windows. Otherwise you can click the **Cancel** button.

Please remember to read the instructions first and then go ahead and carry them out by following the steps indicated in each task.

Starting Windows 95

Switch on your computer and wait until it displays the desktop. Refer to your instructions or manual if this does not appear.

Place the mouse pointer on the [Start] button and click once. This will display the options shown in Figure 1.

Use online Help

With so many commands available, it is important that you are able to access the Help facility to locate and find out more about these commands when you need them. This can be done from the Menu Bar in Excel or directly from the **Start** button as shown below. The three main options are shown on tabs – **Contents** lists the

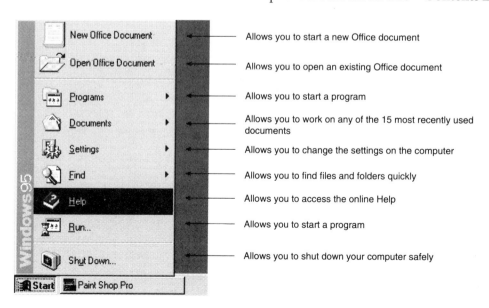

Figure 1 Options

various topics, organised by category, each of which is divided into further subtopics; **Index** allows you to key in the first few letters of a word and then offers you a list of index entries from which further information can be selected; **Find** allows you to search for specific words and phrases in help topics instead of searching for information by category. Where text is underlined, usually in green, you can click on it for a definition.

Now we are going to load the Windows Tour which is an option in the Help facility and spend some time exploring the techniques for starting programs and using the windows. It takes about 10 minutes to complete and is particularly helpful if you have never used Windows before. At this stage, please do not expect to understand and remember everything you are asked to practise. If you have used Windows before it is worth while exploring the alternative topics.

Using online Help

From the desktop, click on the following buttons to select each in turn:

- **Start**
- **Help**

The Help Topics window, similar to the one in Figure 2, will be displayed. Ensure that the Contents tab has been selected:

- [?] Tour: Ten minutes to using Windows
- **Display** – this displays the Tour Window, which now guides you step by step through a range of topics.

When completed, click the following to return to the desktop:

- **Exit Tour**

Help topics are also found in the Excel worksheet under the guise of an **Office Assistant**, shown on the Tool Bar as [?] icon. When you select this icon it will open up a dialogue box similar to the one shown below, from which you can make your selection.

The selections are:

What would you like to do? – You should type in your question here.
Search – Click here to search on topics relating to your question.
Tips – This provides useful tips or suggestions about quick ways of accomplishing tasks.
Options – This allows you to alter features of the Office Assistant such as whether or not to show the tips on screen. The default Office Assistant is called Clippit and you can alter this (using **Options**) to other assistants such as The Genius or Power Pup.

Figure 2 Office assistant

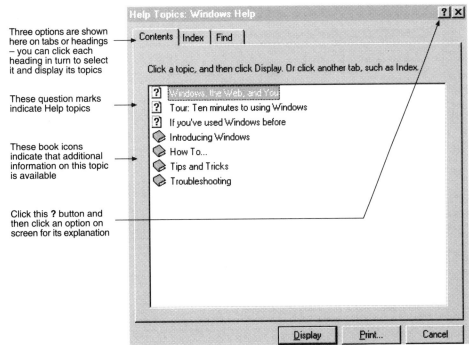

Three options are shown here on tabs or headings – you can click each heading in turn to select it and display its topics

These question marks indicate Help topics

These book icons indicate that additional information on this topic is available

Click this **?** button and then click an option on screen for its explanation

Figure 3 Online Help

Close – This closes the dialogue box but allows the Office Assistant to remain on screen whilst you work. If you prefer, you can return the office assistant to the Tool Bar by selecting the close button at the top right.

Load Excel

Next, let's load Excel and check the different parts of its screen against the information which follows, to make sure that you understand the main elements fully. As you place the mouse pointer on each option and click once to select each option your desktop should display further options. Microsoft Office should appear or perhaps you may even be able to access Excel directly from the Programs option.

Loading Excel

From the desktop, select the following:

*   **Start**

*   **Programs**
*   **Microsoft Office** (if displayed)
*   **Microsoft Excel**

or, if a tool bar is displayed, double-click on the 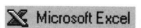 Microsoft Excel icon.

Use Excel

Spreadsheets in Excel are known as *worksheets* or sheets. These are labelled on tabs at the bottom of the screen and are initially given the names Sheet1, Sheet2, Sheet3, etc. These can contain not only spreadsheet information to display numerical data but also other types of sheets such as chart sheets to display data in graphical form and macro sheets to produce data in an automated format. All these separate, but related, sheets are stored in a single file known as a *workbook*. A workbook is initially given the name Book1 and subsequent workbooks will temporarily be called Book2, Book3, etc., until you save them under your chosen filenames. A workbook, or file, can contain as many sheets as available memory will permit, although the default is set so that each workbook initially contains 16 sheets.

The workbook or file in Excel can be thought of as a computerised form of a ring-binder folder. So, for example, you may have a range of ring-binder folders, each concerned with different issues (e.g. a folder for your suppliers, a folder for your customers, a folder for your staff, etc.). In Excel these folders could be set up as separate workbook files, each with a relevant filename such as SUPPLIERS, CUSTOMERS, STAFF, etc. Within each ring-binder folder you may have a number of loose-leaf pages with individual name tabs, e.g. a costing page, a price list, a graph showing sales trends, etc. In Excel these pages could be set up as worksheets, or sheets, each of which can be renamed so that they are more meaningful.

When you load Excel a screen similar to the one in Figure 3 will be displayed. The main elements are explained next.

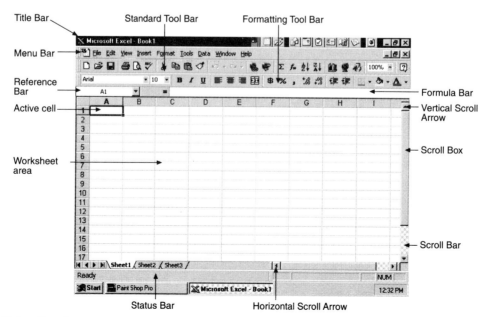

Figure 4 Using Excel

Title Bar – This bar displays the name of the application being used (e.g. Microsoft Excel) and the name of your current document (e.g. Book1 if one has not yet been saved under a chosen filename). If more than one window is open, the Title Bar of the active window (the one on which you are currently working) is a different colour (usually blue) or intensity from the Title Bars of the other inactive windows.

Menu Bar – This bar displays the menu options. Click on any one of these to highlight it and display a pull-down menu with related commands. Click outside it or press Alt to deselect.

Reference Bar – This displays the cell reference (i.e. the column letter and row number) of the selected cell (e.g. A1 as shown in Figure 5).

Formula Bar – This displays the formulae, text or numbers in a selected cell.

Tool Bar – This bar displays icon buttons, or small pictures of frequently used functions. Click on any one of these buttons to perform an action quickly. Position the mouse pointer slowly over an icon to display a description of its function in a **Tool Tip** box. At the same time, a fuller description may be displayed in the Status Bar at the bottom left of the screen. Most of these icon buttons are known as toggle buttons (i.e. click once to select it, then click once again to deselect). When you click on an icon button it appears in a lighter shade as though it has been depressed, to indicate that this function is in operation.

There are many tool bars in Excel but if your system has been set up with the default settings, you will find that usually two are displayed – the **Standard Tool Bar** for common functions such as opening files, printing, etc., and the **Formatting Tool Bar** for functions such as changing font size, style and alignment as well as number formats.

Worksheet area – This is the blank area on screen, where you enter data. It is arranged in a grid of rows and columns. Where a row and a column intersect this is called a *cell*. When you click on a cell to select it, it will be highlighted by a bold border and is known as the *active cell*.

Mouse pointer – You will find that the mouse pointer changes shape depending on where it appears on the worksheet.

When it is positioned inside the worksheet area it appears as a cross ✛. If you click the right mouse button it gives you access to popular editing and formatting commands, such as cut and paste and format cells.

When it is positioned outside the spreadsheet area or at the edge of a selected cell it appears as an arrow 🡔 .

When it is positioned on a cell and you click once to select it, the mouse pointer changes to a blinking vertical bar | in the cell once you begin to type. This is the cursor, or insertion point. As you key in the data, it will appear to the left of this cursor.

When it is positioned on a cell containing data and you double-click to edit it, the mouse pointer changes to an *I* beam. As you key in the data, it will appear to the left of this *I* beam.

When it is positioned between the column headings, e.g. A, B, C, D etc. or row headings, e.g. 1, 2, 3, 4 etc. buttons it changes to a ↔ double-headed arrow.

Status Bar – This displays information about the current status of the document, at the bottom of the screen. When you first start, it will display the word 'Ready' at the bottom left of the screen. When you click on a menu option, command or icon button a description of this may be displayed in the Status Bar. Other functions are also indicated such as Caps, Num, etc., to indicate that Caps Lock or Num Lock are switched on, as explained earlier.

Use Windows controls

Most of the windows that you will use have similar controls and on the Title Bar there is a range of control buttons as shown below (see Figure 4).

Control icon – Click once to display options to shrink or enlarge the window, move it or close it. These commands can also be carried out by using the sizing buttons indicated below, scroll bars or menu.

Close button – Click once to close the window.

Minimise button – Click once to shrink the window to an icon. Double-click on this icon to return it to a window.

Maximise button – Click once to enlarge the window to fill the screen.

Restore button – Appears only when the window is maximised. Click once to restore the window to its previous size and shape.

You may also wish to change the size and shape of a window to make room for other windows on the screen. To do this you must position the mouse pointer on a border so that it changes to an up/down pointing arrow ⬍ and drag the border to expand or contract the sides of the window.

If a window is too small to show all its information at one time, **scroll bars** are automatically placed to the

Figure 5 Title Bar

right or bottom edges. These let you move information, which is not in view, inside the window so you can view the entire contents of a document on screen at a time.

Vertical Scroll Arrow – Click once on a scroll arrow as shown in Figure 3 to move up or down one line at a time.

Scroll Bar – The size of this indicates how much of your total work is in view. As your position changes, the scroll box will move up and down the Scroll Bar.

Horizontal Scroll Arrow – Click once on a scroll arrow – to move across the document to parts which do not fit in the window.

Most of the windows you will use also have a common *menu structure*. Commands can be selected when you position the mouse pointer and click once on a menu option. Alternatively, using the keyboard, you may press Alt and the underlined character. You will also find that some commands have keystrokes indicated – these keyboard shortcuts can be used directly without having to access the Menu Bar. To leave the Menu Bar, click once outside the menu area or press Alt. *Commands* perform actions immediately unless they are followed by symbols:

▶ If a command is followed by ▶ this will offer a further range of options when selected.

… If a command is followed by … this will display a dialogue box when selected.

A *dialogue box* presents a series of additional options from which you can choose, as shown in Figure 5. You can select information by clicking on the option buttons with the mouse or by using the tab or cursor keys.

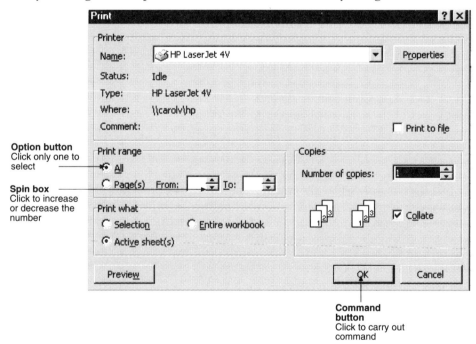

Figure 6 Print dialogue box

Now that you are familiar with the basics, the time has finally come for you to get started on setting up your own worksheet. Don't forget the procedure:

Read … Remember that it is important for you to read and understand the instructions before you

| − | GO | ▼ ▲ |

Go ahead and carry them out!

unit 1
create and save a worksheet

By the end of Unit 1 you should be able to:

- *load Excel*
- *enter text and numbers*
- *save a file*
- *create a new file*
- *move around the worksheet, using the mouse or keyboard*
- *select a range of cells*
- *close a file*
- *generate formulae to add, multiply and divide*
- *save a file under a different name, using Save As*
- *save file changes and exit from Excel with data secure*

Introducing the worksheet

A worksheet is a software program that enables you to enter data and perform calculations, which may range from simple to extremely complex tasks. In order to calculate a row or column of numbers, you enter a formula. Once this is entered, you can change the numbers in the row or column and the formula will automatically recalculate the values. Formulae can be stored in a file and reused. Also, one worksheet can be linked to another so that when numbers in one are changed, this also occurs in the linked worksheet. The use of well planned worksheets can greatly improve the efficiency of any organisation and help with its financial forecasts and planning.

Task 1A

1 If you do not already have Excel on screen, from the desktop, select ;
   Programs; **Microsoft Office** (if displayed); **Microsoft Excel** to load Excel.
2 To ensure that you understand the Excel window and to remind you of the terminology, check back through the information given on page 6, 'Use Excel'.

Enter text and numbers

When you load Excel it automatically displays a worksheet window (known in Excel as a worksheet) ready for data entry. The worksheet is temporarily given the (default) filename of Book1, as indicated in the Title Bar. Information in a worksheet is organised in columns and rows. A vertical line of cells is called a *column*. This is identified by a letter, e.g. A, B, C, etc., which is known as a *column heading button*. A horizontal line of cells is called a *row*. This is identified by a number, e.g. 1, 2, 3, etc., which is known as a *row heading button*. Where a column interacts with a row, this is called a *cell* and is identified by a cell reference, e.g. where column E and row 3 intersect in Figure 1.1 the cell reference is E3.

Entering text and numbers

To enter text and numbers you must click once to select the cell and then key in the data for that cell. When you select a cell, it is known as the *active cell* and is highlighted by a bold border as shown in Figure 1.1, where A1 is the active cell.

When you begin to key in data, three boxes appear to the left of the Formula Bar:

Cancel box – click this if you wish to cancel the entry.

Enter box – click this if you wish to confirm the entry.

Function Wizard box – click this if you wish to follow step-by-step instructions for creating a formula. (Please note that alternatively ▬ **Edit Formula** may appear in place of *fx* **Function Wizard** – which gives you the same step-by-step instructions for creating a formula.)

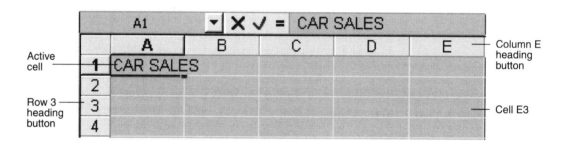

Active cell

Row 3 heading button

Column E heading button

Cell E3

Figure 1.1 A worksheet

As you key in, the data also appears in the Formula Bar as well as in the cell itself, as shown in Figure 1.1. Always check that the data in the Formula Bar is accurate before continuing.

Read through the following carefully before proceeding!

Entering data

- Place the mouse pointer in the desired cell and click to select the cell.
- Key in the data for that cell.
- Click once on the ✔ **Enter** box in the Formula Bar or press ↵ (**Enter**)to confirm entry.

The data will be entered into the cell and the boxes will disappear from the Formula Bar.

When you have keyed in the data, instead of pressing ↵ (**Enter**) each time you could, alternatively, press the cursor arrows on the keyboard, which enter the data into the cell and move you automatically to the next cell.

Amending data

Before confirming your entry, you may amend the data by clicking the *I* beam at the appropriate place in the cell or the Formula Bar.

After confirming your entry, you may amend the data by selecting the cell and clicking the *I* beam at the appropriate place in the cell or the Formula Bar.

If you wish to enter new data, you can simply key this in and it will overwrite what is in the cell.

Cancelling data

Before confirming your entry, you may cancel the data by clicking once on the **Cancel** box in the Formula Bar or by pressing the **Esc** key at the top of the keyboard.

After confirming your entry, you may cancel it by selecting the cell and pressing the **Del** key.

Excel treats text and numbers differently as it expects that you will want to carry out calculations on the numbers. You can tell whether your entry is considered to be text or numbers by the way it is aligned, provided the default has not been altered.

Text

Text is aligned to the left. If a combination of text and numbers is used, Excel treats this as text.

Numbers

Numbers, including dates and times, are aligned to the right.

| − | Task 1B | ▼ ▲ |

Enter the following text and numbers on the new worksheet window:

1 Select cell reference **A1** (column A, row 1) by placing the mouse pointer in the cell and click once (so making it the active cell as indicated by the bold border).

2 Key in the heading: **CAR SALES** – this may overlap into the next cell.

3 Press ↵ **(Enter)**.

4 Select cell reference **A3** (column A, row 3). Key in the following headings in row **3** pressing → (right arrow) after each to move across from cell to cell:

TYPE   JAN   FEB   MAR   APR   MAY   JUN   TOTAL

5 Select cell reference **A5** (column A, row 5). Key in the following information, pressing ↵ **(Enter)** after each one to move you down column A from one cell to the next:

SALOON
COUPE
TOURER
ESTATE
VAN
PICK UP
TOTAL

6 Select cell reference **B5** and, moving from cell to cell down each column, enter the remaining information on to the worksheet as shown in Figure 1.2. It is important that you enter the data in exactly the same cells as shown and it is good business practice, when keying in, to follow copy, i.e. where the information is given in capitals, then you should key it in likewise.

	A	B	C	D	E	F	G	H
1	CAR SALES							
2								
3	TYPE	JAN	FEB	MAR	APR	MAY	JUN	TOTAL
4								
5	SALOON	3	8	10	7	12	11	
6	COUPE	1	1	2	1	2	3	
7	TOURER	10	12	12	15	16	15	
8	ESTATE	8	8	11	12	14	17	
9	VAN	8	12	10	9	7	8	
10	PICK UP	6	7	9	10	9	12	
11	TOTAL							

Figure 1.2   Car sales worksheet

Save a file

When you select the Save option to save a file, the Save As dialogue box, similar to the one in Figure 1.3, will be displayed. At this stage we will save all files to a $3\frac{1}{2}$ inch floppy disk in Drive A, so check now that your disk is inserted in Drive A.

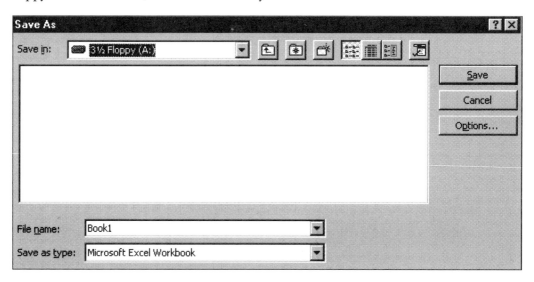

Figure 1.3   Save As dialogue box

Since you have not yet given your file a name, the Save As dialogue box can be accessed by the following steps.

Accessing the Save As dialogue box
- Ensure that your floppy disk is inserted in Drive A.
- From the Menu Bar, select:

File   Save

or, from the Tool Bar, select the 💾 **Save** icon

or, from the keyboard, press **Ctrl + S**.

The Save As dialogue box is displayed on screen. You can select the options in the dialogue box by positioning the mouse pointer and clicking in the text boxes or by using the Tab key on the keyboard.

- **Save in** text box: if **3½ Floppy (A:)** is not already shown, click on the ▼ at the right side of the text box and highlight this drive, where your file is to be saved.

- **Save as type** text box: if **Microsoft Excel Workbook** is not already shown, click on ▼ at the right side of the text box and highlight this option to ensure that your file is saved as an Excel file.

- **File name** text box: a default filename, such as Book1, will appear here. If it is not already selected, i.e. highlighted, usually in blue, select the default filename by placing the mouse pointer at the beginning and click and drag to the end of the name. Key in your chosen filename, e.g. **TASK1C**.

  Filenames can be as long as you wish and may contain spaces, but it is recommended that you use concise and relevant names.

  Don't worry if you pressed the ↵ (**Enter**) key after keying in the filename, as this has the same effect as if you had clicked the **Save** button.

  If you click on ▼ at the right side of the text box by mistake, click anywhere outside the text box to undo this action.

- **Save** button: click this now to save your file (or press the ↵ (**Enter**) key).

  The new filename, e.g. **TASK1C**, appears after Microsoft Excel on the Title Bar.

  Selecting the Save icon will only display the Save As dialogue box when you are saving a *newly created* file.

  If you make changes to a file and save these using the Save icon, Excel will not display the Save As dialogue box again as it knows the filename. It will automatically overwrite the earlier file with the new changed one.

─	Task 1C	▼ ▲

1 Check that a disk is inserted in Drive A and from the Menu Bar, select **File**, **Save**; ensure that the **Save in** text box displays **3½** 🖫 **Floppy (A:)** and in the **File name** text box, key in **TASK1C** to save your file under its new name; click **Save**.

2 Select cell **A15**; key in your name and press **Enter**.
In cell **A16** key in the filename **TASK1C** and press **Enter**.
As you have keyed in new information and made changes to your file, it will have to be saved again to include these details.

3 From the Tool Bar click 🖫 **Save** to save these changes to your file **TASK1C** and check your work with the key.

Create a new file

Sometimes, you may wish to use more than one file at a time. To do this you need to create a new file. This will display a new worksheet window, containing its own range of sheets. The worksheet will be temporarily given a default filename, such as Book2, which is displayed in the Title Bar. The window containing the current file will remain open underneath the new one – just as when you are working with paper files, you might have a current file on your desk and then you might place another new file on top of it. When you select this option from the Menu Bar the New dialogue box, similar to the one in Figure 1.4, will be displayed.

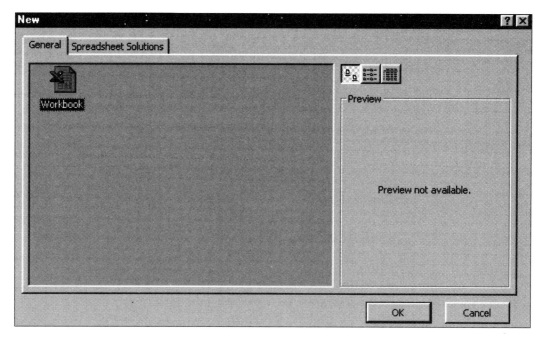

Figure 1.4 New dialogue box

Two tabs are shown in the figure, General – which is the one that you will commonly use – and Spreadsheet solutions – which offers useful templates for you to use such as invoices, orders, etc.

Creating a new file
• From the Menu Bar, select:

<u>F</u>ile   <u>N</u>ew
The New dialogue box is displayed on screen.

• Click **OK**

or, from the Tool Bar, select the ⬜ **New** workbook icon

or, from the keyboard, press **Ctrl + N**.

Task 1D

Create a new file by selecting from the Menu Bar **<u>F</u>ile**, **<u>N</u>ew** and click **OK**. This will open a new worksheet window and the window containing TASK1C will remain underneath this.

Move around the worksheet

To enter text into a cell, you must select it, usually by clicking on it. When you are keying in data it is sometimes quicker to use the following shortcuts.

Moving around the worksheet: shortcuts

To move	*Press*
right one cell	→ **Right arrow** *or* **Tab key**
left one cell	← **Left arrow** *or* **Shift + Tab**

up one cell	↑ **Up arrow**
down one cell	↓ **Down arrow**
to the end of the row	**Ctrl + → Right arrow**
to the beginning of the row	**Home** *or* **Ctrl + ← Left arrow**
to the bottom of the column	**Ctrl + ↓ Down arrow**
to the top of the column	**Ctrl + ↑ Up arrow**
to the end of the worksheet	**Ctrl + End**
to the beginning of the worksheet	**Ctrl + Home**
to a specific cell reference	**Ctrl + G**
or, from the **Menu Bar**, select	**Edit**
	GoTo
in the **Reference** text box	Key in the cell reference and click **OK**, e.g. A11 will move you to the TOTAL cell in TASK1A

To scroll	*Press*
down one screen	**Page down**
up one screen	**Page up**
to the next worksheet	**Ctrl + Page down**
to the previous worksheet	**Ctrl + Page up**
or, from the **Scroll Bar**,	
down the screen	click the ▼ vertical scroll arrow
up the screen	click the ▲ vertical scroll arrow
to the right of the screen	click the ► horizontal scroll arrow
to the left of the screen	click the ◄ horizontal scroll arrow

You will find that the worksheet is extremely large. Rows are numbered from 1 to 65536, whilst columns extend from A to IV (i.e. 256 columns).

Select a range of cells

Sometimes, instead of just one individual cell you need to select a range of cells, particularly if you wish to apply a particular command to more than one cell. A range refers to a block of cells and is identified by a *range reference*, which consists of the cell reference in the top left corner and the cell reference in the bottom right corner of your selection.

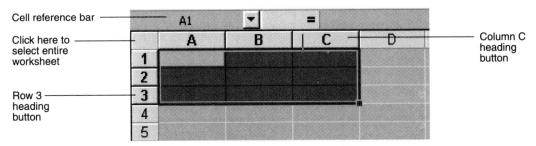

Figure 1.5 Range reference

The range reference **A1:C3** shown in Figure 1.5 includes cells in columns A, B and C and in rows 1, 2 and 3. Notice that the cells which have been selected are highlighted in black and although cell A1 is also included in this selection, it appears in white. This is to indicate to you that cell A1 is the active cell. Sometimes selecting cells with a mouse can be a bit tricky but don't worry – this should improve as your skill at mouse control develops!

Selecting a range
Place the mouse pointer on the cell in the top left corner of the range to be selected. Click and drag to the bottom right corner of the range required. Release the mouse button.

Or, on the keyboard, use the cursor keys (arrows) to move to the cell in the top left corner of the range to be selected. Hold down the Shift key and press the cursor keys to move to the bottom right corner of the range required. Release the Shift and cursor keys.

Deselecting a range
Place the mouse pointer anywhere in the worksheet area and click once.

Or, on the keyboard, press any cursor arrow key.

Selecting an entire column
Place the mouse pointer on the chosen column heading button and click once (click and drag over several columns if required – there is no keyboard equivalent for this).

Or, on the keyboard, use the cursor keys to move to the chosen column and press **Ctrl + Space Bar**.

Selecting an entire row
Place the mouse pointer on the chosen row heading button and click once (click and drag over several rows if required – there is no keyboard equivalent for this).

Or, on the keyboard, use the cursor keys to move to the chosen row and press **Shift + Space Bar**.

Selecting the entire worksheet
Place the mouse pointer on the button to the left of column A heading button and click once.

Or, on the keyboard, press **Ctrl + Shift + Space Bar**.

Selecting several ranges
Using the mouse, select the first range.
Hold down the **Ctrl** key and select the next range.
Continuing to hold down the **Ctrl** key, select further ranges.

▬	Task 1E	▼ ▲

1 We are going to use the new file that you have just created to practise moving around the worksheet and to select a variety of ranges. With the new worksheet window open, select **A1**; type the words **NEW FILE** and press ↵ **(Enter)**.

2 Practise moving around the worksheet by positioning the mouse pointer over each of the following cell references in turn and click once to make it the active cell. Then, practise moving to each of the cells using the keyboard cursor keys as shown previously. Notice how your location is always shown in the cell reference bar (see Figure 1.5) at the top left of the screen.

Select cell reference **A2**   Select cell reference **G5**
Select cell reference **D9**   Select cell reference **H12**
Select cell reference **C7**   Select cell reference **A1**

3 Practise moving around the worksheet using the *scroll bars* to take you beyond the area on your screen and click on each of the following cell references in turn to make it the active cell.

Select cell reference **A130** as follows:

Place the mouse pointer on the ▼ vertical scroll arrow and press and hold down the mouse select button until row **130** appears.
Place the mouse pointer in cell **A130** and click once.

Select cell reference **H4** as follows:

Place the mouse pointer on the ▲ vertical scroll arrow and press and hold down the mouse select button until row **4** appears.
Place the mouse pointer in cell **H4** and click once.

Select cell reference **AA9** as follows:

Place the mouse pointer on the ► horizontal scroll arrow and press and hold down the mouse select button until column **AA** appears.
Place the mouse pointer in cell **AA9** and click once.

Select cell reference **AF46** as follows:

Click the ► horizontal scroll arrow repeatedly until column **AF** appears.

Click the ▼ vertical scroll arrow repeatedly until row **46** appears.
Place the mouse pointer in cell **AF46** and click once.

Select cell reference **A1** as follows:

Place the mouse pointer on the ◄ horizontal scroll arrow and press and hold down the mouse select button until column **A** appears.

Place the mouse pointer on the ▲ vertical scroll arrow and press and hold down the mouse select button until row **1** appears.
Place the mouse pointer in cell **A1** and click once.

4   Now, practise moving to each of the above cells by selecting, from the Menu Bar, **Edit**, **Go to**, then key in the cell reference required and click **OK**. Note your location in the cell reference bar.

5   Select the range of cells from **A1** to **C3** by placing the mouse pointer in cell A1 and click and drag to cell C3 to highlight this range, as shown in Figure 1.5. Release the mouse button. Click once anywhere in the worksheet area to deselect.

6   Now, select the range of cells from **A1** to **C3** by using the cursor keys. Ensure cell **A1** is selected. Hold down the Shift key and press the ↓ (down arrow) twice until you are in cell A3 and then the → (right arrow) twice until you are in cell C3. Release the Shift key. Press any arrow key once to deselect.

7   Select the following using the mouse. Remember to click once anywhere in the worksheet area when you want to deselect.

Select the range **A2–C4** as follows: Click once on A2 and drag to C4.

Select the range **D3–H12** as follows: Click once on D3 and drag to H12.

Select column **B** as follows: Click once on column B heading button.

Select row **9** as follows: Click once on row 9 heading button.

Select the **entire worksheet** as follows: Click the button to the left of column A heading button as shown in Figure 1.5.

Select columns **D**, **E** and **F** as follows: Click column D heading button and drag to E and F.

Select rows **6**, **7**, **8**, **9** and **10** as follows: Click row 6 heading button and drag to row 10.

Select the range **A2–C4** as well as column **B** and row **9** as follows: Select the range A2–C4. Hold down the Ctrl key and click once on column B heading button. Still keeping the Ctrl key held down click once on row 9. Release the Ctrl key.

Click anywhere in the worksheet to deselect.

8   Now try to select each of the above (where you can) using the *keyboard cursor keys* and the *Shift key* as shown previously. Remember to press any cursor key when you want to deselect.

9   Read the following section on how to close a file and then close the file without saving it as follows. From the Menu Bar, select **File**, **Close** and click the **No** button when prompted if you wish to save the changes in Book2. This will close the new file that you have been working on and will reveal again the old file TASK1C which has still been there underneath.

Close a file

This closes the worksheet window and clears the worksheet from the screen.

Closing a file
From the Menu Bar, select:

File   Close

or, from the Title Bar, click the ✖ **Close** button

or, from the keyboard, press **Ctrl + F4**.

If you have made any changes to your files and not saved these, Excel will prompt you to save each document in turn. A dialogue box similar to the one in Figure 1.6 will be displayed on screen.

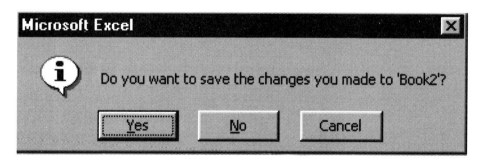

Figure 1.6   Save Changes dialogue box

Saving changes
You can click on one of the following options:

Yes to save the latest changes to your file.
No if you do not want to save the changes you have made.
Cancel if you are not sure and wish to check your document again.

Generate formulae

Formulae are used to carry out calculations on the numbers that you have entered on the worksheet. To indicate to Excel that you wish to use a formula, you must always enter the = sign, followed by the formula. The most commonly used formulae are shown below and can be keyed in using capitals or lower case.

Generating formulae

Formula	Sign	Example
Addition	+	=B5+C5 adds the numbers in these two cells together, *or*
	SUM	=SUM(B5:B10) adds the numbers in this range of cells together.
Subtraction	–	=B5–C5 subtracts the number in C5 from B5.
Multiplication	*	=B5*C5 multiplies the number in B5 by the number in C5, *or*
		=B5*8 multiplies the number in B5 by 8.
Division	/	=B5/C5 divides the number in B5 by the number in C5, *or*
		=B5/8 divides the number in B5 by 8.

As you can see, the addition sign (+) is used to total the numbers in cells, so in TASK1C you could use the formula =B5+B6+B7+B8+B9+B10 to total these numbers. A quicker and more common way of doing this is to identify the range of cells that you wish to total, i.e. from B5 to B10 as shown below.

Totalling a range of cells

• Select the cell where you want the result of your formula to appear, i.e. place the mouse pointer in the appropriate cell and click once.

• Type =.

• Type the formula, e.g. **SUM(B5:B10)**. This will sum or add up the numbers in the range of cells (e.g. from B5 to B10). The range can be shown by keying in the beginning of the range and the end of the range, separated by a : sign.

• Click once on the ✔ **Enter** box in the Formula Bar or press ↵ **(Enter)**.

The total will appear in the cell and the formula that you entered will appear in the Formula Bar. Pressing ↵ **(Enter)** has the additional effect of moving you down to the cell beneath in readiness for you to key in a new entry (Figure 1.7.)

Reference bar —————

Formula bar —————

	COUNT	▾	✗ ✓ =	=SUM(B5:B10)
	A	B	C	D
1	CAR SALES			
2				
3	TYPE	JAN	FEB	MAR
4				
5	SALOON	3	8	10
6	COUPE	1	1	2
7	TOURER	10	12	12
8	ESTATE	8	8	11
9	VAN	8	12	10
10	PICK UP	6	7	9
11	TOTAL	=SUM(B5:B10)		

Select cell where the result is to appear —————

Figure 1.7 Totalling a range of cells

Task 1F ▾ ▲

With **TASK1C** still on screen, enter the following formulae on the worksheet, to calculate the total car sales for each month.

1 Select cell **B11**, i.e. the TOTAL cell for JAN, as shown above.
Key in **=SUM(B5:B10)** (this formula will add up the numbers from B5 to B10).

Click once on the ✔ **Enter** box in the Formula Bar.
As you wish to move across to the cell on the right for your next entry, you will find that instead of clicking on the **Enter** box after entering each formula, it is better to press the right cursor (→).
With cell B11 still selected check now to ensure that the total of 36 appears in cell B11 and the formula =SUM(B5:B10) appears in the Formula Bar.

2 Repeat these steps for the rest of the months, using the following formulae:

In cell **C11**　　Key in **=SUM(C5:C10)**　　Press →
In cell **D11**　　Key in **=SUM(D5:D10)**　　Press →
In cell **E11**　　Key in **=SUM(E5:E10)**　　Press →
In cell **F11**　　Key in **=SUM(F5:F10)**　　Press →
In cell **G11**　　Key in **=SUM(G5:G10)**　　Press →

Now enter the following formulae on the worksheet, to calculate the total sales for each car type.

3 Select cell **H5**, i.e. the TOTAL cell for SALOON.
Key in **=SUM(B5:G5)** (this formula will add up the numbers from B5 to G5).
Press ↵ **(Enter)** – this moves you down to the next cell.

Note that the total of 51 appears in cell H5 and the formula =SUM(B5:G5) appears in the Formula Bar.

4 Repeat these steps for the rest of the car types, using the following formulae:

In cell **H6**　　Key in **=SUM(B6:G6)**　　Press **Enter**
In cell **H7**　　Key in **=SUM(B7:G7)**　　Press **Enter**
In cell **H8**　　Key in **=SUM(B8:G8)**　　Press **Enter**
In cell **H9**　　Key in **=SUM(B9:G9)**　　Press **Enter**
In cell **H10**　　Key in **=SUM(B10:G10)**　　Press **Enter**

Using multiplication and division formulae

As shown earlier, the multiplication sign (*) is used to multiply the numbers in cells and the division sign (/) can be used to divide the numbers in cells. These signs can be found on the numeric keypad (ensure that the Num Lock key is on) as well as on the qwerty keyboard. Try the following exercises to practise using these formulae.

Task 1F (continued) ▾ ▲

Enter the following formulae on the worksheet to calculate the possible *total* car sales per annum (PA), by multiplying the current total for the six months from JAN to JUN by 2.

5 With **TASK1C** still displayed on screen, select cell **I3**; key in **TOTAL PA** and press **Enter**.

6 Select cell **I5**, i.e. the TOTAL PA cell for saloons. Key in **=H5*2** (this formula will multiply the number in cell H5, i.e. the total saloons, by 2).

Press ↵ **(Enter)** – this moves you down to the next cell.

Note that the total of 102 appears in cell H5 and the formula =H5*2 appears in the Formula Bar.

7 Repeat these steps for the rest of the car types, using the following formulae:

In cell **I6**	Key in **=H6*2**	Press **Enter**
In cell **I7**	Key in **=H7*2**	Press **Enter**
In cell **I8**	Key in **=H8*2**	Press **Enter**
In cell **I9**	Key in **=H9*2**	Press **Enter**
In cell **I10**	Key in **=H10*2**	Press **Enter**

Now, enter the following formulae on the worksheet to calculate the *average* number of cars sold each month. To do this you will need to divide the total number of cars sold per month by the number of different types of cars, i.e. 6.

8 Select cell **A12**; key in **AVERAGE** and click once on the ✓ **Enter** box in the Formula Bar.

9 Select cell **B12**, i.e. the AVERAGE cell for JAN. Key in **=B11/6** (this formula will divide the number in cell B11, i.e. the total for Jan, by 6).
Click once on the ✓ **Enter** box in the Formula Bar.
As you wish to move across to the cell on the right for your next entry, you will find that instead of clicking on the **Enter** box after entering each formula, it is better to press the right cursor →).

With cell B12 still selected check now to ensure that the average of 6 appears in cell B12 and the formula =B11/6 appears in the Formula Bar.

10 Repeat these steps for the rest of the months, using the following formulae:

In cell **C12**	Key in **=C11/6**	Press →
In cell **D12**	Key in **=D11/6**	Press →
In cell **E12**	Key in **=E11/6**	Press →
In cell **F12**	Key in **=F11/6**	Press →
In cell **G12**	Key in **=G11/6**	Press →

11 Check that your name is at the bottom of the worksheet and edit the cell beneath to display **TASK1F** instead of TASK1C. Check your work with the key.

12 Read the following section on 'Use Save As' carefully and then save your file under a new filename **TASK1F** as follows. From the Menu Bar, select **File**, **Save As**; ensure that 3½ 🖫 **Floppy (A:)** is displayed in the **Save in** text box; key in **TASK1F** in the **File name** text box.

Use Save As

If you make changes to a file and wish to save the file under a different filename then you must select Save As from the Menu Bar. Use Save As when you wish to

- save a file under a different name
- save selected data within a document
- save a file in a different directory
- save a file in a different file format.

Since you wish to give this file a different name, the Save As dialogue box can be accessed by the following steps.

Accessing the Save As dialogue box
- Ensure that your floppy disk is inserted in Drive A.

- From the Menu Bar, select:

File   **Save As**

The Save As dialogue box is displayed on screen.

Note that selecting the 🖫 **Save** icon would save the changes under the current filename – this icon only displays the Save As dialogue box when you are saving a *newly created* file.

- **Save in** text box: if $3\frac{1}{2}$ **Floppy (A:)** is not already shown, click on ▼ at the right side of the text box and highlight this drive, where your file is to be saved.

- **Save as type** text box: if **Microsoft Excel Workbook** is not already shown, click on ▼ at the right side of the text box and highlight this option to ensure that your file is saved as an Excel file.

- **File name** text box: the current filename, such as TASK1C, will appear here. If it is not already selected, i.e. highlighted, usually in blue, select this name by placing the mouse pointer at the beginning and click and drag to the end of the name. Key in your chosen filename, e.g. **TASK1F**.

- **Save** button: click this now to save your file.

The new filename, e.g. TASK1F appears after Microsoft Excel on the Title Bar. You now have two files saved on the disk in Drive A, i.e. TASK1C and TASK1F, which is an update of your earlier file.

Exit from Excel

I hope you feel that you have made good progress working through the fundamentals of the first unit and now that this has been completed you may wish to end your Excel session. This means that the Excel application will be closed down and you will be returned to the desktop. To exit from Excel, follow the steps below.

Exiting from Excel
From the Menu Bar, select:

File   **Exit**

or, from the Title Bar, click the **Close** button

or, from the keyboard, press **Alt + F4**.

If you still have windows open you may be prompted as to whether you wish to save any changes.

■	Task 1G	▼ ▲

1 Close the file by selecting from the Menu Bar **File**, **Close** and exit from Excel by selecting from the Menu Bar **File**, **Exit**.

2 Don't forget to complete the Record of Progress sheet to indicate that you have finished this unit successfully. If you feel that you would like to do further work to consolidate what you have learned so far, then try Extra Practice Task 1.

Extra Practice Task 1

1 If you do not already have Excel on screen, from the desktop, select **Start**; **Programs**; **Microsoft Office** (if displayed); **Microsoft Excel** to load Excel.

2 Enter the new worksheet window as shown in Figure 1.8 – key it in exactly as it appears, using the same cell references as shown.

	A	B	C	D	E	F	G	H	I
1	CONFECTIONERY SALES								
2									
3	ITEM	JUL	AUG	SEP	OCT	NOV	DEC	TOTAL	TOTAL PA
4									
5	TOFFEES	19	18	11	17	22	23		
6	FUDGE	10	10	11	14	17	18		
7	GUMS	8	7	8	12	11	24		
8	BONBON	14	12	11	12	13	11		
9	MINTS	18	19	20	17	16	15		
10	ROCK	21	24	17	12	11	11		
11	TOTAL								
12	AVERAGE								

Figure 1.8 Worksheet for Extra Practice Task 1

3 Select cell **B11**, i.e. the TOTAL cell for JUL
Key in **=SUM(B5:B10)**
Press → (to calculate the total items sold in July)

4 Repeat these steps for the rest of the months, using the following formulae:

In cell **C11**	Key in **=SUM(C5:C10)**	Press →
In cell **D11**	Key in **=SUM(D5:D10)**	Press →
In cell **E11**	Key in **=SUM(E5:E10)**	Press →
In cell **F11**	Key in **=SUM(F5:F10)**	Press →
In cell **G11**	Key in **=SUM(G5:G10)**	Press →

5 Select cell **H5**, i.e. the TOTAL cell for TOFFEES
Key in **=SUM(B5:G5)** (to calculate the total number of toffees sold)
Press ↵ **(Enter)**

6 Repeat these steps for the rest of the items, using the following formulae:

In cell **H6**	Key in **=SUM(B6:G6)**	Press **Enter**
In cell **H7**	Key in **=SUM(B7:G7)**	Press **Enter**
In cell **H8**	Key in **=SUM(B8:G8)**	Press **Enter**
In cell **H9**	Key in **=SUM(B9:G9)**	Press **Enter**
In cell **H10**	Key in **=SUM(B10:G10)**	Press **Enter**

7 Select cell **I5**, i.e. the TOTAL PA cell for TOFFEES
Key in **=H5*2**
Press ↵ **(Enter)**

8 Repeat these steps for the rest of the items, using the following formulae:

In cell **I6**	Key in **=H6*2**	Press **Enter**
In cell **I7**	Key in **=H7*2**	Press **Enter**
In cell **I8**	Key in **=H8*2**	Press **Enter**
In cell **I9**	Key in **=H9*2**	Press **Enter**
In cell **I10**	Key in **=H10*2**	Press **Enter**

9 Select cell **B12**, i.e. the AVERAGE cell for JUL
Key in **=B11/6**
Press →

10 Repeat these steps for the rest of the months, using the following formulae:

| In cell **C12** | Key in **=C11/6** | Press → |

In cell **D12**	Key in **=D11/6**	Press →
In cell **E12**	Key in **=E11/6**	Press →
In cell **F12**	Key in **=F11/6**	Press →
In cell **G12**	Key in **=G11/6**	Press →

11 Select cell **A15** and key in your name.
Select cell **A16** and key in the filename **EPTASKI**.

12 Check the key to ensure that your work is correct.

13 Check that a disk is inserted in Drive A and from the Menu Bar, select **File**, **Save**; ensure that the **Save in** text box displays **3½ Floppy (A:)** and in the **File name** text box, key in **EPTASK1** to save your file under its new name; click **Save**.

14 Close the file by selecting from the Menu Bar **File**, **Close** and exit from Excel by selecting from the Menu Bar **File**, **Exit**.

15 Don't forget to complete the Record of Progress sheet to indicate that you have finished this task successfully.

■ **YOYO1 (You're On Your Own Task 1)** **▼ ▲**

1 If you do not already have Excel on screen, start up your computer and load Excel.

2 Enter the folowing in the new worksheet window as shown in Figure 1.9 – key it in exactly as it appears, using the same cell references as shown.

	A	B	C	D	E	F	G	H	I
1	WINE SALES								
2									
3	BOTTLE	JUL	AUG	SEP	OCT	NOV	DEC	TOTAL	TOTAL PA
4									
5	CHABLIS	16	17	15	15	15	18		
6	CLARET	20	14	11	14	17	22		
7	MERLOT	28	17	18	22	21	24		
8	HOCK	24	26	27	26	24	28		
9	RIOJA	21	20	22	21	28	31		
10	CHIANTI	23	26	27	22	21	21		
11	TOTAL								
12	AVERAGE								

Figure 1.9 YOYO 1 worksheet

3 Select the **TOTAL** cell for **JUL** and enter a formula to calculate the total bottles for JUL.

4 Repeat this for the rest of the months, from cell **C11** to **G11**.

5 Select the **TOTAL** cell for **CHABLIS** and enter a formula to calculate the total bottles of CHABLIS.

6 Repeat this for the rest of the bottles from cell **H6** to **H10**.

7 Select the **TOTAL PA** cell for **CHABLIS** and enter a formula to calculate the total bottles of CHABLIS sold in a year (**TOTAL*2**).

8 Repeat this for the rest of the bottles from cell **I6** to **I10**.

9 Select the **AVERAGE** cell for **JUL** and enter a formula to calculate the average number of bottles sold in JUL (**TOTAL/6**).

10 Repeat this step for the rest of the bottles from cell **C12** to **G12**.

11 Select cell **A15** and key in **your name**.
Select cell **A16** and key in the filename **YOYO1**.

12 Check they key to ensure that your work is correct.

13 Check that a disk is inserted in Drive A and use **File** from the Menu Bar to save your file under its new name **YOYO1**.

14 Use **File** from the Menu Bar to close the file and exit from Excel.

15 Don't forget to complete the Record of Progress sheet to indicate that you have finished this task successfully.

edit and print a worksheet

By the end of Unit 1 you should be able to:

- *open an existing file*
- *edit, insert and delete data*
- *widen and decrease column width*
- *insert a row or column*
- *use Autosum to total a row or column*
- *delete a row or column*
- *undo an action*
- *print preview*
- *print a worksheet*

Open an existing file

Now that you have created and saved a file, you can open it any time to read it, change it or print it. Excel remembers the names of the last four files you worked on and displays them at the bottom of the list of options under File in the Menu Bar. If the file you want to open is one of those listed you can click on File in the Menu Bar and double-click on the chosen file. Otherwise you will have to select the Open option under File in the Menu Bar. The Open dialogue box will be displayed, similar to the one in Figure 2.1.

Opening an existing file
- Ensure that your floppy disk is inserted in Drive A.

- From the Menu Bar, select:

    File   Open

    Or, from the Tool Bar, select the **Open** icon

    Or, from the keyboard, press **Ctrl/O**.

    The Open dialogue box, similar to the one in Figure 2.1 is displayed on screen. You can select the options in the dialogue box by positioning the mouse pointer and clicking in the text boxes or by using the Tab key on the keyboard.

- **Look in** text box: if $3\frac{1}{2}$ **Floppy (A:)** is not already shown, click on ▼ at the right side of the text box and highlight this drive, where your file should be saved.

    The files in Drive A: will be displayed in the area beneath and the first filename should be highlighted, usually in blue. Each Excel file is preceded by the Excel icon.

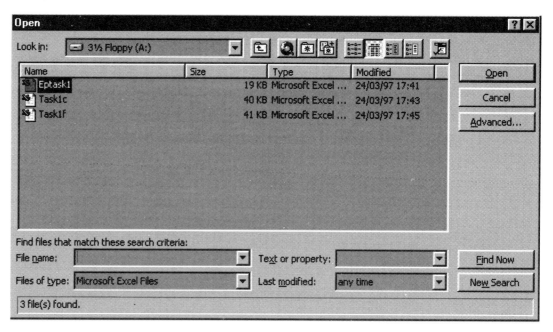

Figure 2.1 Open dialogue box

- Click on the file that you wish to open, e.g. **TASK1F**.

  If the file that you wish to open is not listed, the following text boxes can be used when you need to search for a file. When you have entered a choice into these text boxes you can then click on the **Find Now**, **New Search** or **Advanced** ... buttons.

- **Files of type** text box: if **Microsoft Excel Files** is not already shown, click on ▼ at the right side of the text box and highlight this option to ensure that you are opening an Excel file.

- **File name** text box: if you need to find a file, key in your chosen filename here.

- **Text or property**: if you need to find a file but cannot remember its filename, key in a word that might appear in it and Excel will search for all files containing that word.

- **Last modified**: if you are aware that the file was saved perhaps a week or a month ago, you can click on ▼ at the right side of the text box and highlight the period.

- **Open** button: click this now to open the file (or press ↵ **(Enter)**).

If you click on ▼ at the right side of a text box by mistake, click anywhere outside the text box to undo this action.

The new worksheet file that you have selected, will be opened on to your screen.

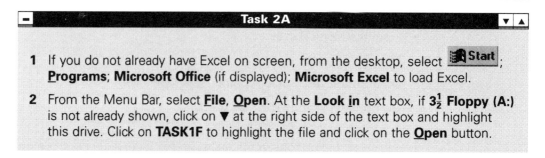

Task 2A

1 If you do not already have Excel on screen, from the desktop, select **Start**; **Programs**; **Microsoft Office** (if displayed); **Microsoft Excel** to load Excel.

2 From the Menu Bar, select **File**, **Open**. At the **Look in** text box, if $3\frac{1}{2}$ **Floppy (A:)** is not already shown, click on ▼ at the right side of the text box and highlight this drive. Click on **TASK1F** to highlight the file and click on the **Open** button.

Edit data

You can edit data if you find that you need to correct a mistake, insert more data or delete data. This is done by first selecting the cell to make it the active cell. Note that the data is displayed in both the cell and in the Formula Bar. Depending on how much you need to change, you can choose one of the following methods.

Typing over an entire entry
- Select the cell by placing the mouse pointer in the appropriate cell and click once.
- Type your new entry.
- Click once on the **Enter** box in the Formula Bar or press ↵ **(Enter)**.

The new data will be entered into the cell, overwriting what was already there.

Deleting an entire entry
- Select the cell by placing the mouse pointer in the appropriate cell and click once.
- Press the **Delete** button on the keyboard.

Editing part of an entry
- Select the cell by placing the mouse pointer in the appropriate cell and click once.
- In the Formula Bar, move the mouse pointer to where you wish to edit so that it changes to an *I* beam and click once

  or double-click to select the cell to edit

  or press **F2** to select the cell to edit.
- Type the new data and/or delete what is not required using the **Delete** button on the keyboard.
- Click once on the **Enter** box in the Formula Bar or press ↵ **(Enter)**.

Task 2B

Using the file **TASK1F** that you have just opened, practise using the above methods of editing data by carrying out the following.

1. Change the entry TOURER to **CAMPER** as follows: Select cell **A7**; key in **CAMPER** and click once on the **Enter** box in the Formula Bar.

2. Edit the title from CAR SALES to **VEHICLE SALES** as follows:
   Select cell **A1**; in the Formula Bar move the mouse pointer to the left of the word **CAR** where it will change to an *I* beam and click once; on the keyboard press the **Delete** button three times to delete the word **CAR**; key in **VEHICLE** and click once on the **Enter** box in the Formula Bar.

3. Edit the VAN sales in APRIL from 9 to **15** as follows:
   Select cell **E9**; key in **15** and click once on the **Enter** box in the Formula Bar.

4. Change the COUPE sales in JAN from 1 to **7** as follows:
   Select cell **B6**; key in **7** and click once on the **Enter** box in the Formula Bar.

5. Delete the entry PICK UP and key in **TRUCK** in its place as follows:
   Select cell **A10**; on the keyboard press the **Delete** button once; key in **TRUCK** and click once on the **Enter** box in the Formula Bar.

6. Edit the cell containing the filename TASK1F to **TASK2B** as follows:
   Select cell **A16**; in the Formula Bar move the mouse pointer to the left of the **1F** in the word TASK1F where it will change to an *I* beam and click once; on the keyboard press the **Delete** button twice to delete the letters 1F; key in **2B** and click once on the **Enter** box in the Formula Bar.

7. From the Menu Bar, select **File, Save As**; ensure that the **Save in** text box displays $3\frac{1}{2}$ **Floppy (A:)** and in the **File name** text box, key in **TASK2B** to save your file under its new name and click **Save**.

Change column width

Sometimes the text that you enter is wider than the worksheet column, or when ##### appears in a cell instead of numbers, this indicates that the column is too narrow for the entry. All columns have been set up with a default or preset width, usually 8.43 characters wide. A character can be a letter, number, space or symbol.

Changing column width

*   Place the mouse pointer on the column heading button of the column you wish to change and click once to select it.

*   From the Menu Bar, select:

    Forma<u>t</u>   <u>C</u>olumn   <u>W</u>idth

*   Type the number of characters required into the Column Width box. (The number that appears in the standard Column width box is the average number of digits 0–9 of the standard font that fit in a cell.)

*   Click **OK** or press **Enter** *or,*

*   place the mouse pointer to the right edge of the chosen column heading button until it changes to a double-headed arrow (Figure 2.2)

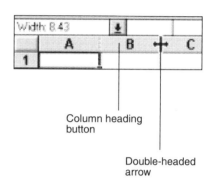

Column heading button

Double-headed arrow

Figure 2.2   Changing the column width

*   click (note the current width shown in the reference bar) and drag to the required width *or* double-click for the cell width to widen automatically.

Task 2B (continued)

Practise the above methods for changing the column width on the following.

8   Select cell **A5** and change the entry SALOON to **SALOON 4DR**.
Select column **A** heading button to highlight the column.
From the Menu Bar, select **Format, Column, Width**.
Key in **12** to ensure the column is widened sufficiently to display this entry and click **OK**. Click anywhere to deselect.

9   Decrease the width of column **H** to fit the word **TOTAL** as follows:
Place the mouse pointer over the line between column **H** and **I** heading buttons at the top of the worksheet. When it changes to a double-headed arrow, drag the mouse to the left until the column is decreased to fit the word TOTAL.

10   Select cell **A9** and change the entry VAN to **HATCHBACK 5DR**.
Widen the column as follows:
Place the mouse pointer over the line between column **A** and **B** heading buttons at the top of the worksheet. When it changes to a double-headed arrow, double-click for the cell width to widen automatically.

11   Now place the mouse pointer over the line between column **B** and **C** heading buttons at the top of the worksheet. When it changes to a double-headed arrow, double-click for the cell width to widen automatically. Continue to do the same for the rest of the columns from **C** to **I**.

12   From the Tool Bar, click 🖫 **Save** to save these changes to your file **TASK2B** and check your work with the key.

Insert a row/column

When a new row is inserted it appears *above* the active cell. All the other rows are moved down and the cell references are adjusted automatically. Similarly, when a new column is inserted it appears to the *left* of the active cell; the other columns move across to the right and cell references are adjusted automatically.

Inserting a row/column

*   Place the mouse pointer on the row/column heading button of the row/column you wish to change and click once to select it (Figure 2.3).

*   From the Menu Bar, select:

    Insert   **Rows** or **Columns**

    The new row or column will be inserted.

If the new row or column is inserted *within* a range referred to in a formula then it will be included in the calculation. You need to check that the new row or column is included, otherwise you will have to amend the formula.

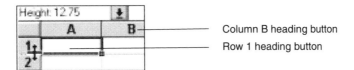

Column B heading button
Row 1 heading button

Figure 2.3   Inserting a row/column

Task 2C		▼ ▲

1   With **TASK2B** still displayed, make the following changes:
Select cell **G3** and change the entry JUN to **JUL**.

2   Insert a new column between MAY and JUL as follows:
Click column **G** heading button at the top to select the entire column.
From the Menu Bar, select **Insert, Columns**.
A new column is inserted between MAY and JUL.
The column containing JUL moves across and cell references adjust.

3   Select cell **G3**; key in **JUN** and press ↵ **(Enter)**. Key the following details in the new column:

    2   0   1   8   5   6

4   Select cell **I5**. Notice how the vehicle-type total has changed automatically to include this new column – remember the formula for the vehicle-type total included *all* the columns in this range, so you do *not need to amend* the formula.

5   In the TYPE column, insert a new row between TRUCK and TOTAL as follows:
Click row **11** heading button at the left to select the entire row.
From the Menu Bar, select **Insert, Rows**.
A new row is inserted between TRUCK and TOTAL.
The row containing TOTAL moves down and cell references adjust.

6   Select cell **A11**; key in **CABRIOLET** and press ▶ (right cursor arrow).
Key in the following details in the new row:

    0   0   6   6   6   6   6

7   Select cell **B12**. Notice that the monthly totals have *not* changed to include this new row – this is because the formula for the monthly total was only for the

range of cells B5–B10, so you *must amend* the formula. Read on to find out how!

8 Check that your name is keyed in at the bottom of the worksheet and edit the cell beneath to display **TASK2C** instead of TASK2B.

9 From the Menu Bar, select **File**, **Save As**; ensure that the **Save in** text box displays $3\frac{1}{2}$ **Floppy (A:)** and in the **File name** text box, key in **TASK2C** to save your file under its new name and click **Save**.

Use Autosum to total a row/column

In Unit 1 you learned how to total a range of cells by typing in a formula. This can also be done a quicker way using the Autosum button. When you click this, Excel looks above and then to the left of the active cell for a range of cells to total. This may result in blank cells being included if they occur in this range.

Using Autosum

*   Place the mouse pointer on the cell where you want the total to appear and click once to select it.

*   From the Tool Bar, select:

    Σ **Autosum** button

    The range of cells to be added appears in the cell and in the Formula Bar. If this is the range that you wish to total then you can confirm this as follows.

*   Click the ✔ **Enter** box or press ↵ **(Enter)**.

    Since Excel guesses the range of cells you want to sum, occasionally this may not necessarily be the range you want. If you want to sum a different range of cells:

    either cancel the process and start again as follows:

    In the Formula Bar, click the ✘ **Cancel** box.
    Ensure that the cell where you want the total to appear is selected.
    Drag the mouse across the chosen range to highlight it.
    Click the Autosum button and check that the formula is correct.
    Click the ✔ **Enter** box or press ↵ **(Enter)**.
    Click anywhere or use the cursor arrow keys to deselect the cells

    or edit the formula as follows:

    In the Formula Bar, position the mouse pointer to the right of the opening bracket (so that it changes to an *I* beam and click once.
    Press the **Delete** button several times to delete the contents inside the brackets.
    Key in the chosen range.
    Click the ✔ **Enter** box or press ↵ **(Enter)**.

▬	Task 2C (continued)	▼ ▲

10 With **TASK2C** still displayed, select cell **B12**.
    From the Tool Bar, select the Σ **Autosum** button by clicking on it.
    In the Formula Bar, check that the range displays **=SUM(B5:B11)** to include the new row, and click the ✔ **Enter** box.

11 Select cell **C12**.
    From the Tool Bar, select the Σ **Autosum** button.
    In the Formula Bar, check that the range displays **=SUM(C5:C11)** to include the new row and click the ✔ **Enter** box.

12 Recalculate the rest of the totals in row **12** (from **D12** to **H12**) in the same way.

13 Select cell **I 11** to insert a TOTAL for **CABRIOLET**. Try the other method of using the Autosum button, i.e. click <u>on</u> **I 11** and drag the mouse to highlight the range from **I 11** to **B11**. Click on the **Σ Autosum** button; in the Formula Bar check that the formula displays **=SUM(B11:H11)**; press ↵ **(Enter)** and click anywhere to deselect the cells.

14 The figures for the AVERAGE are no longer required. Select cell **B13** and drag the mouse to highlight the range to **H13**; press the **Delete** button. You will find that this only deletes the contents of the cells. If you wish to delete an entire row then you must select from the Menu Bar as shown below.

15 From the Tool Bar, click 🖫 **Save** to save these changes to your file **TASK2C** and check your work with the key.

Delete a row/column

When a row/column is to be deleted you must select the chosen row/column heading button so that the entire row/column including all its contents will be deleted.

Deleting a row/column
- Select the row/column heading button of the row/column that you want to delete.
- From the Menu Bar, select:

<u>E</u>dit   <u>D</u>elete

Undo an action

Excel has an Undo function which reverses or undoes the last thing you did, e.g. if you deleted a row, inserted a column, made text bold, etc., and decided that you had made a mistake, then you could use Undo. To undo recent actions one at a time, click Undo. To undo several actions at once click the arrow next to Undo and select from the list. Excel revises the selected action and all actions above it. If you decide you did not want to undo an action, click the Redo 🔁 icon in the Tool Bar or select from Edit in the Menu Bar.

Undoing an action
From the Menu Bar, select:

<u>E</u>dit   <u>U</u>ndo

or, from the Tool Bar, select the **Undo** icon

or, from the keyboard, press **Ctrl/Z**.

Note that from the Edit, Undo menu option, the description of the Undo feature reflects the last action you have taken.

▬   **Task 2D**   **▼ ▲**

1 With **TASK2C** still displayed, click row **11** heading button at the left to select the entire row. Delete this row, containing information on the CABRIOLET, as follows: From the Menu Bar, select **Edit, Delete**.
Notice how the other rows move up, the cell references adjust automatically and how the totals recalculate.

2 Click column **B** heading button to select the entire column.
   Delete this column, containing information on JAN, as follows:
   From the Menu Bar, select **Edit**, **Delete**.
   Notice how the other columns move left, the cell references adjust automatically
   and how the totals recalculate.

3 Undo the delete action that you have just taken on column **B** as follows:
   From the Menu Bar, select **Edit**, **Undo Delete**.
   Notice that column **B** containing JAN has now been restored to its former position
   and the cells and totals appear as they did before.

4 Click column **G** heading button to select the entire column.
   Delete this column, containing information on JUN, as follows:
   From the Menu Bar, select **Edit**, **Delete**.

5 Select cell **G3** and amend the entry JUL to **JUN**.

6 Check that your name is keyed in at the bottom of the worksheet and edit the cell
   beneath to display **TASK2D** instead of TASK2C.

7 From the Menu Bar, select **File**, **Save As**; ensure that the **Save in** text box
   displays 3½ **Floppy (A:)** and in the **File Name** text box, key in **TASK2D** to save
   your file under its new name and click **Save**

Print Preview

Once you have completed your worksheet you will probably want to print it out.
Before this, however, it is always a good idea to check what it will look like on the
page, and using Print Preview will give you the opportunity to see if there are any
layout changes that you might want to make. When you select Print Preview your
screen should look similar to the one in Figure 2.4.

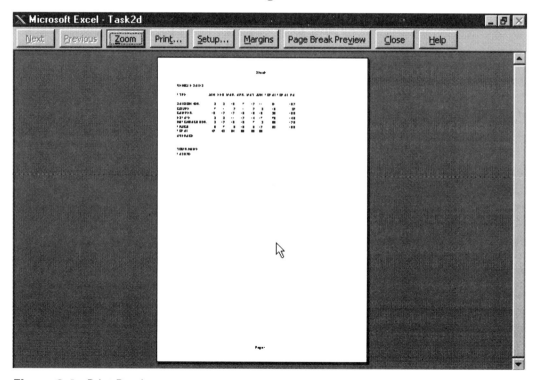

Figure 2.4 Print Preview

There are a range of features on this option but, for now, we will just use it to check
the appearance of your worksheet.

Using Print Preview
- From the Menu Bar, select:

    <u>F</u>ile   **Print Pre<u>v</u>iew**

    or, from the Tool Bar, select the **Print Preview** icon.

    The Print Preview screen is displayed on screen, as shown in Figure 2.4. Note that the mouse pointer changes to a small magnifying glass when it is over the page. Position this on the area that you wish to view more closely. Click the mouse once to zoom in and click once again to zoom out.

    If you click the **Print** button, the Print dialogue box will be displayed or you can just click the Close button to return to your worksheet.

- Click **<u>C</u>lose**.

Print a worksheet

Once you are satisfied with the appearance of your worksheet you can select Print from the File option on the Menu Bar to display a Print dialogue box similar to the one in Figure 2.5. At this stage, we will just use the standard default print settings, i.e. to print one copy of the selected sheet on an A4 portrait sheet. You will also find that the default is set up to print the worksheet sheet name and the page number.

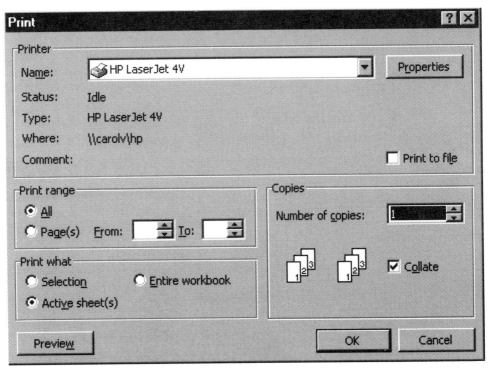

Figure 2.5 Print dialogue box

The options are as follows:

Printer – The name of the current printer is displayed with other details such as status, type, the port to which it is connected and comment.

<u>P</u>rint What – Selected sheet – i.e. the worksheet on which you are currently working is the default. Choose Entire Workbook if you want to print all the files in that workbook or Selection if you want to print only a selected range of the worksheet, in which case you will first have to select the range.

<u>C</u>opies – **1** is the default. You can increase or decrease the number of copies of the worksheet by keying in the number or clicking on the up or down arrow.

Page Range – **All** is the default. You can select **Pages** and key in a range of page numbers if desired.

Printing a worksheet
- From the Menu Bar, select:

<u>F</u>ile   **P<u>r</u>int**

or, from the Tool Bar, select the 🖨 **Print** icon

or, from the keyboard, press **Ctrl/P**.

The Print dialogue box is displayed on screen, as shown in Figure 2.5.

- Click **OK** or press ↵ **(Enter)** to accept the default settings. Unless you have altered the default settings you will find that your worksheet is displayed with the worksheet name, e.g. Sheet 1, and the page number, e.g. Page 1.

Task 2D (continued)

8 With **TASK2D** still displayed on screen, from the Menu Bar, select <u>F</u>ile, **Print Pre<u>v</u>iew** to check the appearance of your worksheet. Click once at the top left of the page to zoom in and click once again to zoom out. Try this on different parts of the page to see its effect. Click the **<u>C</u>lose** button when finished.

9 Check your work with the key.

10 From the Tool Bar, select the 🖨 **Print** icon to print a copy of the worksheet.

11 Close the file by selecting from the Menu Bar **<u>F</u>ile**, **<u>C</u>lose** and exit from Excel by selecting from the Menu Bar **<u>F</u>ile**, **E<u>x</u>it**.

12 Don't forget to complete the Record of Progress sheet to indicate that you have finished this unit successfully. If you feel that you would like to do further work to consolidate what you have learned so far, then try Extra Practice Task 2.

Extra Practice Task 2

1 If you do not already have Excel on screen, from the desktop, select ▓**Start**; **Programs**; **Microsoft Office** (if displayed); **Microsoft Excel** to load Excel.

2 From the Menu Bar, select **<u>F</u>ile**, **<u>O</u>pen**. At the **Look <u>i</u>n** text box, if $3\frac{1}{2}$ **Floppy (A:)** is not already shown, click on ▼ at the right side of the text box and highlight this drive. Click on **EPTASK1.XLS** to highlight the file and click on the **<u>O</u>pen** button.

3 Edit the data as follows:
Select cell **A9** and change the entry MINTS to **MINTOS**.
Select cell **A1** and edit the title from CONFECTIONERY SALES to **SALES OF CONFECTIONERY**.
Select cell **B6** and edit the FUDGE sales in JUL from 10 to **16**.
Select cell **G10** and change the ROCK sales in DEC from 11 to **5**.
Select cell **A8** and delete the entry BONBON and key in **JELLIES** instead.

4 Select cell **A10** and change the entry ROCK to **LIQUORICE**.
Select column **A** heading button.
From the Menu Bar, select **Format**, **Column**, **Width**.
Key in **11** and press ↵ **(Enter)**.

5 Select cell **A5** and change the entry TOFFEES to **BUTTER TOFFEES**.
Place the mouse pointer over the line between column **A** and **B** heading buttons. When it changes to a double-headed arrow, double-click for the cell width to widen automatically.

6 Now place the mouse pointer over the line between column **B** and **C** heading buttons at the top of the worksheet. When it changes to a double-headed arrow,

double-click for the cell width to widen automatically. Continue to do the same for the rest of the columns from **C** to **I**.

7   Select cell **G3** and change the entry DEC to **JAN**.
    Insert a new column between NOV and JAN as follows:
    Click column **G** heading button at the top to select the entire column.
    From the Menu Bar, select **Insert**, **Column**.

8   Select cell **G3** and key in the following details in the new column:
    DEC   22   18   15   12   10   9

9   Insert a new row between LIQUORICE and TOTAL as follows:
    Click row **11** heading button at the left to select the entire row.
    From the Menu Bar, select **Insert**, **Row**.

10 Select cell **A11** and key the following details in the new row:
    TREACLE TOFFEE   24   18   18   18   30   24   24

11 Include the figures of the new row in the monthly TOTAL as follows:
    Click on cell reference **B12** to select it.
    From the Tool Bar, select the **Σ Autosum** button.
    Check that the range includes the new row, i.e. **=SUM(B5:B11)** and click the ☑
    Enter box.
    Click on cell reference **C12** to select it.
    From the Tool Bar, select the **Σ Autosum** button.
    Check that the range includes the new row, i.e. **=SUM(C5:C11)** and click the ☑
    Enter box.
    Recalculate the rest of the totals in row **12** (from **D12** to **H12**) in the same way.

12 Move to cell reference **I 11** to insert a TOTAL for TREACLE TOFFEE. Try the other method of using the Autosum button, i.e. click on **I 11** and drag the mouse to highlight the range from **I 11** to **B11**. Click on the **Σ Autosum** button; in the Formula Bar check that the formula displays **=SUM(B11:H11)**; click the **Enter** box or press ↵ **(Enter)**; click anywhere to deselect cells.

13 Click column **B** heading button to select the entire column.
    Delete this column containing information on JUL as follows:
    From the Menu Bar, select **Edit**, **Delete**.
    Undo the delete action that you have just taken on column **B** as follows:
    From the Menu Bar, select **Edit**, **Undo Delete**.

14 Click column **G** heading button to select the entire column.
    Delete this column containing information on DEC as follows:
    From the Menu Bar, select **Edit**; **Delete**.

15 Select cell **G3** and amend the entry JAN to **DEC**.

16 Click row **11** heading button to select the entire row.
    Delete this row, containing information on TREACLE TOFFEE, as follows:
    From the Menu Bar, select **Edit**, **Delete**.

17 Select cell **A15** and key in your name.
    Select cell **A16** and key in the filename **EPTASK2**.

18 With **EPTASK1** still displayed on screen, from the Menu Bar, select **File**, **Print Preview** to check the appearance of your worksheet. Click once to zoom in and once again to zoom out. Click **Close** when finished. Check the key to ensure that your work is correct.

19 Check that a disk is inserted in Drive A and from the Menu Bar, select **File**, **Save As**; ensure that the **Save in** text box displays $3\frac{1}{2}$ 🖫 **Floppy (A:)** and in the **File name** text box, key in **EPTASK2** to save your file under its new name; click **Save**.

20 From the Tool Bar, select the 🖨 **Print** icon to print a copy of the worksheet.

21 Close the file by selecting from the Menu Bar **File**, **Close** and exit from Excel by selecting from the Menu Bar **File**, **Exit**.

22 Don't forget to complete the Record of Progress sheet to indicate that you have finished this task successfully.

1 If you do not already have Excel on screen, start up your computer and load Excel.

2 Open the file **YOYO1**.

3 Edit the data as follows:

Delete the entry HOCK and key in **SHIREZ** instead.
Edit the title from WINE SALES to **SALES OF POPULAR WINES**.
Edit the CLARET sales in JUL from 20 to **14**.
Change the CHIANTI sales in DEC from 21 to **27**.
Change the entry SHIREZ to **SHIRAZ**.

4 Change the entry CHIANTI to **SEMILLON**.
Select column **A** heading button and, using the Menu Bar, widen the column to display the data fully.

5 Change the entry SHIRAZ to **SHIRAZ CABERNET**.
Place the mouse pointer over the line between column **A** and **B** heading buttons so that it changes to a double-headed arrow and widen the column to display the data fully.

6 Now place the mouse pointer over the line between column **B** and **C** heading buttons at the top of the worksheet so that it changes to a double-headed arrow and adjusts the column automatically. Continue to do the same for the rest of the columns from **C** to **I**.

7 Change the entry DEC to **JAN**.
Insert a new column between NOV and JAN.

8 Key the following details in the new column (G):

DEC   19   23   25   27   29   20

9 Insert a new row between SEMILLON and TOTAL.

10 Key in the following details in the new row (11):

CHARDONNAY   36   30   30   36   30   30   30

11 Include the figures of the new row in the monthly TOTAL for JUL using the **Autosum** button; check that the range includes the new row. Recalculate the rest of the totals in row **12** (from **C12** to **H12**) in the same way.

12 Insert a TOTAL for CHARDONNAY (to do this, drag the mouse to highlight the range from **B11** to **I11** and use the **Autosum** button).

13 Delete the column containing information on **JUL**.

Undo the delete action that you have just taken on this column.

14 Delete the column containing information on **DEC**.

15 Amend the entry JAN to **DEC**.

16 Delete the row containing information on **CHARDONNAY**.

17 Select cell **A15** and key in **your name**.
Select cell **A16** and key in the filename **YOYO2**.

18 With **YOYO2** still displayed on screen, using the Menu Bar, display **Print Preview** to check the appearance of your worksheet. Check the key to ensure your work is correct.

19 Check that a disk is inserted in Drive A and use **File** from the Menu Bar to save your file under its new name **YOYO2**.

20 Using the Tool Bar, print a copy of the worksheet.

21 Use **File** from the Menu Bar to close the file and exit from Excel.

22 Don't forget to complete the Record of Progress sheet to indicate that you have finished this task successfully.

unit

3 manipulate a worksheet and use display features

By the end of Unit 3 you should be able to:

- *format data to change alignment, font size and style*
- *clear cells*
- *change row height*
- *format numbers to integers, decimals and currency*
- *extend the worksheet*
- *insert multiple rows or columns*
- *replicate entries – formulae and data*
- *select a range of text to cut, move, copy and paste*
- *select a range of text to drag and drop*
- *generate new values*
- *display formulae*

Format data

To format data means to apply different attributes to one or more cells so that the appearance of the data is changed, e.g. alter the alignment so that the data is centred, change the font size/style to make it stand out or change figures to appear to two decimal places preceded by a £ sign. You will have noticed from your previous printouts that the appearance of your worksheet is not very well balanced, mainly because the default settings in Excel align text to the left and numbers to the right.

You will find that the quickest method of formatting data is by using the Tool Bar – remember that, just as with other Tool Bar icons, you can position the mouse pointer slowly over any of the icons to display a description of its function in a Tool Tip box. Although there is a range of options on the Formatting Tool Bar, we shall just use a few at this stage.

Before formatting data, you must select the cell or range of cells you wish to format. If you are not sure how to do this then refer back to page 15 – 'Select a range of cells'. When you select a range of cells you can apply a range of formatting functions whilst the cells are still highlighted. When you are finished with the range, click once outside it to deselect.

It is usual practice not to format the worksheet until you are sure about the general layout and after you have completed entering data/formulae.

Changing alignment
- Ensure that the cell or range of cells to be aligned has been selected.

- From the Menu Bar, select:

F<u>o</u>rmat   **C<u>e</u>lls**

The Format Cells dialogue box is displayed, on which there are six tabs for formatting different aspects of cells.

- Select the **Alignment** tab. The Format Cells dialogue box should be similar to the one in Figure 3.1.

This dialogue box can also be accessed by selecting the cell or cells, clicking the right mouse button and selecting the menu option **<u>F</u>ormat cells...** from the pop-up list.

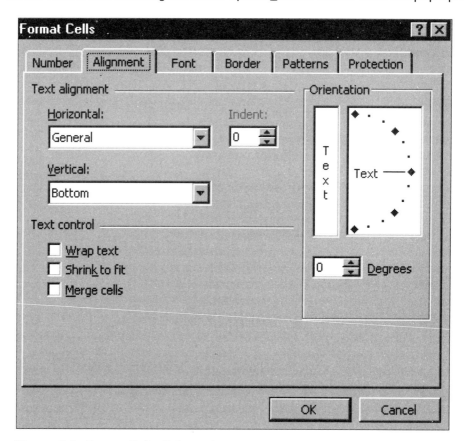

Figure 3.1 Format Cells dialogue box

- Select the alignment required.

- Click **OK**

    or, from the Tool Bar, select one of the following:

Align Left   **Centre**   **Align Right**   **Centre Across Columns**

- Click outside the highlighted range to deselect it.

When you select a button from the Tool Bar, notice how it appears in a lighter shade – this is to indicate that the function has been applied to the current data. If you want to revert to the original format click the button again to reverse the process.

These types of buttons are called *toggle buttons*. This means that if you click once, the function will be applied; if you click once again it will be switched off.

Clear cells

When you have applied a number of formats to a particular cell or range of cells, it is quicker to clear out the attributes using the following method.

Clearing cells
- Select the cell or range of cells to be cleared.

- From the Menu Bar, select:

    Edit   **Cle**a**r**

- Select one of the following:

    All   to remove formulae, formatting and data
    Formats   to remove formatting only
    Contents   to remove formulae and data only
    Notes   to remove only notes that have been attached to a cell.

▬	Task 3A	▼ ▲

1 Open **TASK2D** and try each of the following for practice, noting the effects of the changes.

   Select the range of cells by highlighting from **A3** to **A12**:

   - Right align these headings by selecting from the Menu Bar **F**o**r**mat, **C**e**l**ls, **Alignment** and from the **Horizontal** column, select the **Right** button; click **OK**.
   - With the range **A3–A12** still highlighted, centre these headings by clicking once on the ☰ **Centre** icon on the Tool Bar.

   Deselect, i.e. click once outside the highlighted area.

2 Select the range of cells by highlighting from **A1** to **I1** (column I, row 1) and try the following:

   - Centre the main heading across these cells by clicking once on the ▦ **Centre Across Columns** icon on the Tool Bar.
   - Click on the **B** **Bold** icon to embolden the main heading and then **deselect**.

3 Select cells **A15** and **A16**; click on the ☰ **Centre** icon on the Tool Bar; then **deselect**.

4 Select the range of cells by highlighting from **A3** to **A12** and clear the formats, so as to display the default settings, as follows. From the Menu Bar, select **E**dit, **Cle**a**r**, **F**ormats.

5 Select the range **B3** to **I3** (column I, row **3**); right align these headings by clicking once on the ☰ **Align Right** icon on the Tool Bar.

Change font size/style

A range of different fonts is available and these can be displayed in a variety of sizes and styles, such as bold, italic and underline. Very large sizes will depend on the ability of your printer to support them (see Figure 3.2).

Font – when you click here a drop down list, from
which you can choose a range of fonts, is displayed

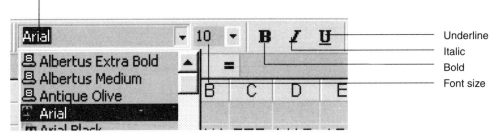

Figure 3.2   Font size and style

Changing font size/style

• Ensure that the chosen cell or range of cells to be formatted has been selected.

• From the Menu Bar, select:

Format   Cells

The Format Cells dialogue box is displayed, on which there are six tabs for formatting different aspects of cells.

• Select the **Font** tab. The Format Cells dialogue box should be similar to the one in Figure 3.3.

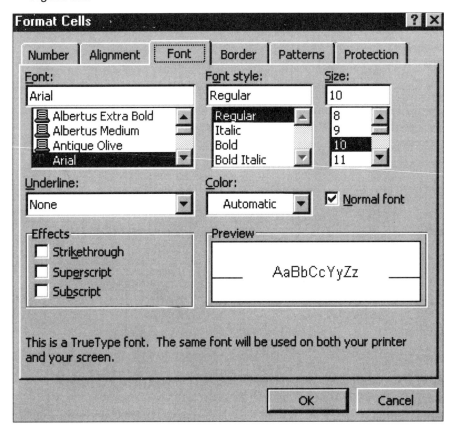

Figure 3.3   Format Cells dialogue box

Select the options required. A **Preview** of how your data will appear is displayed, as shown in Figure 3.3.

• Click **OK**

or, from the Tool Bar, click on the ⬛ to the right of the font/size box to display the options and then click on the desired font/size to highlight and select it.

Click on one or more of the following to select the required style:

Bold   **Italic**   **Underline**

• Click outside the highlighted range to deselect it.

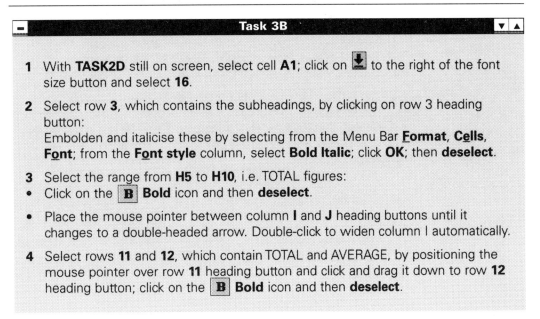

Task 3B

1 With **TASK2D** still on screen, select cell **A1**; click on the button to the right of the font size button and select **16**.

2 Select row **3**, which contains the subheadings, by clicking on row 3 heading button:
Embolden and italicise these by selecting from the Menu Bar **Format**, **Cells**, **Font**; from the **Font style** column, select **Bold Italic**; click **OK**; then **deselect**.

3 Select the range from **H5** to **H10**, i.e. TOTAL figures:
• Click on the **B** Bold icon and then **deselect**.

• Place the mouse pointer between column **I** and **J** heading buttons until it changes to a double-headed arrow. Double-click to widen column I automatically.

4 Select rows **11** and **12**, which contain TOTAL and AVERAGE, by positioning the mouse pointer over row **11** heading button and click and drag it down to row **12** heading button; click on the **B** Bold icon and then **deselect**.

Change row height

All rows have been set up with a default or preset height, usually 12.75. As I am sure you will have noticed, when you increased the size of the text in a row, Excel automatically increased the height of the row to accommodate this. However, if you wish, you may also set the row to a specific height. When selecting rows or ranges, if you choose the wrong one by mistake, just click anywhere to deselect.

Changing row height
• Place the mouse pointer on the row heading button of the row you wish to change and click once to select it.

• From the Menu Bar, select:

Format   **Row**   **Height**

• Type the height required into **Row Height** box.

• Click **OK** *or* press ↵ **(Enter)** *or*

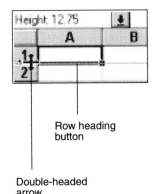

Row heading button

Double-headed arrow

• place the mouse pointer on the bottom edge of the chosen row heading button until it changes to a double-headed arrow.

• Click (note the current height shown in the reference bar) and drag to the required height *or* double-click for the row height to increase automatically to accommodate the tallest cell entry.

Figure 3.4 Changing the row height

Task 3C

1 With **TASK2D** still on screen, double the width of row **15** by placing the mouse pointer on the bottom edge of row **15** heading button until it changes to a double-headed arrow. Drag downwards until the row is double the height of the others – note the height shown in the reference bar should have increased from 12.75 to about 25.5.

2 Select row **15** heading button to highlight the entire row and from the Menu Bar, select **Format**, **Row**, **Height**. Key in **12.75**; click **OK**.

3 The entry TRUCK should be **OFF ROADER**. Please amend.

4 The TOTAL PA is no longer required so delete this column by selecting column **I** heading button to highlight the entire column; from the Menu Bar, select **Edit**, **Delete**. Deselect. In cell **I3** (column **I**, row **3**) key in a new column heading **COST**; click the ✔ **Enter** box in the Formula Bar. This will automatically appear in bold and italics as you have formatted this row earlier. Next, right align this by clicking once on the 🔲 **Align Right** icon on the Tool Bar.

5 Enter the following figures in column I, pressing the ↓ down cursor arrow key to move you down from cell to cell:

in row **5** (SALOON 4DR)   **10499**
in row **6** (COUPE)   **17000**
in row **7** (CAMPER)   **20500**
in row **8** (ESTATE)   **12499**
in row **9** (HATCHBACK 5DR) **10500**
in row **10** (OFF ROADER)   **25500**

6 Since the heading has only been centred across columns **A** to **H** and as there will be many more alterations to the worksheet, it is simpler to left align as follows:

Select **A1**; click the 🔲 **Align Left** icon on the Tool Bar.

Let us also make the rest of the worksheet consistent as follows:

Select **A15** and **A16**; click the 🔲 **Align Left** icon on the Tool Bar.

7 Select cell **H11** and calculate the overall **TOTAL** number of cars by clicking on the Σ **Autosum** button; ensure that **=SUM(H5:H10)** is displayed in the Formula Bar (if not, key in this formula); click the ✔ **Enter** box in the Formula Bar.

8 Select cell **H12** and key in the formula **=H11/6** to calculate the average number of vehicles sold in this period; click the ✔ **Enter** box in the Formula Bar.

9 The sales of the **COUPE** are inaccurate and need to be altered. Amend by keying in the following, pressing the → right cursor arrow key to move you across from cell to cell in row 6:

JAN	FEB	MAR	APR	MAY	JUN
3	6	6	7	10	9

This changes the average number and since you clearly cannot have 0.17 of a vehicle, this needs to be rounded to the nearest integer (i.e. whole number). Next you will find out how to format the numbers so that the appearance of your worksheet is consistent.

10 Change the filename in **A16** from TASK2D to **TASK3C**.

11 From the Menu Bar, select **File**, **Print Preview** to check the appearance of your worksheet and to ensure that it corresponds with the key. Click once to zoom in and once again to zoom out. Click **Close** when finished.

12 From the Menu Bar, select **File**, **Save As** and save the file as **TASK3C**.

13 From the Tool Bar, select the 🖨 **Print** icon to print a copy of the worksheet.

Format numbers

As with changing alignment, font size and style, you also have to select the chosen cell or range of cells to be formatted when you wish to format numbers.

Formatting numbers
- Ensure that the chosen cell or range of cells to be formatted has been selected.

- From the Menu Bar, select:

    F**o**rmat   C**e**lls

    The Format Cells dialogue box is displayed, on which there are six tabs for formatting different aspects of cells.

- Select the **Number** tab. The Format Cells dialogue box should be similar to the one in Figure 3.5.

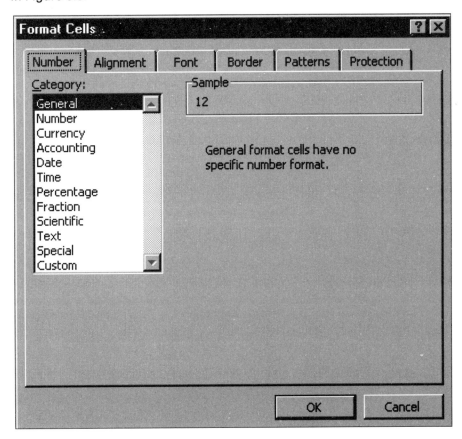

Figure 3.5 Format Cells dialogue box

The default is set at **General** in the **C**ategory box, the entries of which have no specific number format. If you wish to display other categories with specific number formats then the appropriate category needs to be selected, which will display additional option boxes (e.g. **Decimal Places, S**ymbol). The potential appearance of the value in the cell is shown in the **Sample** box. If the category selected does not display your requirements, then the **Custom** category can be selected by selecting **Custom** from **C**ategory box and clicking in the **T**ype box as indicated and if you wish to change the options to display other information such as symbols or format codes, e.g. $ sign, you can type the sign directly into the **T**ype box or select from a drop down list.

- Select the options required – some common ones are as follows:

    Display in integer format:
    From **C**ategory, select **Number**   From **D**ecimal Places, select **0**

Display to two decimal places:
From **Category**, select **Number**   From **Decimal Places**, select **2**

Display in currency format:
From **Category**, select **Currency**

To two decimal places:
From **Decimal Places**, select **2**

To the nearest pound:
From **Decimal Places**, select **0**   From **Symbol**, select **£ English (British)**

· Click **OK**

Or, from the Tool Bar, click one of the following to select the required format:

Currency Style	Percent Style	Comma Style	Decrease Decimal	Increase Decimal

Currency Style   This displays currency to two decimal places, e.g. £2.25.
Percent Style   This displays the value as a percentage, e.g. 22%
Comma Style   This inserts commas in values over 999, e.g. 2,345.21.
Increase Decimal   This adds one decimal place, e.g. 2,345.216.
Decrease Decimal   This removes one decimal place, e.g. 2,345.21 (click twice to remove two decimal places e.g. to round the value 2,345.21 to an integer or whole number, i.e. 2345).

· Click outside the highlighted range to deselect it.

Removing number format

· Select the cell or cells that are to be unformatted.

· From the Menu Bar, select:

Fo**rmat**   **C**e**lls**

The Format Cells dialogue box is displayed.

· Select the **Number** tab:

From **Category** select **All**   From **Format Codes** select **General**.

When you require cell contents to be displayed with a £ sign, do not be tempted to key this in from the keyboard, as Excel will recognise it as text and you will be unable to perform any calculations on the data. Always use **F**o**rmat**, **C**e**lls** from the Menu Bar to display currency symbols.

Task 3D

1 With **TASK3C** still on screen, select **H12**, the **AVERAGE** figure. From the Menu Bar, select **F**o**rmat**, **C**e**lls**, **Number**. From **Category** select **Number**, from **Format Codes** select **0**; click **OK**. The average should now be displayed in integer (i.e. whole number) format.

2 Position the mouse pointer on **I5** (column **I**, row **5**); click and drag it to **I10** to select the range containing the data on **COST**. From the Tool Bar click on **Currency Style** to apply the currency format.

3 The cells will fill with ###### to indicate that the column is not wide enough. Position the cursor between columns **I** and **J** heading buttons until it changes to a double-headed arrow. Double-click to widen the column automatically.

4 The default for the **Currency style** icon is shown to two decimal places but as this is not required for such large amounts of money, change the format to display integers as follows. The range from **I5** to **I10** should still be highlighted. If not, select this range now; from the Menu Bar, select **F**o**rmat**, **C**e**lls**, **Number**. From the **Category** box select **Currency**; from **Decimal places**, select **0** from **Symbol**, select **£ English (British)**.

5   In **A16** change the filename to **TASK3D**.

6   From the Menu Bar, select **File**, **Print Preview** to check the appearance of your worksheet and to ensure that it corresponds with the key. Click once to zoom in and once again to zoom out. Click **Close** when finished.

7   From the Menu Bar, select **File**, **Save As** and save the file as **TASK3D**.

8   From the Tool Bar, select the 🖨 **Print** icon to print a copy of the worksheet.

Extend the worksheet

You will often find that you need to extend a worksheet as and when additional information becomes available. This will require you to insert extra rows or columns, add data, check that current formulae and formatting attributes include the new data and, if not, adjust accordingly. In Unit 2 you were shown how to insert a single row or column – refer back to page 29 ('Insert a row/column') if you want to refresh your memory on how this is done. Use the method shown below if you need to insert more than one row or column.

When you extend the worksheet you may have to select across a range which extends beyond the immediate data in the window on your screen. Sometimes this can be tricky if you have not fully mastered control of the mouse. You may find it easier to use the scroll bars to move the section you are working on on to the screen. Alternatively, from the keyboard, once you have selected the first cell, hold down the Shift key and use the cursor keys. To avoid dragging the range too far it is always advisable, if you can, to start your selection from the right or the bottom of the worksheet and drag it to the left or upwards.

Insert multiple rows/columns

When you need to insert more than one row or column you must first highlight the number required by selecting the appropriate number of heading buttons. Formulae will automatically update to include these new rows or columns if they are inserted *within* the range specified. You must always check your formulae after you have inserted rows or columns as you will need to amend formulae to include the new rows or columns if they have been inserted *outside* the range.

Inserting multiple rows/columns
*   Place the mouse pointer on the row/column heading button where the new row/column is to be inserted.

    Inserting several rows:
    Click and drag downwards over the number of row heading buttons required

    Or

    Inserting several columns:
    Click and drag to the right over the number of column heading buttons required.

*   From the Menu Bar, select:

    Insert   Rows or Columns

    The new rows or columns will be inserted.

> **Task 3E**
>
> 1 With **TASK3D** still on screen, insert two new rows between COUPE and SALOON 4DR by clicking on row 6 heading button and also drag downwards to select row **7**; from the Menu Bar, select **Insert**, **Rows**. Select cell **A6** and key in **CABRIOLET**; press ↵ **(Enter)** to move to cell **A7** and key in **HATCHBACK 3DR**; press ↵ **(Enter)**.
>
> 2 Insert three new columns between JUN and TOTAL by clicking on column **H** heading button and also drag across to select columns **I** and **J**; from the Menu Bar, select **Insert**, **Columns**. In each new column, key in the following, pressing the → right cursor arrow key to move you across from cell to cell; select cell **H3** and key in **JUL**; select cell **I3** and key in **AUG**; select **J3** and key in **SEP**.
>
> 3 When you alter the column width it is important that this is done as accurately as possible so that the worksheet is not extended over a larger area than necessary. Try the following to see the effect excessive column width might have on your work. Place the mouse pointer between **A** and **B** column heading buttons until it appears as a double-headed arrow and double-click to widen column **A** to fit the car-type names and the title. Select column **K** heading button; from the Menu Bar, select **Format**, **Column**, **Width**; key in **14**; click **OK**; click anywhere to deselect.
>
> 4 From the Menu Bar, select **File**, **Print Preview** to check the appearance of your worksheet; click once on the top right of the page to zoom in – you will find that only the TOTAL column is displayed; click once again to zoom out; click **Next** to view the information which has extended to page 2; click **Close**. You will find that a vertical dashed line has appeared between columns **K** and **L**. This indicates that your worksheet extends to a further page. In order to make it all fit on one page, you can decrease the column widths, as follows. Position the mouse pointer between column **L** and column **M** heading buttons until it appears as a double-headed arrow; double-click to make the column adjust to the size of its largest entry. Next, position the mouse pointer between column **K** and column **L** heading buttons until it appears as a double-headed arrow; double-click to make the column adjust to the size of its largest entry. The dashed line should now appear to the right of column **L**, indicating that you are close to the edge of the page.
>
> 5 In **A18** change the filename to **TASK3E**.
> 6 From the Menu Bar, select **File**, **Print Preview** to check the appearance of your worksheet and to ensure that it corresponds with the key. Click once to zoom in and once again to zoom out. Click **Close** when finished.
>
> 7 From the Menu Bar, select **File**, **Save As** and save the file as **TASK3E**.
> 8 From the Tool Bar, select the 🖨 **Print** icon to print a copy of the worksheet.

Replicate formulae and data

To replicate simply means to copy, and this is a term that is often associated with copying formulae. Earlier in Unit 1 (page 21) you *keyed in* the formula for the TOTAL car types for JAN. Once this formula is entered you can simply copy it across the TOTAL cells for the rest of the months and Excel will automatically input the correct formulae to calculate the different totals in each different column. When you select a cell to be copied, its contents and formats will also be copied to the range of cells that you select. The method shown below is one of a number of ways of copying formulae and data.

Replicating formulae and data
- Select the cell to be copied.

- Click and drag the mouse across the range required to highlight it.

- From the Menu Bar, select:

  Edit   F**i**ll

  and choose one of the following:

  Down if the range is below *or* press **Ctrl/D**
  Right if the range is to the right *or* press **Ctrl/R**
  Up if the range is above
  Left if the range is to the left.

  A quicker method of copying formulae and data across to other cells is to position the mouse at the edge of the active cell until it changes to a **+** (cross). Then click and drag the mouse across the range required to copy the cell contents across.

Task 3F

1 With **TASK3E** still on screen, in cell **B6** key in **2**; click the ✔ **Enter** box in the Formula Bar. As there were only two cars sold per month from JAN to JUN you can use the **Fill** command to copy this across as follows. Select **B6**; click and drag to **G6** to highlight this range; from the Menu Bar, select **E**dit, F**i**ll, **R**ight. The figure 2 should be copied into each column.

2 In cell **B7** key in **5**; click the ✔ **Enter box** in the Formula Bar. As five cars were sold per month from JAN to JUN you can use the **Fill** command to copy this across as follows. Select **B7**; click and drag to **G7**; from the Menu Bar, select **E**dit, F**i**ll, **R**ight. The figure 5 should be copied into each column.

3 In cell **H6** key in **3**; click the ✔ **Enter** box in the Formula Bar. Copy this across to **SEP** as follows. Position the mouse pointer at the bottom right edge of the active cell (**H6**) until it changes to a ✛ (cross); click and drag the mouse to **J6**; release the mouse button; the figure 3 should be copied into the next two cells.

4 In cell **H7** key in **6**; click the ✔ **Enter** box in the Formula Bar. Copy this across to **SEP** as follows. Position the mouse pointer at the bottom right edge of the active cell (**H7**) until it changes to a ✛ (cross); click and drag the mouse across to **J7**; release the mouse button. The figure 6 should be copied into the next two cells.

5 As the other figures are not yet available for the rest of the cars, projected figures are to be used for JUL, AUG and SEP. The figures for the SALOON 4DR are to be based on the CABRIOLET. Select the range from **H6** to **J6** and drag it upwards to extend the range to include from **H5** to **J5**; from the Menu Bar, select **E**dit, F**i**ll, **U**p. The figure 3 should be copied upwards.

6 The projected figures for the other cars will be based on the HATCHBACK 3DR. Select the range from **H7** to **J7** and drag it downwards to extend the range to include from **H7** to **J12**, as indicated in Figure 3.6; from the Menu Bar, select **E**dit, F**i**ll, **D**own. The figure 6 should be copied downwards.

7 Select cell **K5**. You will find that the formula which appears in the Formula Bar does not include the three new columns, as these were added outside the original range of the formula. From the Tool Bar, select the **Autosum** icon; check that the formula **=SUM(B5:J5)** is displayed; click the ✔ **Enter** box in the Formula Bar.

8 This new formula now needs to be copied down the column since the rest will also need updating. With cell **K5** still selected, click and drag down to **K13**; from the Menu Bar, select **E**dit, F**i**ll, **D**own. Click in some of the cells in column **K** to see how the formula has now been adjusted.

9 Select cell **G13**. Since the two new rows inserted were *within* the range of the formula, the figures for these have been included in the calculation. Click **G13** and drag to **J13**; from the Menu Bar, select **E**dit, F**i**ll, **R**ight.

10 Select cell **K14**. Since two more car types have been included the total now needs to be divided by 8 to find the **AVERAGE**. Key in **=K13/8**; click the ✔ **Enter** box in the Formula Bar.

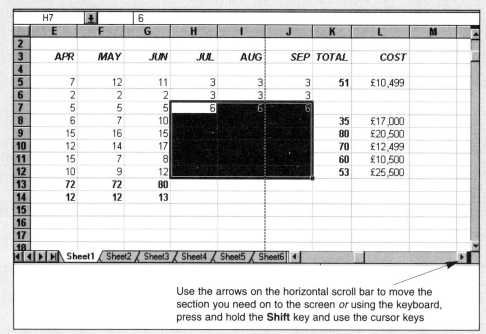

H7	↓		6						
	E	F	G	H	I	J	K	L	M
2									
3	*APR*	*MAY*	*JUN*	*JUL*	*AUG*	*SEP*	*TOTAL*	*COST*	
4									
5	7	12	11	3	3	3	51	£10,499	
6	2	2	2	3	3	3			
7	5	5	5	6	6	6			
8	6	7	10				35	£17,000	
9	15	16	15				80	£20,500	
10	12	14	17				70	£12,499	
11	15	7	8				60	£10,500	
12	10	9	12				53	£25,500	
13	72	72	80						
14	12	12	13						
15									
16									
17									
18									

Sheet1 / Sheet2 / Sheet3 / Sheet4 / Sheet5 / Sheet6

Use the arrows on the horizontal scroll bar to move the section you need on to the screen *or* using the keyboard, press and hold the **Shift** key and use the cursor keys

Figure 3.6   Replicating data

11 You now need to copy the new AVERAGE formula across the other cells. Select cell **K14**; click and drag to **B14**; from the Menu Bar, select **Edit**, **Fill**, **Left**.

12 In cell **L6** key in **19999** and in cell **L7** key in **10000**. Because you previously formatted this column for currency, the new data appears similar to the rest.

13 In **A18** change the filename to **TASK3F**.

14 From the Menu Bar, select **File**, **Print Preview** to check the appearance of your worksheet and to ensure that it corresponds with the key. Click once to zoom in and once again to zoom out. Click **Close** when finished.

15 From the Menu Bar, select **File**, **Save As** and save the file as **TASK3F**.

16 From the Tool Bar, select the 🖨 **Print** icon to print a copy of the worksheet.

Cut, copy and paste

Another method for copying or moving data is to use the Cut, Copy and Paste commands. These can be selected from the Menu Bar Edit option, from the Tool Bar Cut, Copy or Paste icons or from the keyboard. Data can be copied or moved around the current worksheet, to other worksheets and to other applications.

When you use the Cut command, Excel *moves* the data from the cell or cells that you have selected and places it on a clipboard, which is a temporary memory storage place. The original information is physically removed from its location and will be pasted to a new location.

When you use the Copy command, Excel takes a *copy* of the data in the cell or cells that you have selected and places it on a clipboard. The original information remains where it is and a copy of it can be pasted to a new location.

The information on the clipboard can be used again and again until you cut or copy something else – this will then replace the previous information as the clipboard can only store one piece of information at a time. As the clipboard is a temporary memory storage place, its contents will be lost when you exit Windows. If there is something that you need to use at a later stage, this will need to be pasted to a new file and saved to disk.

Cutting (moving) and pasting data
- Select the cell or cells containing the data to be cut (moved).
- From the Menu Bar, select:

<u>E</u>dit   Cu<u>t</u>

or, from the Tool Bar, select the ✂ **Cut** icon

or, from the keyboard, select **Ctrl/X**.

The range which is to be cut is highlighted by a wavering dashed line. The message 'Select destination and press ENTER or choose Paste' appears at the bottom of the screen in the Status Bar. The data will be physically removed from its original location and placed on the clipboard.

- Select the cell at the top left corner of the area where you want the data to appear. Although you do not need to select the entire paste area, you do need to ensure that the area to which you move or copy data is the same size.
- From the Menu Bar, select:

<u>E</u>dit   <u>P</u>aste

or, from the Tool Bar, select the 📋 **Paste** icon

or, from the keyboard, select **Ctrl/V**.

- Click anywhere to deselect.

Don't forget, if you select the wrong item, click anywhere to deselect. If you cut, copy or paste incorrectly, use the Undo function by either selecting from the Menu Bar **<u>E</u>dit**, **<u>U</u>ndo**, *or* from the Tool Bar the ↺ **Undo** icon, *or* from the keyboard press **Ctrl/Z**.

Copying and pasting data
- Select the cell or cells containing the data to be copied.
- From the Menu Bar, select:

<u>E</u>dit   <u>C</u>opy

or, from the Tool Bar, select the 📋 **Copy** icon

or, from the keyboard, select **Ctrl/C**.

The range which is to be copied is highlighted by a wavering dashed line. The message 'Select destination and press ENTER or choose Paste' appears at the bottom of the screen in the Status Bar. A copy will be taken of the data and placed on the clipboard, leaving the original information where it is.

- Select the cell at the top left corner of the area where you want the data to appear. Although you do not need to select the entire paste area, you do need to ensure that the area to which you move or copy data is the same size.
- From the Menu Bar, select:

<u>E</u>dit   <u>P</u>aste

or, from the Tool Bar, select the 📋 **Paste** icon

or, from the keyboard, select **Ctrl/V**.

- Click anywhere to deselect.

The range that has been copied will remain highlighted by a wavering dashed line (enabling you to paste further copies elsewhere) until you and begin to key new data into the worksheet again.

Cut, Copy and Paste can also be accessed by selecting a cell or cells, clicking the right mouse button and selecting the required menu option from the pop up menu.

Drag and drop

Using the mouse, you can also move and copy data within the worksheet by the drag and drop method.

Dragging and dropping

• Select the cell or cells containing the data to be moved or copied.

• Click and drag to select the range.

• Release the mouse.

• *To move data*:
  Position the mouse pointer at the edge of the cell or range of cells so that it changes from a ✛ (cross) to a 🔖 (pointer arrow).

  Click and drag the range to the new location.

  Or

• *To copy data*:
  Press and hold down the **Ctrl** button on the keyboard and position the mouse pointer at the edge of the cell or range of cells so that it changes from a ✛ (cross) to a 🔖 (pointer arrow).

  Click and drag the range to the new location.

When you click, note the explanation at the bottom left of the screen, informing you to 'Drag to move cells' or 'Drag to copy cell contents'. Note also that as you move the range it appears as a grey outline block as shown in Figure 3.7.

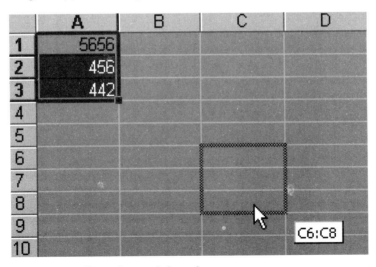

Figure 3.7 Dragging and dropping

Task 3G

As you know, you have saved your most recent file TASK3F to the disk in Drive A. The worksheet on your screen is a *copy* of this file. You are now going to work on this copy of TASK3F on your screen, to practise the use of cut, copy and paste. When you have finished, you will close this copy of TASK3F but not save the changes. Your original file will still be safely stored on your disk and will be unaffected by this work.

1 Practise cut, copy and paste as follows:
   - Select the range from **A3** to **J3**; click ✂ **Cut**; select **A2**, click 📋 **Paste**; deselect by clicking anywhere.
   - Select cell **A13**, click ⎘ **Copy**; select cell **M3**, click 📋 **Paste**. With cell **M3** still selected, position the mouse pointer at the edge of this cell so that it changes to a ↖ (pointer arrow); click and drag to cell **A15**.
   - Select cell **A17**; press the **Delete** button on the keyboard to delete its contents.
   - Select the range from **A5** to **A12**; position the mouse pointer at the edge of this range so that it changes to a ↖ (pointer arrow); click and drag to **A20–A27**.
   - Select the range from **A20** to **A27**; position the mouse pointer at the edge of this range so that it changes to a ↖ (pointer arrow); click and drag it back to **A5–A12**. **Deselect**.
   - Select cell **A18**. Position the mouse pointer at the edge of this cell so that it changes to a ↖ (pointer arrow); click and drag it to cell **B17**. You will find that it extends across the next two columns. If these columns contained information then the task name would not be completely displayed and you would have to widen its column accordingly.

2 From the Menu Bar, select **File**, **Close**; when the dialogue box prompts you to 'Save changes in TASK3F?' click **No**. The file will be closed and cleared from your screen.

Generate new values

You will often need to generate new values by adding, subtracting, multiplying or dividing certain items by others. We are now going to consider some more complicated formulae to enable you to do this. First we will create a new workbook and then copy some of the contents from TASK3F into it, to avoid having to key in the same information.

Task 3H

1 Open the file **TASK3F** by clicking on the 📂 **Open** icon on the Tool Bar. From the Open dialogue box, select the file **TASK3F** and click **OK**.

2 Select the range from **A1** *down to* **L12** and from the Tool Bar click the ⎘ **Copy** icon.

3 From the Tool Bar, select 🗋 **New** workbook to open a new file.

4 Ensure that cell **A1** is selected and click 📋 **Paste** to paste the copy on the new workbook. **Deselect**.

   You will notice that the worksheet is pasted on to the new workbook according to the default settings of that workbook, i.e. the column width is 8.43. However it retains the alignment, character size and font formatting.

5 Click column **A** heading button; from the Menu Bar, select **Format, Column, Width**; key in **16** to ensure the column is widened sufficiently to display the cell entries; click **OK**.

6 Select the range from **B1** *down to* **K12**; from the Menu Bar, select **Edit, Clear, All** to clear out the contents.

7 Select the range **L3–L12**; position the mouse pointer at the edge of this range so that it changes to a ☐ (pointer arrow); click and drag to **E3–E12**; **deselect**.

8 Key in the data in Figure 3.8 exactly as it appears.

	A	B	C	D	E	F	G	H
1	**VEHICLE SALES**							
2								
3	*TYPE*	TOTAL	TOTAL	ANNUAL	*COST*	STOCK	SELLING	PROFIT
4		JAN-JUN	JUL-DEC	TOTAL	PRICE	VALUE	PRICE	PER CAR
5	SALOON 4DR	51	63		£10,499		11999	
6	CABRIOLET	12	14		£19,999		22999	
7	HATCHBACK 3DR	30	49		£10,000		11499	
8	COUPE	35	38		£17,000		19499	
9	CAMPER	80	67		£20,500		21999	
10	ESTATE	70	63		£12,499		14499	
11	HATCHBACK 5DR	60	59		£10,500		11999	
12	OFF ROADER	53	46		£25,500		28499	
13	TOTAL							
14	AVERAGE							
15								

Figure 3.8   Generating new values – Task 3H

9 Select the range **A3** *down to* **H4**; position the mouse pointer at the edge of this range so that it changes to a ☐ (pointer arrow); click and drag to **A2–H3**; **deselect**.

10 Select cell **E2**; from the Menu Bar, select **Edit, Clear, Formats**.

11 Select the range **B2–H3**. From the Tool Bar, select the following icons:

 Bold   **Italic**   **Align Right**

12 The ANNUAL TOTAL is calculated by *adding* the TOTAL JAN-JUN to TOTAL JUL-DEC. Select cell **D5** and enter the formula **=B5+C5**. Click the ✔ **Enter** box in the Formula Bar.

13 Replicate (i.e. copy) this formula down to **D12** as follows to display the ANNUAL TOTAL for the other car types. Select cell **D5**; click and drag downwards to **D12** to highlight the range; click **Edit, Fill, Down**.

14 The STOCK VALUE is calculated by *multiplying* the ANNUAL TOTAL by the COST PRICE. Select cell **F5** and enter the formula **=D5*E5**. Click the ✔ **Enter** box in the Formula Bar.

15 Replicate this formula down to **F12** as follows to display the STOCK VALUE for the other car types. Select cell **F5**; click and drag downwards to **F12** to highlight the range; click **Edit, Fill, Down**.

16 To ensure consistency in the layout of the cells containing currency, position the mouse pointer on column **E** heading button and click and drag to select *also* **F**, **G** and **H** heading buttons. From the Menu Bar, select **Format, Cells, Number**. From the **Category** box select **Currency**; from **Decimal places**, select **0**; from **Symbol**, select **£ English (British)**.

17 You will now need to widen some of these columns. Position the mouse pointer between **F** and **G** column heading buttons until it changes into a double-headed arrow and double-click.

18 The PROFIT PER CAR is calculated by *subtracting* the COST PRICE from the SELLING PRICE. Select cell **H5** and enter the formula **=G5-E5**. Click the ✔ **Enter** box in the Formula Bar.

19 Replicate this formula down to **H12** as follows to display the PROFIT PER CAR for the other car types. Select cell **H5**; click and drag towards to **H12** to highlight the range; click **Edit, Fill, Down**; deselect.

20 Select cell **B13** and from the Tool Bar click on the Σ **Autosum** icon to total the TOTAL JAN–JUL for all the car types. Check that the formula **=SUM(B5:B12)** is displayed. Click the ✔ **Enter** box in the Formula Bar.

21 Replicate this formula across to **H13** as follows to display the rest of the totals in row 13. Select the range from **B13** to **H13**; click **Edit, Fill, Right**. Select the range from **E13** to **H13**; format for currency as follows. From the Menu Bar, select **Format, Cells, Number**. From the **Category** box select **Currency**; from **Decimal places**, select **0**; from **Symbol**, select **£ English (British)**. Position the mouse pointer between **F** and **G** column heading buttons until it changes into a double-headed arrow and double-click to widen column F.

22 The AVERAGE number of cars sold in JAN–JUN is calculated by *dividing* the TOTAL by the number of car types, i.e. 8. Select cell **B14** and enter the formula **=B13/8**. Click the ✔ **Enter** box in the Formula Bar.

23 Replicate this formula across to **D14** as follows to display these average figures also. Select cell **B14**; click and drag across to **D14** to highlight the range; click **Edit, Fill, Right**. With this range still highlighted change the numbers to integers by clicking three times on the Decrease Decimal button. The numbers should now appear as integers (i.e. whole numbers).

24 Select cell **A16** and enter your name; select cell **A17** and enter the filename **TASK3H**.

25 From the Menu Bar, select **File, Print Preview** to check the appearance of your worksheet and to ensure that it corresponds with the key. Click once to zoom in and once again to zoom out. Click **Close** when finished.

26 From the Menu Bar, select **File, Save As** and save the file as **TASK3H**.

27 From the Menu Bar, select **File, Print** to print a copy of the worksheet.

Display formulae

The default setting in Excel displays the data or results of formulae in cells rather than the actual formulae themselves. It is only when a specific cell is selected that its formula can be seen in the Formula Bar. Sometimes you may need to view and print out the formulae of all the cells and this can be done as follows.

Displaying formulae
- From the Menu Bar, select:

Tools   **Options**

The Options dialogue box, similar to the one in Figure 3.9, will be displayed.

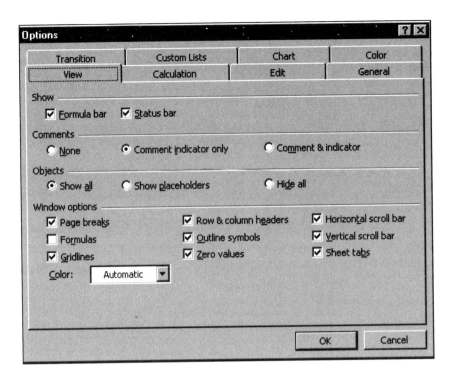

Figure 3.9   Options dialogue box

- Select the **View** tab.

- From the **Window Options** column click on the checkbox beside **Formulae** to display √.

- Click **OK.**

The formulae will now be shown in the cells and the columns will be widened automatically to display them fully. Please note that if text in a cell should extend across another column this will appear truncated when formulae are displayed.

You can print this display by following the usual method for printing (see page 33).

If you wish to turn off the formulae and display just the data again, follow the instructions above and from the **Window Options** click on the checkbox beside **Formulae** to remove the √.

Task 3 I

1   With **TASK3H** still on screen, from the Menu Bar, select **Tools**, **Options** and click the **View** tab; from the **Window Options** column click on the checkbox beside **Formulae** to display √ and click **OK**. Your worksheet will now be shown with all the formulae displayed and the columns will be widened automatically to accommodate this.

2   Select cell **A17** and amend the filename TASK3H to **TASK3I**.

3   From the Menu Bar, select **File**, **Print Preview** to check the appearance of your worksheet and to ensure that it corresponds with the key. Click once to zoom in and once again to zoom out. You will find that it spreads across three pages and you will have to select the **Next** and **Previous** buttons at the top left of the screen to look at each page. In the next unit you will be shown how to get it to fit on to one page but this is not required at this stage. Click **Close** when finished.

4   From the Menu Bar, select **File**, **Save As** and save the file as **TASK3I**.

5 From the Menu Bar, select **File**, **Print** to print a copy of the worksheet.

6 From the Menu Bar, select **File**, **Close** to close the file. The file TASK3F which was behind the TASK3I worksheet window is now revealed again. From the Menu Bar, select **File**, **Close** to close the file and then select **File**, **Exit** to exit from Excel.

Don't forget to complete the Record of Progress sheet to indicate that you have finished this unit successfully. If you feel that you would like to do further work to consolidate what you have learned so far, then try Extra Practice Task 3A and B.

Extra Practice Task 3A ▼ ▲

1 Open **EPTASK2**; select the range of cells **A3–A12**; right align these headings by selecting from the Menu Bar **Format**, **Cells**, **Alignment** and from the **Horizontal** column, select the **Right** button; click **OK**; with the range **A3–A12** still selected, centre these headings by clicking once on the ▤ **Centre** icon; **deselect**, i.e. click once outside the highlighted area.

2 Select the range of cells **A1–I1**; centre the main heading across these cells by clicking one on the ▦ **Centre Across Columns** icon on the Tool Bar; click on the ▣ **Bold** icon to embolden the main heading; then **deselect**.

3 Select cells **A15** and **A16**; click on the ▤ **Centre** icon on the Tool Bar; then **deselect**.

4 Select the range of cells **A3–A12** and clear the formats as follows. From the Menu Bar, select **Edit**, **Clear**, **Formats**.

5 Select cell **A1**; click on to the right of the Font Size button and select **16** to increase the font size to make the title longer.

6 Select row **3** by clicking on row **3** heading button; embolden and italicise these headings by selecting from the Menu Bar **Format**, **Cells**, **Font**; from the **Font style** column, select **Bold Italic**; click **OK**; then **deselect**.

7 Select the range from **H5** to **H10**, i.e. TOTAL figures; click on the ▣ **Bold** icon; then **deselect**; place the mouse pointer between column **I** and **J** heading buttons until it changes to a double-headed arrow and double-click to widen column I automatically.

8 Select rows **11** and **12**, which contain TOTAL and AVERAGE, by positioning the mouse pointer over row **11** heading button and click and drag it down to row **12** heading button; click on the ▣ **Bold** icon; then **deselect**.

9 Double the width of row **15** by placing the mouse pointer on the bottom edge of row **15** heading button until it changes to a double-headed arrow. Drag downwards until the row is double the height of the others – note the height shown in the reference bar should have increased from 12.75 to about 25.5. Don't worry if it is not exact – just keep practising your mouse control!

10 Select row **15** heading button to highlight the entire row and from the Menu Bar, select **Format**, **Row**, **Height**. Key in **12.75**; click **OK**.

11 The entry LIQUORICE should be **ROCK**. Please amend.

12 The TOTAL PA is no longer required so delete the column containing this data as follows. Select column **I** heading button to highlight the entire column; from the Menu Bar, select **Edit**, **Delete**. **Deselect**.

13 In cell **I3** key in a new column heading, **COST**; click once on the ✔ **Enter** box in the Formula Bar. This will automatically appear in bold and italics as you have formatted this row earlier. With cell **I 3** still selected, right align this by clicking once on the ▤ **Align Right** icon on the Tool Bar.

14 Enter the following figures in column **I**, pressing the ↓ down cursor arrow key to move you down from cell to cell:

in row **5** (BUTTER TOFFEES)	**0.75**
in row **6** (FUDGE)	**0.65**
in row **7** (GUMS)	**0.55**
in row **8** (JELLIES)	**0.65**
in row **9** (MINTOS)	**0.65**
in row **10** (ROCK)	**0.45**

15 Since the heading has only been centred across columns **A–H** and as there will be many more alterations to the worksheet, it is simpler to left align it is as follows. Select **A1**; click the ▤ **Align Left** icon on the Tool Bar. Let us also make the rest of the worksheet consistent as follows. Select **A15** and **A16**; click the ▤ **Align Left** icon on the Tool Bar.

16 Select cell **H11** and calculate the overall **TOTAL** packs of confectionery by clicking on the ∑ **Autosum** button; ensure that **=SUM(H5:H10)** is displayed in the Formula Bar (if not, key in this formula); click once on the ✔ **Enter** box in the Formula Bar.

17 Select cell **H12** and key in the formula **=H11/6** to calculate the average number of packets sold in this period; click once on the ✔ **Enter** box in the Formula Bar.

18 The sales of packets of **FUDGE** are inaccurate and need to be altered. Amend as follows. Press the → right cursor arrow key to move you across from cell to cell:

JUL	AUG	SEP	OCT	NOV	DEC
11	**12**	**17**	**17**	**20**	**22**

19 Select the range **B12–H12**, the AVERAGE figures. From the Menu Bar, select **Format**, **Cells**, **Number**. From **Category** select **Number**, from **Decimal Places** select **0**; click **OK**.

20 Position the mouse pointer on **I5**; click and drag it to **I 10** to select the range containing the data on **COST**. From the Menu Bar, select **Format**, **Cells**, **Number**. From the **Category** box select **Currency**; from the **Symbol** box select **£ British (English)**; from **Decimal Places** select **2**; click **OK**; deselect.

21 Insert two new rows between **FUDGE** and **BUTTER TOFFEES** by clicking on row **6** heading button and also drag downwards to select row **7**; from the Menu Bar, select **Insert**, **Rows**. Select cell **A6** and key in **NUTTY TOFFEES**; select cell **A7** and key in **NUTTY FUDGE**.

22 Insert three new columns between **DEC** and **TOTAL** by clicking on column **H** heading button and also drag across to select columns **I** and **J**; from the Menu Bar, select **Insert**, **Columns**. Enter the following data, pressing the → right cursor arrow key to move you across from cell to cell as follows. Select cell **H3** and key in **JAN**; select cell **I3** and key in **FEB**; select **J3** and key in **MAR**.

23 Place the mouse pointer between **A** and **B** column heading buttons until it appears as a double-headed arrow and double-click to widen column A to fit the confectionery names and the title. From the Menu Bar, select **File**, **Print Preview**; click once on the top right of the page to zoom in; notice that not all the columns are shown; click once again to zoom out; click **Next** to view the information which has extended to page 2; click **Close**.

24 You will find that a vertical dashed line has appeared between columns **J** and **K**. This indicates that your worksheet now extends to a second page. In order to make it all fit on one page, you can decrease column **A** width as follows. Click column **A** heading button to select the entire column; from the Menu Bar, select **Format**, **Column**, **Width**; key in **17** to ensure the column is sufficiently wide to display the cell entries; click **OK**; **deselect**.

25 In cell **B6** key in **20**; click the ✔ **Enter** box in the Formula Bar. As there were only 20 packs sold per month from JUL to DEC, you can use the **Fill** command to copy this across as follows. Select **B6**; click and drag to **G6**; from the Menu Bar, select **Edit**, **Fill**, **Right**. The figure 20 should be copied into each column.

26 In cell **B7** key in **15**; click the ✔ **Enter** box in the Formula Bar. As there were 15 packs sold per month from JUL to DEC, you can use the **Fill** command to copy this across as follows. Select **B7**; click and drag to **G7**; from the Menu Bar, select **Edit**, **Fill**, **Right**. The figure 15 should be copied into each column.

27 In cell **H6** key in **13**; click the ✔ **Enter** box in the Formula Bar. Copy this across to **MAR** as follows. Position the mouse pointer at the bottom right edge of the active cell (**H6**) until it changes to a ⊕ (cross); click and drag the mouse across to **J6**; then, release the mouse button. The figure 13 should be copied into the next two cells.

28 In cell **H7** key in **16**; click the ✔ **Enter** box in the Formula Bar. Copy this across to **MAR** as follows. Position the mouse pointer at the bottom right edge of the active cell (**H7**) until it changes to a ⊕ (cross); click and drag the mouse across to **J7**; then, release the mouse button. The figure 16 should be copied into the next two cells.

29 As the other figures are not yet available, projected figures are to be used for **JAN**, **FEB** and **MAR**. The figures for the **BUTTER TOFFEES** are to be based on the **NUTTY TOFFEES**. Select the range from **H6** to **J6** and drag it upwards to extend the range to include **H5–J5**; from the Menu Bar, select **Edit**, **Fill**, **Up**. The figure 13 should be copied upwards.

30 The projected figures for the other items will be based on the **NUTTY FUDGE**. Select the range from **H7** to **J7** and drag it downwards to extend the range to include from **H12** to **J12**; from the Menu Bar, select **Edit**, **Fill**, **Down**. The figure 16 should be copied downwards.

31 Select cell **K5**. You will find that the formula which appears in the Formula Bar does not include the three new columns. From the Tool Bar, select the Σ **Autosum** icon; check that the formula **=SUM(B5:J5)** is displayed; click once on the ✔ **Enter** box in the Formula Bar.

32 This new formula now needs to be copied down the column. With **K5** still selected, click and drag down to **K13**; from the Menu Bar, select **Edit**, **Fill**, **Down**. Click in some of the cells in column **K** just to see how the formula has now been adjusted.

33 Select cell **G13**. Since the two new rows inserted were *within* the range of the formula, the figures for these have been included in the calculation. Click **G13** and drag to **J13**; from the Menu Bar, select **Edit**, **Fill**, **Right**.

34 Select **B14**. Since two more confectionery types have been included the total now needs to be divided by 8 to find the **AVERAGE**. Key in **=B13/8**; click once on the ✔ **Enter** box in the Formula Bar.

35 You now need to copy the new **AVERAGE** formula across the other cells. Select cell **B14**; click and drag to **K14**; from the Menu Bar, select **Edit**, **Fill**, **Right**.

36 In cell **L6** key in **0.80** and in cell **L7** key in **0.70**. Notice how the new data appears similar to the rest because you previously formatted this column for currency.

37 In **A18** amend the filename to **EPTASK3A**. From the Menu Bar, select **File**, **Print Preview** to check the appearance of your worksheet and to ensure that it corresponds with the key. Click once to zoom in and once again to zoom out. Click **Close** when finished.

38 From the Menu Bar, select **File**, **Save As** and save the file as **EPTASK3A**.

39 From the Tool Bar, select the 🖨 **Print** icon to print a copy of the worksheet.

–   **Extra Practice Task 3B**   ▲ ▼

1 With **EPTASK3A** still on screen, select the range from **A1** *down to* **L12** and from the Tool Bar click the 📋 **Copy** icon.

2 From the Tool Bar, select 🗋 **New** workbook to open a new file.

3 Ensure that cell **A1** is selected and click 📋 **Paste** to paste the copy on the new workbook. **Deselect**.

4 Click column **A** heading button; from the Menu Bar, select **Format**, **Column**, **Width**; key in **17**; click **OK**; click anywhere to deselect.

5 Select the range from **B1** *down to* **K12**; from the Menu Bar, select **Edit**, **Clear**, **All** to clear out the contents.

6 Select the range **L3–L12**; position the mouse pointer at the edge of this range so that it changes to a ▨ (pointer arrow); click and drag to **E3–E12**; **deselect**.

7 Key in the data in Figure 3.10 exactly as it appears.

	A	B	C	D	E	F	G	H
1	**SALES OF CONFECTIONERY**							
2								
3	*ITEM*	TOTAL	TOTAL	ANNUAL	*COST*	STOCK	SELLING	PROFIT
4		JAN–JUN	JUL–DEC	TOTAL	PRICE	VALUE	PRICE	PER PACK
5	BUTTER TOFFEES	88	110		£0.75		0.85	
6	NUTTY TOFFEES	96	120		£0.80		0.9	
7	NUTTY FUDGE	92	90		£0.70		0.8	
8	FUDGE	106	99		£0.65		0.75	
9	GUMS	80	70		£0.55		0.6	
10	JELLIES	85	73		£0.65		0.75	
11	MINTOS	110	105		£0.65		0.75	
12	ROCK	98	90		£0.45		0.5	
13	TOTAL							
14	AVERAGE							
15								

Figure 3.10   Data – Extra Practice Task 3B

8 Select the range **A3–H4**; position the mouse pointer at the edge of this range so that it changes to a ▨ (pointer arrow); click and drag to **A2–H3**; **deselect**.

9 Select cell **E2**; from the Menu Bar, select **Edit**, **Clear**, **Formats**.

10 Select the range **B2–H3**. From the Tool Bar, select the following icons

         B   *I*   ≣

     Bold   **Italic**   **Align Right**

11 The ANNUAL TOTAL is calculated by *adding* the TOTAL JAN–JUN to TOTAL JUL–DEC. Select cell **D5** and enter the formula **=B5+C5**. Click once on the ✔ **Enter** box in the Formula Bar.

12 Replicate (i.e. copy) this formula down to D12 as follows to display the ANNUAL TOTAL for the other confectionery items. Select cell **D5**; click and drag downwards to **D12** to highlight the range; click **Edit**, **Fill**, **Down**.

13 The STOCK VALUE is calculated by *multiplying* the ANNUAL TOTAL by the COST PRICE. Select cell **F5** and enter the formula **=D5*E5**. Click once on the ✔ **Enter** box in the Formula Bar.

14 Replicate this formula down to F12 as follows to display the STOCK VALUE for the other confectionery items. Select cell **F5**; click and drag downwards to **F12** to highlight the range; click **Edit**, **Fill**, **Down**.

15 To ensure consistency in the layout of the cells containing currency, position the mouse pointer on column **E** heading button and click and drag to select also **F**, **G** and **H** heading buttons. From the Menu Bar, select **Format**, **Cells**, **Number**. From the **Category** box select **Currency**; from the **Symbol** box select **£ English (British)**; from **Decimal places** select **2** – this may already be displayed – and click **OK**; **deselect**.

16 Position the mouse pointer between **H** and **I** column heading buttons until it changes into a double-headed arrow and double-click.

17 The PROFIT PER PACK is calculated by *subtracting* the COST PRICE from the SELLING PRICE. Select cell **H5** and enter the formula **=G5-E5**. Click once on the ✔ **Enter** box in the Formula Bar.

18 Replicate this formula down to **H12** as follows to display the PROFIT PER PACK for the other confectionery items. Select cell **H5**; click and drag downwards to **H12** to highlight the range; click **Edit**, **Fill**, **Down**. **Deselect**.

19 Select cell **B13** and from the Tool Bar click on the Σ **Autosum** icon to total the TOTAL JAN–JUN for all the item types. Check that the formula **=SUM(B5:B12)** is displayed; click once on the ✔ **Enter** box in the Formula Bar.

Replicate this formula across to **H13** as follows to display the rest of the totals in row **13**. Select the range from **B13** to **H13**; click **Edit**, **Fill**, **Right**. Select the range from **E13** to **H13**. Format for currency as follows. From the Menu Bar, select **Format**, **Cells**, **Number**; from the **Category** box select **Currency**; from the **Symbol** box select **£ English (British)**; from **Decimal Places** select **2** – this may already be displayed – and click **OK**; **deselect**.

20 The AVERAGE number of packs sold in JAN–JUN is calculated by *dividing* the TOTAL by the number of confectionery items, i.e. 8. Select cell **B14** and enter the formula **=B13/8**. Click once on the ✔ **Enter** box in the Formula Bar.

21 Replicate this formula across to **D14** as follows to display these average figures also. Select cell **B14**; click and drag across to **D14** to highlight the range; click **Edit**, **Fill**, **Right**. With this range still highlighted change the numbers to integers by clicking three times on the **Decrease Decimal** icon.

22 In cell **A16** and enter your name; select cell **A17** and enter the filename **EPTASK3B**.

23 From the Menu Bar, select **File**, **Print Preview** to check the appearance of your worksheet and to ensure that it corresponds with the key. Click once to zoom in and once again to zoom out. Click **Close** when finished.

24 From the Menu Bar, select **File**, **Save As** and save the file as **EPTASK3B**.

25 From the Tool Bar, select the 🖨 **Print** icon to print a copy of the worksheet.

26 From the Menu Bar, select **Tools**, **Options** and click the **View** tab; from the **Window Options** column click on the checkbox beside **Formulas** to display √ and click **OK**. Your worksheet will now be shown with all the formulae displayed and the columns will be automatically widened to accommodate this. You will find that if text in column A extends across into the next column, this will appear truncated when the formulae are displayed.

27 Select cell **A17** and amend the filename EPTASK3B to **EPTASK3C**.

28 From the Menu Bar, select **File**, **Print Preview** to check the appearance of your worksheet and to ensure that it corresponds with the key. Click once to zoom in and once again to zoom out. You will find that it spreads across three pages and you will have to select the **Next** and **Previous** buttons at the top left of the screen to look at each page. In the next unit you will be shown how to get it to fit on to one page but this is not required at this stage. Click **Close** when finished.

29 From the Menu Bar, select **File**, **Save As** and save the file as **EPTASK3C**.

30 From the Tool Bar, select the **Print** icon to print a copy of the worksheet.

31 From the Menu Bar, select **File**, **Close** to close the file. The file EPTASK3A which was behind EPTASK3C worksheet window is now revealed again. From the Menu Bar, select **File**, **Close** to close the file and then select **File**, **Exit** to exit from Excel.

Don't forget to complete the Record of Progress sheet to indicate that you have finished this unit successfully.

▬ YOYO3A (You're On Your Own Task 3A) ▼ ▲

1 Open **YOYO2**; select the range of cells **A3–A12** and, using the Menu Bar, right align these headings; with the range **A3–A12** still selected, using the Tool Bar, centre these headings.

2 Select the range of cells **A1–I1** and, using the Tool Bar, centre the main heading across these cells and embolden it.

3 Select cells **A15** and **A16** and, using the Tool Bar, centre the data.

4 Select the range of cells **A3–A12** and, using **Edit** from the Menu Bar, clear the formats.

5 Select cell **A1** and use the Tool Bar to clear the formats and then change the font size of the heading to 16.

6 Select row **3** and, using the Menu Bar, embolden and italicise these headings.

7 Select the range containing the **TOTAL** bottle figures and, using the Tool Bar, embolden these figures; place the mouse pointer between column **I** and **J** heading buttons until it changes to a double-headed arrow and widens column **I** automatically.

8 Select rows containing the **TOTAL** and **AVERAGE** figures for each month and, using the Tool Bar, embolden the data.

9 Double the width of row **15** by placing the mouse pointer on the bottom edge of row **15** heading button until it changes to a double-headed arrow and increase it so the height shown in the reference bar increases from 12.75 to about **25.5**.

10 Select row **15** heading button to highlight the entire row and, using **Format** from the Menu Bar, format the row to a height of **12.75**.

11 The entry SEMILLON should be **SAUVIGNON**. Please amend.

12 The **TOTAL PA** is no longer required so delete the column containing this data.

13 In cell **I3** key in a new column heading, **COST**; this will automatically appear in bold and italics as you have formatted this row earlier. With cell **I3** still selected, using the Tool Bar, right align this data.

14 Enter the following figures in column **I**:
in row 5 **CHABLIS**   5.30
in row 6 **CLARET**   3.30

in row 7 **MERLOT**	1.90
in row 8 **SHIRAZ CABERNET**	2.60
in row 9 **RIOJA**	4.60
in row 10 **SAUVIGNON**	2.60

15 Since the heading has only been centred across columns **A–H** and as there will be many more alterations to the worksheet, using the Tool Bar, simply left align it and also make the rest of the worksheet consistent by selecting **A15** and **A16** and left align the data in these cells.

16 Select the appropriate cell and calculate the overall **TOTAL** bottles of wine using **Autosum**.

17 Select the appropriate cell and key in a formula to calculate the average number of bottles sold in this period (**TOTAL/6**).

18 The sales of bottles of **CLARET** are inaccurate and need to be altered. Please amend as follows:

JUL	AUG	SEP	OCT	NOV	DEC
21	16	17	18	20	24

19 Select the range containing **AVERAGE** figures and, using **Format** from the Menu Bar, format the numbers to integer (no decimal places).

20 Select the range containing the data on **COST** and, using **Format** from the Menu Bar, format the numbers for **Currency** to two decimal places.

21 Use **Insert** from the Menu Bar to insert two new rows between **CHABLIS** and **CLARET** (remember first to click on row **6** heading button and also drag downwards to select row **7**). Select cell **A6** and key in **BEAUJOLAIS**; select cell **A7** and key in **BURGUNDY**.

22 Use **Insert** from the Menu Bar to insert three new columns between **DEC** and **TOTAL** (remember first to click on column **H** heading button and also drag across to select columns **I** and **J**). Enter the following data: select cell **H3** and key in **JAN**; select cell **I3** and key in **FEB**; select **J3** and key in **MAR**.

23 Place the mouse pointer between **A** and **B** column heading buttons until it appears as a double-headed arrow and widen column **A** to fit the bottles names and the title. Use **File** from the Menu Bar to display **Print Preview**.

24 You will find that a vertical dashed line has appeared between the final columns. This indicates that your worksheet now extends to a second page. In order to make it all fit on one page, alter the column widths using the Menu Bar to ensure columns are sufficiently wide to display the data.

25 In cell **B6** key in **20**; as 20 bottles were sold per month from **JUL** to **DEC** use the **Fill** command (from **Edit** on the Menu Bar) to copy this across. The figure 20 should be copied into each column.

26 In cell **B7** key in **25**; as 25 bottles were sold per month from **JUL** to **DEC** use the **Fill** command (from **Edit** on the Menu Bar) to copy this across. The figure 25 should be copied into each column.

27 In cell **H6** key in **23**: copy this across to **MAR** by positioning the mouse pointer at the edge of the active cell until it changes to a ✚ (cross); click and drag across to **J6**; the figure 23 should be copied into the next two cells.

28 In cell **H7** key in **26**; copy this across to **MAR** by positioning the mouse pointer at the edge of the active cell until it changes to a ✚ (cross); click and drag across to **J7**; the figure **26** should be copied into the next two cells.

29 As the other figures are not yet available, projected figures are to be used for **JAN**, **FEB** and **MAR**. The figures for the **CHABLIS** are to be based on the **BEAUJOLAIS**. Select the range from **H6** to **J6** and drag it upwards to extend the range to include **H5–J5**; use the **Fill** command (from **Edit** on the Menu Bar) to copy the figure 23 upwards.

30 The projected figures for the other items will be based on the **BURGUNDY**. Select the range from **H7** to **J7** and drag it downwards to extend the range to include from **H12** to **J12**; use the **Fill** command (from **Edit** on the Menu Bar) to copy the figure 26 downwards.

31 Select cell **K5**. You will find that the formula which appears in the Formula Bar does not include the three new columns. From the Tool Bar use **Autosum** to ensure that the new formula includes the three new columns.

32 This new formula now needs to be copied down the column. With **K5** still selected, click and drag down to **K13**; use the **Fill** command (from **Edit** on the Menu Bar) to copy the formula downwards. Click in some of the cells in column **K** just to see how the formula has now been adjusted.

33 Select cell **G13**. Since the two new rows inserted were *within* the range of the formula, the figures for these have been included in the calculation. Click **G13** and drag to **J13**; use the **Fill** command (from **Edit** on the Menu Bar) to copy this formula to the right.

34 Select **B14**. Since two more rows have been included, alter the formula to calculate the average (**TOTAL/8**).

35 You now need to copy the **AVERAGE** formula across the other cells from cell **B14** to **K14**; use the **Fill** command (from **Edit** on the Menu Bar) to copy this formula to the right.

36 In cell **L6** key in **2.60** and in cell **L7** key in **3.30**. Notice how the new data appears similar to the rest because you previously formatted this column for currency.

37 In **A18** amend the filename to **YOYO3A**. Use **File** from the Menu Bar to display **Print Preview** to check the appearance of your worksheet and to ensure that it corresponds with the key.

38 Use **File** from the Menu Bar to save the file as **YOYO3A**.

39 Using the Tool Bar, print a copy of the worksheet.

□   **YOYO3B (You're On Your Own Task 3B)**   **▼ ▲**

1 With **YOYO3A** still on screen, select the range from **A1** *down to* **L12** and, using the Tool Bar, copy this range.

2 Using the Tool Bar, open a new file.

3 Ensure that cell **A1** is selected and paste the copy on the new workbook.

4 Click column **A** heading button; using the Menu Bar, format the column width to display the data fully.

5 Select the range from **B1** *down to* **K12**; using the Menu Bar, clear out the contents.

6 Select the range **L3–L12**; position the mouse pointer so that it changes to a (pointer arrow); drag **E3–E12**.

7 Key in the data shown in Figure 3.11 exactly as it appears.

	A	B	C	D	E	F	G	H
1	SALES OF POPULAR WINES							
2								
3	*BOTTLE*	TOTAL	TOTAL	ANNUAL	*COST*	STOCK	SELLING	PROFIT
4		JAN-JUN	JUL-DEC	TOTAL	PRICE	VALUE	PRICE	PER BOTTLE
5	CHABLIS	96	138		£5.30		13.25	
6	BEAUJOLAIS	120	138		£2.60		6.5	
7	BURGUNDY	150	156		£3.30		8.25	
8	CLARET	116	156		£3.30		8.25	
9	MERLOT	130	156		£1.90		4.75	
10	SHIRAZ CABERNET	155	156		£2.60		6.5	
11	RIOJA	143	156		£4.60		11.5	
12	SAUVIGNON	146	156		£2.60		6.5	
13	TOTAL							
14	AVERAGE							

Figure 3.11   YOYO 3B data

8   Select the range **A3–H4**; position the mouse pointer so that it changes to a (pointer arrow); drag the range to **A2–H3**.

9   Select cell **E2**; using the Menu Bar, clear the formats of this cell.

10 Select the range **B2–H3**. Using the Tool Bar, alter the data to bold italic and align right.

11 The annual total is calculated by adding the total Jan–Jun to the total Jul–Dec. Select **ANNUAL TOTAL** for **CHABLIS** and enter the appropriate formula.

12 Using **Edit** from the Menu Bar, replicate (i.e. copy) this formula down to **D12** to display the **ANNUAL TOTAL** for the other bottles (remember first to select cell **D5** and click and drag downwards to **D12** to highlight the range).

13 The stock value is calculated by multiplying the annual total by the cost price. Select **STOCK VALUE** for **CHABLIS** and enter the appropriate formula.

14 Using **Edit** from the Menu Bar, replicate this formula down to **F12** to display the **STOCK VALUE** for the other bottles (remember first to select cell **F5** and click and drag downwards to **F12** to highlight the range).

15 To ensure consistency in the layout of the cells containing currency, position the mouse pointer on column **E** heading button and click and drag to select also **F**, **G** and **H** heading buttons. Using **Format** from the Menu Bar, format the numbers for currency (displaying the £ sign) to two decimal places.

16 Position the mouse pointer between **H** and **I** column heading buttons until it changes into a double-headed arrow and widen column **H** to display the data fully.

17 The profit per bottle is calculated by subtracting the cost price from the selling price. Select **PROFIT PER BOTTLE** for **CHABLIS** and enter the appropriate formula.

18 Using **Edit** from the Menu Bar, replicate this formula down to **H12** to display the **PROFIT PER BOTTLE** for the other bottles (remember first to select cell **H5** and click and drag downwards to **H12** to highlight the range).

19 Select the **TOTAL** for TOTAL JAN-JUN and, from the Tool Bar, use **Autosum** to total the TOTAL JAN-JUN for all the bottles. Using **Edit** from the Menu Bar, replicate this formula across to **H13** to display the rest of the totals in row 13 (remember first to select the range from **B13** to **H13**). Select the range from **E13** to **H13** and use **Format** from the Menu Bar to format the numbers for currency (displaying the £ sign) to two decimal places.

20 The average number of packs sold in Jan–Jun is calculated by dividing the total by the number of bottles, i.e. 8. Select **AVERAGE** for **TOTAL JAN-JUN** and enter the appropriate formula.

21 Using **Edit** from the Menu Bar, replicate this formula to display the average figures in the rest of the columns (remember first to select the range from **B14** to **D14**). With the range still highlighted, use the Tool Bar to change the numbers to integer.

22 In cell **A16** enter your name; select **A17** and enter the filename **YOYO3B**.

23 Use **File** from the Menu Bar to display **Print Preview** to check the appearance of your worksheet and to ensure it corresponds with the key.

24 Use **File** from the Menu Bar to save the file as **YOYO3B**.

25 Using the Tool Bar, print a copy of the worksheet.

26 Use **File** from the Menu Bar to display the formulae. Your worksheet will now be shown with all the formulae displayed and the columns will be widened automatically to accommodate this. You may find that if text in column **A** extends across into the next column it will appear truncated when formulae are displayed.

27 Amend the filename YOYO3B to **YOYO3C**.

28 Use **File** from the Menu Bar to display **Print Preview** to check the appearance of your worksheet and to ensure that it corresponds with the key. In the next unit you will be shown how to get it to fit on to one page but this is not required at this stage.

29 Use **File** from the Menu Bar to save the file as **YOYO3C**.

30 Using the Tool Bar, print a copy of the worksheet.
31 Use **File** from the Menu Bar to close the file. The file YOYO3A which was behind YOYO3C worksheet window is now revealed again. Use **File** from the Menu Bar to close the file and then exit from Excel.

Don't forget to complete the Record of Progress sheet to indicate that you have finished this unit successfully.

Congratulations! You have now completed all the work necessary for you to be able to do the RSA Stage 1 CLAIT (spreadsheet) examination. Turn now to Section A Consolidation and work through the mock assignments to prepare you for your examination. There are no helpful suggestions about which menu/Tool Bar options or keyboard strokes you might use but you are allowed to refer to the Memory Jogger to meet CLAIT objectives and any notes that you might have made.

If you do not wish to do the examination preparation for CLAIT, then move on now to Unit 4.

consolidation

RSA CLAIT (Spreadsheets)

The CLAIT scheme was developed to encourage anyone to use computers and information technology effectively in common applications found in business and the home. It is designed so that anyone, whatever his or her age, can experience in a practical way the operations and use of computer and information technology.

The scheme is made up of 14 applications including spreadsheets. The mock assignments which follow will prepare you for the spreadsheet application in CLAIT.

Assessment

Assessment of the Spreadsheet Module is through an assignment, which is made up of practical tasks using a spreadsheet application, such as MS Excel. There are four elements of certification:

1 Create a spreadsheet and enter data.
2 Edit and manipulate a spreadsheet.
3 Use spreadsheet display features.
4 Save a spreadsheet, print its contents and exit application.

For each of these elements, there are assessment objectives. Assessment objectives are the operations you *must* be able to do to prove your ability, and the performance criteria define the level of accuracy to which these objectives must be carried out.

A maximum of three data entry errors in text is permitted, but numeric information must be entered with 100% accuracy.

Exam tips

1 An assignment must be completed within a two-hour period.

2 All instructions must be followed exactly.

3 The spreadsheet files should be saved under filenames that are concise and meaningful. The filenames below can be used for your assignments (e.g. SMOCKP1 is composed of S for spreadsheet, MOCK for mock, P1 for printout 1):

	Mock 1	*Mock 2*	*Final*
Spreadsheet Printout 1	SMOCK1P1	SMOCK2P1	SFINALP1
Spreadsheet Printout 2	SMOCK1P2	SMOCK2P2	SFINALP2
Spreadsheet Printout 3	SMOCK1P3	SMOCK2P3	SFINALP3

4 Make sure you key in your name and filename on each spreadsheet before you save and print it.

5 When an assignment has been completed, the printouts should be assembled in the correct order and handed to the tutor with the copy of the assignment.

6 There are two mock assignments to prepare you for the final assignment. The spreadsheet assignment for Mock 2 should not be commenced until Mock 1 has been checked for accuracy. Your printouts should match the keys exactly – otherwise you may fail an objective and therefore fail the entire assignment.

7 If you are not successful in the first assignment, a second completely fresh attempt is permitted.

8 You should not speak to anyone when you are working on an assignment and must not ask your tutor any questions.

9 You are permitted to use you own notes, centre-prepared manuals or manufacturers' manuals.

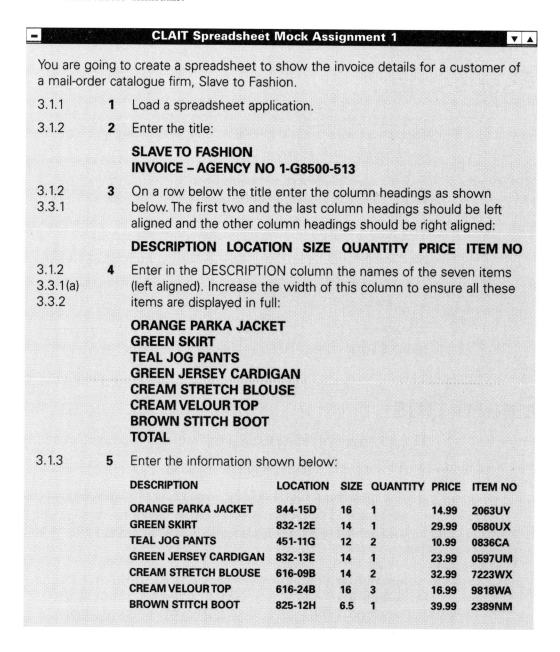

■	CLAIT Spreadsheet Mock Assignment 1	▼ ▲

You are going to create a spreadsheet to show the invoice details for a customer of a mail-order catalogue firm, Slave to Fashion.

3.1.1	**1**	Load a spreadsheet application.
3.1.2	**2**	Enter the title:

SLAVE TO FASHION
INVOICE – AGENCY NO 1-G8500-513

3.1.2 3.3.1	**3**	On a row below the title enter the column headings as shown below. The first two and the last column headings should be left aligned and the other column headings should be right aligned:

DESCRIPTION LOCATION SIZE QUANTITY PRICE ITEM NO

3.1.2 3.3.1(a) 3.3.2	**4**	Enter in the DESCRIPTION column the names of the seven items (left aligned). Increase the width of this column to ensure all these items are displayed in full:

ORANGE PARKA JACKET
GREEN SKIRT
TEAL JOG PANTS
GREEN JERSEY CARDIGAN
CREAM STRETCH BLOUSE
CREAM VELOUR TOP
BROWN STITCH BOOT
TOTAL

3.1.3	**5**	Enter the information shown below:

DESCRIPTION	LOCATION	SIZE	QUANTITY	PRICE	ITEM NO
ORANGE PARKA JACKET	844-15D	16	1	14.99	2063UY
GREEN SKIRT	832-12E	14	1	29.99	0580UX
TEAL JOG PANTS	451-11G	12	2	10.99	0836CA
GREEN JERSEY CARDIGAN	832-13E	14	1	23.99	0597UM
CREAM STRETCH BLOUSE	616-09B	14	2	32.99	7223WX
CREAM VELOUR TOP	616-24B	16	3	16.99	9818WA
BROWN STITCH BOOT	825-12H	6.5	1	39.99	2389NM

3.1.4(a)	6	Use a formula to calculate the total PRICE of the items.
3.2.2	7	Replicate this formula so that the total QUANTITY is displayed.
3.3.3(a)	8	Set the format for the SIZE column to display integer.
3.4.1 3.4.2	9	Save and print the spreadsheet.
3.2.1(a)	10	There are two errors in the data. Amend as follows: The size of the TEAL JOG PANTS should be **14** The GREEN SKIRT should read **GREEN STRETCH SKIRT**
3.2.1(b)	11	The LOCATION column does not need to be shown on the invoice. Delete this column.
3.2.3	12	Insert a new row between BROWN STITCH BOOT and CREAM VELOUR TOP and enter the information below: **WHITE JOG PANTS 14 1 10.99 0801BL**
3.2.3 3.3.1(b)	13	Insert a new column between the PRICE and the ITEM NO column to display the total costs of each of the items. Use the heading COST which should be right aligned.
3.2.4	14	Use a formula to calculate the COST for the ORANGE PARKA JACKET by multiplying the QUANTITY by the PRICE.
3.2.2	15	Replicate this formula so that the COST for the rest of the items is displayed. Ensure that an appropriate formula is used in the TOTAL row of COST to sum the values in this column.
3.3.3(b)	16	Set the format for the PRICE column and the TOTAL COST column to display two decimal places.
3.4.1 3.4.2	17	Save and print the spreadsheet.
3.1.4(b)	18	Produce a printout to show the formulae for the TOTAL row and the TOTAL COST column. Ensure that all formulae are displayed in full.
3.4.3	19	Save your file and exit from the spreadsheet application with data secure.

CLAIT Spreadsheet Mock Assignment 2

You are going to create a spreadsheet to show the quarterly sales of fabrics in a department store.

3.1.1	1	Load a spreadsheet application.
3.1.2	2	Enter the title: **QUARTERLY SALES FIGURES – FABRICS**
3.1.2 3.3.1	3	On a row below the title enter the column headings as shown below. The first column headings should be left aligned and the other column headings should be right aligned: **FABRIC DESCRIPTION JAN FEB MAR QT CP(M) SP(M)** QT is the abbreviation used for QUARTERLY TOTAL CP(M) is the abbreviation used for COST PRICE (PER METRE) SP(M) is the abbreviation used for SELLING PRICE (PER METRE)

3.1.2 3.3.1(a) 3.3.2	**4**	Enter in the first column the names of the seven fabrics (left aligned). Increase the width of the first column only to ensure all these headings are displayed in full:

FIONULA
ORLA STRIPE
AISLIN
TARA LATTICE
FIONA
ELLEN BRIAR
DEIRDRE PLAID

3.1.3	**5**	Enter the information shown below:

FABRIC DESCRIPTION	JAN	FEB	MAR	QT	CP(M)	SP(M)
FIONULA	**17**	**18**	**16**		**5.70**	**9.50**
ORLA STRIPE	**8**	**13**	**12**		**5.75**	**9.50**
AISLIN	**10**	**15**	**16**		**5.75**	**8.95**
TARA LATTICE	**7**	**5**	**4**		**5.25**	**7.50**
FIONA	**6**	**9**	**9**		**5.95**	**7.95**
ELLEN BRIAR	**16**	**15**	**12**		**6.00**	**8.50**
DEIRDRE PLAID	**20**	**18**	**16**		**5.50**	**9.00**

3.1.4(a)	**6**	Use a formula to calculate the total quarterly sales (QT) for the FIONULA fabric.
3.2.2	**7**	Replicate this formula so that the total quarterly sales (QT) for the rest of the fabrics listed under FABRIC DESCRIPTION are displayed.
3.3.3(b)	**8**	For only the columns showing QT, CP(M) and SP(M) set the format to display two decimal places.
3.4.1 3.4.2	**9**	Save and print the spreadsheet.
3.2.1(a)	**10**	There are two errors in the data. Amend as follows: The ORLA STRIPE figure for JAN should be **12** The AISLIN fabric should read **AISLIN TARTAN**
3.2.1(b)	**11**	The TARA LATTICE fabric has been discontinued. Delete this row.
3.2.3 3.3.1(b)	**12**	Insert a new column between the QT column and the CP(M) column to display the profit margin on each of the fabrics. Use the heading PROFIT which should be right aligned.
3.2.4	**13**	Use a formula to calculate the PROFIT per metre for FIONULA by subtracting CP(M) from SP(M).
3.2.2	**14**	Replicate this formula so that the PROFIT for the rest of the fabrics listed under FABRIC DESCRIPTIONS is displayed.
3.3.3(a)	**15**	Set the format for the QT column to display integer.
3.4.1 3.4.2	**16**	Save and print the spreadsheet.
3.1.4(b)	**17**	Produce a printout to show the formulae for the QT and PROFIT columns. Ensure that all formulae are displayed in full.
3.4.3	**18**	Save your file and exit from the spreadsheet application with data secure.

unit

4 worksheet design and data analysis

By the end of Unit 4 you should be able to:

- *design a worksheet and present it in a consistent layout*
- *build more complex formulae including the use of percentages*
- *generate formulae, by pointing*
- *find and amend erroneous formulae, including circular references*
- *use functions to generate values*
- *use the Function Wizard*
- *alter the page setup, including margins and column tabs*
- *insert, edit and remove headers and footers*
- *alter sheet options, including column headings displayed on each page*
- *insert and remove page breaks*
- *print a range of information from selected cells*

Worksheet design and data analysis

Having completed Section A you now know the basics of creating, saving, editing and manipulating a worksheet, using Excel. A worksheet package such as Excel is a very powerful application and to use it properly you must first design the worksheet by planning what information you need to produce from your data. Data comprises facts and figures collected from various sources both from within an organisation and from outside it. Information is data which, as a result of analysing and processing, has been assembled into a concise format that will enable decision-making.

In the RSA IBT Stage II examination and indeed at work, you will be provided with a range of data from which you must extract what is relevant to enable you to present useful information. In the examination, it is important that you read the question carefully, highlight the key requirements and then extract the relevant data. Similarly at work, you must identify the key requirements and extract the data needed to produce useful information in an appropriate format that will be easily understood by decision-makers and management.

When you design a worksheet to present information it is good business practice to ensure that the design or layout is consistent in appearance, e.g. headings aligned with the contents in the rest of the column, related figures displayed in the same format such as all in integer, decimal, currency, etc., and font size/style used appropriately to enhance and not to detract (by overuse) from the worksheet information. You also need to ensure that any new rows/columns inserted also comply with the standard format. In this unit the objectives will be achieved by the use of a scenario.

Task 4A

Imagine you work in a community leisure complex where there are 18 employees. Initially you are required to design a worksheet that will help in the wages calculations. The data you require is given in Figure 4.1 in the form of time sheets. You must read the questions very carefully and it will probably help if you underline or highlight the key requirements before you extract the specified data.

Your worksheet should display the wages for full-time instructors for week 32. All staff with weekly hours of 35 or more are classified as full-time employees; those with weekly hours of less than 35 are classified as part time. You will need to organise your data to show the staff names, weekly hours and overtime hours. Formulae to calculate the gross, tax, NI (national insurance) and net for each employee should be inserted. You will also be expected to provide a total for each of these calculations as well as the overall total wages bill.

1 Load Excel and, in cell **A1** of the new worksheet, key in the following title:

SPERRIN VIEW COMMUNITY CLUB – WAGES FOR WEEK 32

2 Study the details on the time sheets in Figure 4.1 and extract the names of the full-time instructors for week 32. Enter these names into column **A**; enter their weekly hours into column **B**; enter their overtime into column **C**. Your worksheet should be set out similar to the one below and must include the following, although headings can be abbreviated:

NAME	WEEKLY HOURS	OVER- TIME	GROSS	TAX	NI	NET

TOTAL

Ensure that

NAME appears in cell **A3**.
The **name of the first** full-time instructor appears in cell **A6**.
TOTAL appears in cell **A16**.

3 Once you have entered the text and data, it should look like Figure 4.2 – if not, read the questions again carefully to find where you went wrong and amend it so that it appears the same. Also ensure that

- column **A** is widened sufficiently to display the staff names as follows. Select column **A** heading button; from the Menu Bar, select **Format**, **Column**, **Width**; key in **13** to ensure the column is sufficiently widened to display the longest name; click **OK**; click anywhere to **deselect**.

WEEK 32	TIME SHEET		WEEK 32	TIME SHEET
NAME:	Vera Brown		**NAME:**	Sean Dawson
GRADE:	Instructor		**GRADE:**	Supervisor
WEEKLY HRS:	40		**WEEKLY HRS:**	40
OVERTIME:	5.5		**OVERTIME:**	0

WEEK 32	TIME SHEET		WEEK 32	TIME SHEET
NAME:	Paul Gibson		**NAME:**	Mike Green
GRADE:	Instructor		**GRADE:**	Instructor
WEEKLY HRS:	40		**WEEKLY HRS:**	40
OVERTIME:	7		**OVERTIME:**	7.5

WEEK 32	TIME SHEET		WEEK 32	TIME SHEET
NAME:	Keith Daley		**NAME:**	Gary Boyle
GRADE:	Instructor		**GRADE:**	Instructor
WEEKLY HRS:	30		**WEEKLY HRS:**	40
OVERTIME:	7.5		**OVERTIME:**	0

WEEK 32	TIME SHEET		WEEK 32	TIME SHEET
NAME:	Adrian Lang		**NAME:**	Jean Timms
GRADE:	Instructor		**GRADE:**	Supervisor
WEEKLY HRS:	35		**WEEKLY HRS:**	40
OVERTIME:	0		**OVERTIME:**	7.5

WEEK 32	TIME SHEET		WEEK 32	TIME SHEET
NAME:	Mark Robinson		**NAME:**	Brian Bradley
GRADE:	Manager		**GRADE:**	Instructor
WEEKLY HRS:	40		**WEEKLY HRS:**	40
OVERTIME:	0		**OVERTIME:**	9.5

WEEK 32	TIME SHEET		WEEK 32	TIME SHEET
NAME:	Jake Johnston		**NAME:**	Pat Jones
GRADE:	Instructor		**GRADE:**	Instructor
WEEKLY HRS:	40		**WEEKLY HRS:**	30
OVERTIME:	7.5		**OVERTIME:**	9

WEEK 32	TIME SHEET		WEEK 32	TIME SHEET
NAME:	John Knight		**NAME:**	Bob Dunn
GRADE:	Supervisor		**GRADE:**	Instructor
WEEKLY HRS:	35		**WEEKLY HRS:**	40
OVERTIME:	5.5		**OVERTIME:**	5.5

WEEK 32	TIME SHEET		WEEK 32	TIME SHEET
NAME:	Kevin Barrat		**NAME:**	Martin Grey
GRADE:	Instructor		**GRADE:**	Instructor
WEEKLY HRS:	40		**WEEKLY HRS:**	40
OVERTIME:	2.5		**OVERTIME:**	7.5

WEEK 33	TIME SHEET		WEEK 33	TIME SHEET
NAME:	Angela Black		**NAME:**	Jackie Horrocks
GRADE:	Instructor		**GRADE:**	Supervisor
WEEKLY HRS:	40		**WEEKLY HRS:**	40
OVERTIME:	0		**OVERTIME:**	0

Figure 4.1 Time sheets

- the text in the first column is left aligned as follows. Select column **A** heading button to highlight the entire column and from the Tool Bar, select ▤ **Align Left**.

- the other column headings are right aligned as follows. Position the mouse pointer on the cell containing **WEEKLY**; click and drag down to highlight a range including the row containing **HOURS**, whilst also dragging across to include the other columns as far as **NET**; from the Tool Bar, select ▤ **Align Right**.

- the weekly and overtime hours are displayed to **one** decimal place as follows. Select the column heading buttons of the columns containing **WEEKLY HOURS** and **OVERTIME** to highlight both columns. From the Menu Bar, select **Format**, **Cells**, **Number**. From **Category** select **Number** and in the **Decimal Places** spin box select **1**; click **OK**.

- any monetary amounts are displayed to **two** decimal places as follows. Select the column heading buttons of the columns containing **GROSS**, **TAX**, **NI**, **NET** to highlight these columns. From the Menu Bar, select **Format**, **Cells**, **Number**. From **Category** select **Number** and in the **Decimal Places** spin box select **2**; click **OK**.

4 Select cell **A25** and enter your name; select cell **A26** and enter the filename **TASK4A**.

5 From the Menu Bar, select **File**, **Save**; ensure that the **Save in** text box displays Drive **A** and in the **File name** text box key in **TASK4A**; click **Save** to save the worksheet using a unique filename.

	A	B	C	D	E	F	G
1	SPERRIN VIEW COMMUNITY CLUB - WAGES FOR WEEK 32						
2							
3	NAME	WEEKLY	OVER-	GROSS	TAX	NI	NET
4		HOURS	TIME				
5							
6	Vera Brown	40.0	5.5				
7	Paul Gibson	40.0	7.0				
8	Adrian Lang	35.0	0.0				
9	Jake Johnston	40.0	7.5				
10	Kevin Barrat	40.0	2.5				
11	Mike Green	40.0	7.5				
12	Gary Boyle	40.0	0.0				
13	Brian Bradley	40.0	9.5				
14	Bob Dunn	40.0	5.5				
15	Martin Grey	40.0	7.5				
16	TOTAL						

Figure 4.2 Week 32 wages

Build more complex formulae

In Unit 1 you were shown how to generate simple formulae using mathematical operators such as multiply, divide, add and subtract. If you wish to build more complex formulae involving several mathematical operators and a number of different cells or values, then you need to use brackets to ensure that the calculations are performed in the order required. Excel performs multiplication and division before addition and subtraction unless you indicate otherwise by the use of brackets. In the formula =6+4*2+5+3 the result will be 22 because Excel will multiply the 4 and the 2 first. However, in the formula =(6+4)*2+5+3 the result will be 28 because here Excel will add the 6 and the 4 together before performing the multiplication.

Although you can use a combination of cell references and values in formulae, it is always best to use cell references where possible as this means that the results will automatically update when the contents of the cell references are changed, e.g. the formula =B6*10.25 would result in the cell contents of B6 always being multiplied by 10.25; whereas the formula =B6*C6 where C6 contained the value 10.25 would allow you to change the value to, say, 12.25 so that you could make projections to find what effect increasing the value might have.

Using percentages

We will also be using percentages in the next exercise, which can simply be keyed with the figure and the % sign on your keyboard, e.g.:

The formulae D6*25% would calculate 25% of the cell contents in D6.

The formula D6*125% would increase the cell contents of D6 by 25%, i.e. it would calculate 25% of the cell contents in D6 and add this to 100% of the cell contents in D6, so making 125%.

Enter formulae by pointing

When you build more complex formulae you may need to use cells which are beyond the immediate screen area. You will probably find that it is better to enter these cell references by pointing. This is obviously an easier and quicker method than keying in the formulae. It is also a more accurate method because when you point to the actual cell reference, Excel enters it for you, which reduces the occurrence of keyboarding errors. From now on when you have to enter a formula you can use either this method or the earlier method of keying in the formula. It's your choice – the results will still be the same!

Entering formulae by pointing

- Select **the cell where you want the result** of your formula to appear, i.e. place the mouse pointer in the appropriate cell and click once.
- Type the **=** sign.
- Select the **cell which forms the first part** of the formula by clicking once or using the cursor keys, e.g. for the formula =B3+C3 you would select cell B3.
- Key in the **mathematical operator**, e.g. the + sign.
- Select the **next cell** required (or if using a value, key in the value), e.g. C3.
- Continue building the formula with mathematical operators and cell references or values until complete.
- Click the **Enter** box in the Formula Bar or press the **Enter** key.

▬	Task 4B	▼ ▲

Now you are ready to build more complex formulae to help with the wages calculations for the Sperrin View Community Club staff.

1 Staff are paid £10.25 per hour and £12.50 per overtime hour. Using the appropriate formula, generate the **GROSS** (WEEKLY HOURS multiplied by 10.25)

+ (OVERTIME multiplied by 12.5) for the first employee. Replicate this formula for each of the other employees.

If you are not sure, follow these instructions (using the 'keying in' method). Select cell **D6** and key in the formula **=(B6*10.25)+(C6*12.50)** ensuring that it appears exactly like this in the Formula Bar; click the ✔ **Enter** box in the Formula Bar.

With cell **D6** still selected, click and drag to **D15** to highlight this range; from the Menu Bar, select **Edit**, **Fill**, **Down** to copy this formula down to the other cells.

2 The income is to be taxed at a basic rate of 25%. Using the appropriate formula, generate the **TAX** (GROSS multiplied by 25%) for the first employee. Replicate this formula for each of the other employees.

If you are not sure, follow these instructions (using the 'pointing' method). Select cell **E6**; key in **=** and then select cell **D6** (using either the mouse to point and click once or the ← left cursor arrow key); key in ***25%** and ensure that the formula **=D6*25%** appears exactly like this in the Formula Bar; click the ✔ **Enter** box in the Formula Bar.

With cell **E6** still selected, click and drag to **E15** to highlight this range; from the Menu Bar, select **Edit**, **Fill**, **Down** to copy this formula down to the other cells.

3 The NI is to be calculated at a rate of 7%. Using the appropriate formula, generate the **NI** (GROSS multiplied by 7%) for the first employee. Replicate this formula for each of the other employees.

If you are not sure, follow these instructions (using the 'keying in' method). Select cell **F6** and key in the formula **=D6*7%** ensuring that it appears exactly like this in the Formula Bar; click the ✔ **Enter** box in the Formula Bar.

With cell **F6** still selected, click and drag to **F15** to highlight this range; from the Menu Bar, select **Edit**, **Fill**, **Down**.

4 Using the appropriate formula, generate the **NET** (GROSS minus TAX minus NI) for the first employee. Replicate this formula for each of the other employees.

If you are not sure, follow these instructions (using the 'pointing' method). Select cell **G6**; key in **=** and then select cell **D6**; key in **–** and then select cell **E6**; key in **–** and then select cell **F6**; ensure that the formula **=D6-E6-F6** appears exactly like this in the Formula Bar; click the ✔ **Enter** box in the Formula Bar.

With cell **G6** still selected, click and drag to **G15** to highlight this range; from the Menu Bar, select **Edit**, **Fill**, **Down**.

5 On the **TOTAL** row, using the appropriate formulae, generate **TOTALS** for the columns WEEKLY HOURS, OVERTIME and NET *only.*

If you are not sure, follow these instructions.

Select cell **B16** and from the Tool Bar, select the Σ **Autosum** icon; check that the formula **=SUM(B6:B15)** appears in the Formula Bar; click the ✔ **Enter** box in the Formula Bar.

With cell **B16** still selected, from the Tool Bar, select the ▣ **Copy** icon; select cell **C16** and from the Tool Bar, select the ▣ **Paste** icon; select cell **G16** and from the Tool Bar, select the ▣ **Paste** icon.

6 Select cell **A26** and amend the filename to **TASK4B**.

7 From the Menu Bar, select **File**, **Print Preview** to check the appearance of your worksheet and to ensure that it corresponds with the key. Click once to zoom in and once again to zoom out. Click **Close** when finished.

8 From the Menu Bar, select **File**, **Save As** and save the worksheet to the disk in Drive A, using a unique filename, e.g. **TASK4B**.

9 From the Tool Bar, select the ⎙ **Print** icon to print a copy of the worksheet.

Amend errors in formulae

When you are dealing with more complex formulae you may find that your results are sometimes not what you expected. In some cases Excel can identify what you have done wrong but in other cases it cannot. At examination level, you are expected to detect and amend erroneous formulae, so it is vitally important that you check all formulae carefully. It is also useful to make a rough estimate in your head of what you expect the result to be, i.e. round it up to the nearest unit, tens or thousands, etc.

Amending errors in formulae
Some typical errors occur as follows:

- *Simply entering a wrong cell reference.* This will probably only be picked up by you, i.e. by careful checking of your formulae. So it is extremely important to get the formula right to begin with, before you start copying it to other cells.

- *Simply keying in the wrong word*, e.g. SIM instead of SUM. Excel will pick this up and display the error message **#NAME?** in the affected cell or cells. You will need to select the cell and amend the entry.

- *Inserting a new row or column which is outside the range specified in the formula.* This needs to be picked up by you, i.e. by careful checking of your formulae when you make any new insertions.

- *Deleting a row or column which contains cells that are referred to in a formula.* Excel will pick this up and display the error message **#REF!** in the affected cell or cells. You will need to select the cell and amend the formula accordingly. In the screen shot in Figure 4.3, column C was deleted, causing the GROSS column to shift across from column D to column C, thereby producing an incalculable formula. The erroneous part of the formula is indicated by **#REF!** within the formula in the Formula Bar.

- *Entering a formula which contains the cell reference of the cell itself*, e.g. if the formula =B3+C3 was entered into cell C3 Excel would not be able to arrive at a result because when it adds B3 to C3 the result in C3 will change and therefore the formula will recalculate B3 plus C3 again, resulting in a new figure C3, which will then be recalculated again and again, and so it goes into a circular loop – this is

	B	C	D	E	F
VIEW COMMUNITY CLUB - WAGES FOR WEEK 32					
	WEEKLY HOURS	GROSS	TAX	NI	NET
ꞁ	40.0	#REF!	#REF!	#REF!	#REF!
ın	40.0	#REF!	#REF!	#REF!	#REF!
g	35.0	#REF!	#REF!	#REF!	#REF!
;ton	40.0	#REF!	#REF!	#REF!	#REF!
at	40.0	#REF!	#REF!	#REF!	#REF!
ꞁ	40.0	#REF!	#REF!	#REF!	#REF!

Figure 4.3 Error message #REF!

called a *circular reference* and when it occurs Excel will display a dialogue box similar to the one in Figure 4.4. A Help dialogue box may also be displayed to explain how you can locate the error. You will then need to edit the formula to ensure that it does not contain the cell in which the formula calculation is to be carried out.

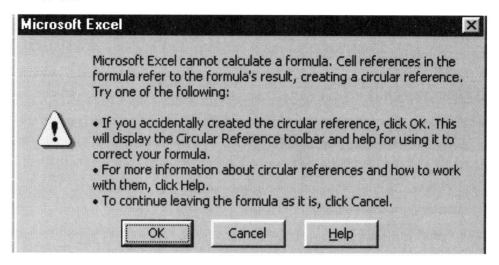

Figure 4.4   Circular reference dialogue box

Task 4C

With Task 4B still on screen, try the following to practise dealing with erroneous formulae:

1   Select cell **B16**; position the mouse pointer in the Formula Bar so that it changes to an *I* beam; click once and amend the word SUM to **SIM**; click the ✔ **Enter** box in the Formula Bar; note the error message **#NAME?** displayed.

2   With cell **B16** still selected, click once in the Formula Bar and amend the word SIM to **SUM**; click the ✔ **Enter** box in the Formula Bar.

3   Select column **C** heading button; from the Menu Bar, select **Edit, Delete**; note the error message **#REF!** displayed in all the cells with formulae which contain reference to the column you have just deleted. In the Formula Bar, the location of this error is also identified so that you will more easily be able to amend it.

4   From the Menu Bar, select **Edit, Undo Delete** *or* from the Tool Bar, select the ↶ **Undo** icon.

5   Select cell **B16**; click once in the Formula Bar and amend the formula from =SUM(B6:B15) to **=SUM(B6:B16)**, i.e. it includes the cell itself; click the ✔ **Enter** box in the Formula Bar; note the dialogue box informing you that you have created a circular reference; click **OK**; click once in the Formula Bar and amend the formula to **=SUM(B6:B15)**; click the ✔ **Enter** box in the Formula Bar.

6   Keith Daley's weekly hours were entered incorrectly into the time sheets. He worked **40** weekly hours and **7.5** overtime hours. Extend the worksheet by inserting a new row above Vera Brown and adding the new details, as follows. Select row **6** heading button; from the Menu Bar, select **Insert, Rows**; select cell **A6** and key in **Keith Daley**; select cell **B6** and key in **40.0**; select cell **C6** and key in **7.5**.

7   Replicate the necessary formulae and ensure that the display is consistent, as follows. Select cell **D7** and click and drag across to **G7** and upwards to extend the range to include the new row, i.e. from **D6** to **G6**; from the Menu Bar, select **Edit, Fill, Up**. The formulae will be copied up and as you formatted the entire columns earlier to two decimal places, the results should be consistent with the rest of the worksheet.

> **8** Correct any erroneous formulae as follows. Select cell **B17** and note from the Formula Bar that the range does not include the new row **6**; click once in the Formula Bar and amend the formula to **=SUM(B6:B16)**; click the ✅ **Enter** box in the Formula Bar; select cell **C17**; click once in the Formula Bar and amend the formula to **=SUM(C6:C16)**; click the ✅ **Enter** box in the Formula Bar; select cell **G17**; click once in the Formula Bar and amend the formula to **=SUM(G6:G16)**; click the ✅ **Enter** box in the Formula Bar. (Alternatively, you could have copied the new formula from **B17** and pasted it to **C17** and **G17**.)

Use functions to generate values

A function is a formula which has already been set up to perform a useful calculation. Earlier in Unit 1 you were introduced to the SUM function which was used to add together all the values in a range of cells. Excel offers many function categories including financial, mathematical and statistical as well as a wide range of function names. We shall consider a few of the simpler and more common ones.

As with a formula, functions must start with the = sign; followed by the function name in capital letters; followed by a set of brackets, containing the cell reference or references of a range of cells that are to be calculated. This reference, in brackets, is known as the function's *argument*. It can contain numbers, cell references or more complex formulae. When more than one argument is used then commas must be used to separate them. As with a formula, if you increase the range by inserting new rows or columns of data within the range, the function will automatically adjust to include these.

Using functions to generate values

- Select the **cell where you want the result** of your function to appear, i.e. place the mouse pointer in the appropriate cell and click once.

- Type the = sign.

- Type the function. Some common ones are

AVERAGE	calculates the average of the values in the range of cells
COUNT	calculates the number of numeric values in the range of cells
COUNTA	calculates the number of cells containing data
MAX	gives the maximum value in the range of cells
MIN	gives the minimum value in the range of cells

  You can use either lower or upper case to key in the function as Excel displays it in upper case. It is probably best to key in functions in lower case because if Excel does not convert it to upper case then you will know that it is incorrect.

  Alternatively, you can use the Function Wizard which allows you to choose the function from a list which it then pastes into the active cell, as shown later.

- Select the **beginning of the range** by keying it in or pointing to it and the **end of the range**, separated by a : sign and **enclosed in brackets**, e.g. AVERAGE(B5:B10).

- Click the ✅ **Enter** box in the Formula Bar or press **Enter**.

Task 4D

With Task 4B still on screen; practise using some of these functions now on your Sperrin View Community Club spreadsheet by generating new values which will enable the manager of the community club to analyse the staffing hours.

1 In **A19** key in **AVERAGE**; in **A20** key in **HIGHEST**; in **A21** key in **LOWEST**; in **A23** key in **NO OF EMPLOYEES**; place the mouse pointer between column **A**

and column **B** heading buttons until it becomes a double-headed arrow and then drag to the right to widen column **A** to display these entries fully.

2 Use the **AVERAGE** function to calculate the average weekly hours as follows. Select cell **B19**; key in **=AVERAGE(** and enter the range by either keying in **B6:B16** *or* by pointing to B6 and clicking and dragging to highlight the range to **B16**; key in **)** and ensure the formula **=AVERAGE(B6:B16)** is displayed in the Formula Bar; click the ✔️ **Enter** box in the Formula Bar.

3 Replicate this formula across the other columns as follows. With cell **B19** still selected, click and drag across to **G19**; from the Menu Bar, select **Edit, Fill, Right**.

4 With the range **B19–G19** still selected, format these cells for integer as follows: from the Menu Bar choose **Format, Cells, Number**; from **Category**, select **Number**; from **Decimal Places**, select **0**; click **OK**.

5 Use the **MAX** function to calculate the highest number of weekly hours as follows. Select cell **B20**; key in **=MAX(** and enter the range **B6:B16**; key in **)** and ensure the formula **=MAX(B6:B16)** is displayed in the Formula Bar; click the ✔️ **Enter** box in the Formula Bar.

6 Use the **MIN** function to calculate the lowest number of weekly hours as follows. Select cell **B21**; key in **=MIN(** and enter the range **B6:B16**; key in **)** and ensure the formula **=MIN(B6:B16)** is displayed in the Formula Bar; click the ✔️ **Enter** box in the Formula Bar.

Use the Function Wizard

As there are so many different functions and as it would be difficult to remember all the different names or syntax, Excel has provided a Function Wizard. This is a sequence of dialogue boxes to take you through the stages of building the formula, step by step.

Using the Function Wizard

- Select the **cell where you want the result** of your function to appear, i.e. place the mouse pointer in the appropriate cell and click once.

- Type the **=** sign.

- From the Menu Bar, select:

  Insert   Function ...

  or, from the Tool Bar, select the 🔧 **Function Wizard** icon

The Function Wizard dialogue box is displayed, similar to the one in Figure 4.5.

- From **Function Category** select the category, usually **Most Recently Used**. Function names are grouped by category, e.g. the category **Date and Time** will list the function names associated with this. The default may be set to display the category **Most Recently Used** which will list the most recently used function names. If you can't find a specific function, select **All** in the **Function Category** box and all available functions will be listed in the **Function Name** box.

- From **Function Name** select the name of the function, e.g. AVERAGE.

  When you select a function name, the syntax and a brief description of it is given at the bottom of the dialogue box. You can also click on [?] in the dialogue box if you want further explanation of the function.

- Click **OK**. The next dialogue box is displayed, similar to the one in Figure 4.6. In this example the argument (i.e. information that you want the function to use in its

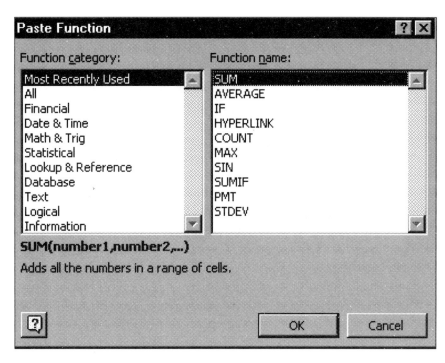

Figure 4.5 Function Wizard dialogue box

calculations) has been inserted by selecting the adjacent range A1:A4, so the Function Wizard will average the value of these cells.

- If the argument does not refer to the range you wish to be used in the calculation, insert the argument into the **number1** text box by keying it in or in your worksheet click and drag to highlight the range.

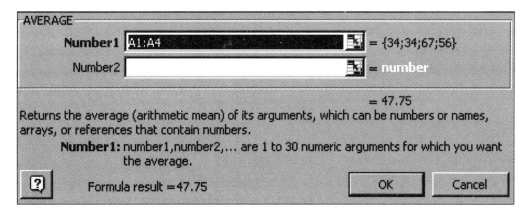

Figure 4.6 AVERAGE dialogue box

If the Function Wizard dialogue box is in the way, place the mouse pointer on its Title Bar and click and drag it aside until the range on the worksheet can be seen.

If the function requires more than one argument, click in the **number2** text box and insert it – note that a **number3** text box is also displayed if required.

- Click **OK**.

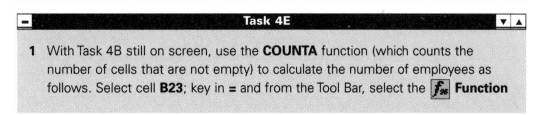

Task 4E

1 With Task 4B still on screen, use the **COUNTA** function (which counts the number of cells that are not empty) to calculate the number of employees as follows. Select cell **B23**; key in **=** and from the Tool Bar, select the ▒ **Function**

Wizard icon; from **Function Category** select **All**; from **Function Name** select **COUNTA**; click **OK** and in **value1** text box key in **A6:A16** and click **Finish**; ensure the formula **=COUNTA(A6:A16)** is displayed in the Formula Bar; click the ✔ **Enter** box in the Formula Bar.

2   The manager of the community club is considering an increase from 35 to 40 weekly hours for all full-time staff. In order to make a projection on the effect this might have, amend as follows. Select cell **B9** and increase Adrian Lang's weekly hours from 35 to **40**; select cell **A24** and key in **PROJECTION**; select cell **B24** and key in the new **TOTAL** figure for **NET**, which the formulae in the worksheet should automatically calculate to 3576.8.

3   As this increase is only a projection, return the worksheet to its original values, as follows. Select cell **B9**; key in **35** and note the effect this has on the TOTAL figure for NET.

4   Select cell **A28** and amend the filename to **TASK4E**.

5   From the Menu Bar, select **File**, **Print Preview** to check the appearance of your worksheet and to ensure that it corresponds with the key. Click once to zoom in and once again to zoom out. Click **Close** when finished.

6   From the Menu Bar, select **File**, **Save As** and save the worksheet to the disk in Drive A, using a unique filename, e.g. **TASK4E**.

7   From the Tool Bar, select the 🖨 **Print** icon to print a copy of the worksheet.

8   From the Menu Bar, select **File**, **Close** to close the worksheet.

Page Setup

As explained in Unit 2, the default settings in Excel produce a printout of your worksheet in A4 portrait style, showing the worksheet name and the page number. You can alter these by using the Page Setup option. We are going to look first at the Page and Margins features within this option.

Using Page Setup
- From the Menu Bar, select:

  File   **Page Setup**

  or, from the Tool Bar, select the 🔍 **Print Preview** icon.

  From the Preview window, select **Setup** ...

- Click on the **Page** tab. A Page Setup dialogue box, similar to the one in Figure 4.7, will be displayed. It may vary slightly depending on the type of printer you have. In **Page Setup** there are four tabs, each with different options.

- In the **Page** tab, select the options of your choice, orientation probably being one of the most used options.

  In the **Orientation** row, select one of the following buttons:

  Portrait for A4 size 210 × 297 mm (with the shorter edge at the top)
  or
  Landscape for A4 size 297 × 210 mm (with the longer edge at the top).

  In the **Scaling** box you can increase or reduce the size of the printed image.
  In the **Paper size** box you can select the appropriate paper size that you are using.
  In the **Print quality** box you can select the intensity of your print.

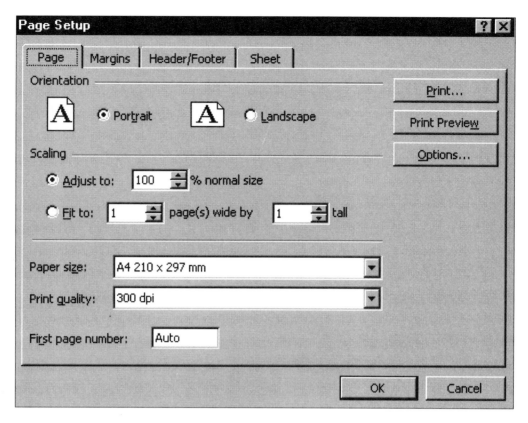

Figure 4.7 Page Setup dialogue box

Further options relating to the printer are available by selecting the **Options** button and this is available on all these tabs in **Page Setup**.

- Click on the **Margins** tab. A dialogue box, similar to the one in Figure 4.8, will be displayed.

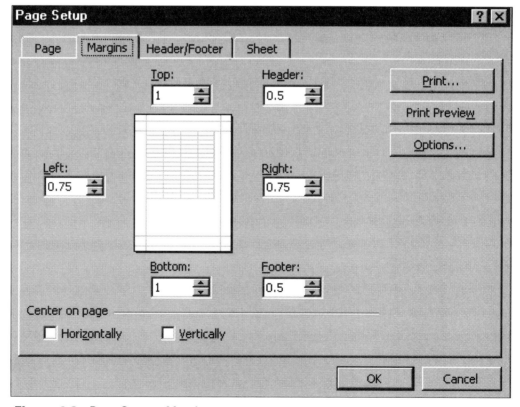

Figure 4.8 Page Setup – Margins

- Select the options of your choice.

  You may sometimes need to alter the *top, bottom, left* or *right margins* or the *header/footer* position to get more information on the page. These can be decreased or increased by clicking on the spin buttons at the side or by keying in the amount. You may also wish to centre your work on the page either *horizontally* or *vertically*. As you enter the changes, the Preview will display what the page layout will look like.

- Click **OK**.

Changing margins and columns from Print Preview

You can also alter the margins and column tabs from the Print Preview screen, as shown below and, as this is more visual, it is sometimes the preferred method.

- From the Menu Bar, select:

  File   Print Preview

  or, from the Tool Bar, select the [icon] **Print Preview** icon.

- From the Preview window, select **Margins**. The Preview window should be displayed, similar to the one in Figure 4.9.

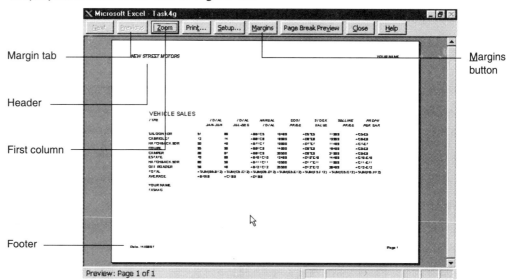

Figure 4.9 Preview window

- Position the mouse pointer at any of the column or margin tabs until it becomes a double-headed arrow and click and drag to alter the widths of the columns or margins.

- Click the **Margins** button again to switch this display off.

- Click **Close** when finished.

Task 4F

1 From the Menu Bar, select **File, Open** and open the file **TASK3I.XLS**.

2 From the Menu Bar, select **File, Page Setup**; click the **Page** tab; from the Orientation row click the **Landscape** button so that more information can be displayed across the page; click the **Print Preview** button; click the **Next** and **Previous** buttons in the Print Preview window to see the worksheet on both pages.

3 From the Print Preview window click the **Margins** button to display the column and margin tabs; position the mouse pointer at the **first column tab** as indicated in the screen shot in Figure 4.9 until it becomes a double-headed

arrow; click and drag to decrease the column width to fit the longest entry (i.e. **VEHICLE SALES**) in the column; continue to do this for all the columns so that the entire worksheet fits on to one page; when you are finished click the **Margins** button to switch off the display.

4   From the Print Preview window select the **Setup** button and from the Page Setup dialogue box, click on the **Margins** tab; practise clicking on the spin boxes to increase and decrease the amounts in each of the text boxes, noting that the Preview indicates to you the part of the worksheet that you are altering; ensure that the settings are as follows before proceeding – **Top 1   Bottom 1   Left 0.75   Right 0.75   From Edge Header   0.5   Footer 0.5**; in the **Center on Page** option click the checkboxes against **Horizontal** and **Vertical** to ensure that √ appears against each of these centring options; click **OK**; click **Close**.

Headers and footers

A header is an identical piece of information which appears at the top of each page. It may be the name of a company, the title of the workbook or a reference for the worksheet. A footer is an identical piece of information which appears at the bottom of each page. This might be the page number, the date or the filename. The default in Excel is set up to print the worksheet sheet name as a header and the page number as a footer. (Please note that this default might not appear on your screen as it depends on how the default settings have been applied.) Headers and footers only need to be keyed in once and will be printed automatically, within the top and bottom margins, on all the pages in the workbook. Headers and footers can also be edited if the text or alignment needs to be changed.

Inserting/editing headers and footers

• From the Menu Bar, select:

   File   Page Setu**p**

   or, from the Tool Bar, select the [icon] **Print Preview** icon.

   From the Preview window, select **Setup** ...

• Click on the **Header/Footer** tab. A dialogue box, similar to the one in Figure 4.10, will be displayed.

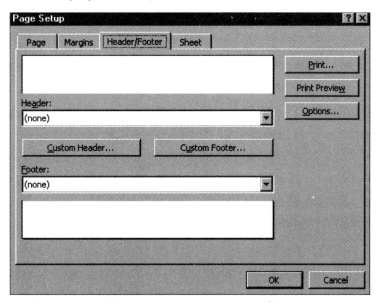

Figure 4.10   Page Setup – Header/Footer

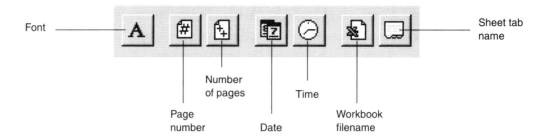

Figure 4.11 Customising headers and footers

• Select the options of your choice.

You can choose a predefined header or footer from drop-down lists in the **He_a_der** and **_F_ooter** text boxes or you can create your own headers or footers by selecting either **_C_ustom Header** or **C_u_stom Footer**. If you choose to customise your own header or footer a dialogue box (as shown in Figure 4.13) will be displayed, which permits you to enter text in three sections of the worksheet, i.e. the left, centre and right sections. You will be presented with a series of buttons, as shown in Figure 4.11.

To alter the *font,* select the text and click the Font icon to display the Font dialogue box.

To use the other functions, position the cursor in the text box and click the desired button. These will enter *codes* in the text boxes as follows:

&[Page]	inserts current page number	**&[Pages]**	inserts total number of pages
&[Date]	inserts current date	**&[Time]**	inserts current time
&[File]	inserts workbook filename	**&[Tab]**	inserts sheet tab name

To edit the text:
click once in the text box where data is to be edited
delete unwanted data
key in new data

Removing headers and footers
• From the Menu Bar, select:

_F_ile   **Page Set_u_p**

or, from the Tool Bar, select the [🔍] **Print Preview** icon.

From the Preview window, select **_S_etup ...**

• Click on the **Header/Footer** tab to display the Header/Footer dialogue box.

• Select the ▼ at the side of the **He_a_der** text box to display a drop-down list of predefined headers.

• Select **None**.

• Select the ▼ at the side of the **_F_ooter** text box to display a drop-down list of predefined headers.

• Select **None**.

Altering the sheet options
• Click on the **Sheet** tab. A dialogue box, similar to the one in Figure 4.12, will be displayed.

• Select the options of your choice.

Enter the required range into the **Print _A_rea** text box to print only a selected area of the worksheet. If you wish to print non-adjacent ranges, key in the range references with a comma separating each (e.g. **E1:E14, A1:A14**). At the right end of the **Print _A_rea** and **Print Titles** text boxes are **Collapse Dialogue** buttons. These temporarily move the **Page Setup** dialogue box so that you can enter the range by selecting cells in the worksheet. When you finish, click the button again to display the entire dialogue box.

Enter the required range into the **Print Titles** text box if you wish row or column titles to appear on each page e.g. **A1:G3**.

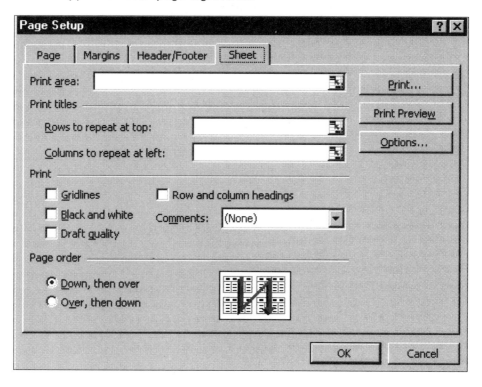

Figure 4.12 Page Setup – Sheet

Click on the checkboxes to select any of the options in **Print**. A √ indicates that the function is on and a blank checkbox indicates that the function is off.

Click on the **Page Order** of your choice for multiple pages to be printed.

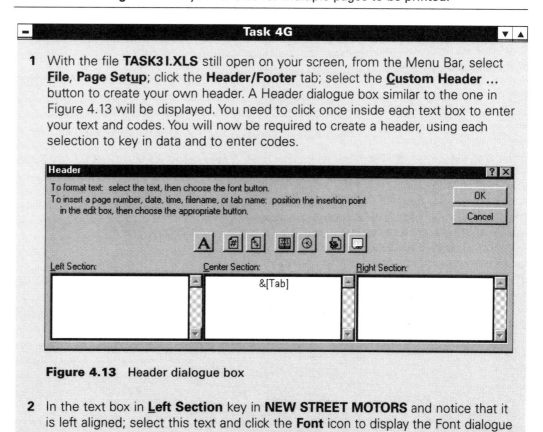

Figure 4.13 Header dialogue box

2 In the text box in **Left Section** key in **NEW STREET MOTORS** and notice that it is left aligned; select this text and click the **Font** icon to display the Font dialogue

box; from **Font Style** select **Bold Italic** and from **Size** select **12**; click **OK**; in the text box in **Centre Section** select (if necessary) the default code **&[Tab]** (used to insert the sheet tab name); and press the Delete key on the keyboard to remove the sheet tab name; in the text box in **Right Section** key in **YOUR NAME** and notice that it is right aligned; click **OK**. This will return you to the **Header/Footer** tab window.

3 Select the **Custom Footer ...** button to create your own footer. A Footer dialogue box similar in layout to the one in Figure 4.13 will be displayed. In the text box in **Left Section** key in **Date:** and press the Space Bar on the keyboard; click the **Date** icon to insert the current date code; in the text box in **Centre Section** select (if necessary) the default code **&[Page]** and press the Delete key on the keyboard to remove the page number code; in the text box in **Right Section** key in **Page** and press the Space Bar on the keyboard; click the **Page** icon to insert the current page number; click **OK**. This will return you to the **Header/Footer** tab window.

4 Select the **Print Preview** button to see how your worksheet now looks and to check this with the key; select **Close** when finished.

5 Select cell **A17** and enter the filename **TASK4G**.

6 From the Menu Bar, select **File**, **Save As** and save the worksheet using a unique filename, e.g. TASK4G.

7 From the Tool Bar, select the 🖨 **Print** icon to print a copy of the worksheet.

8 From the Menu Bar, select **File**, **Close** to close the worksheet.

— | Task 4H | ▼ ▲

1 Open the file **TASK4E**. From the Menu Bar, select **File**, **Page Setup**; click the **Header/Footer** tab; select the ▼ at the side of the **Header** text box to display a drop-down list of predefined headers; select **None**.

2 Select the ▼ at the side of the **Footer** text box to display a drop-down list of predefined headers; select **None**; click **OK**.

3 From the Menu Bar, select **File**, **Print Preview** to check the appearance of your worksheet and to ensure that it corresponds with the key. Click once to zoom in and once again to zoom out. Click **Close** when finished.

4 Select cell **A27** and amend the filename to **TASK4H**.

5 From the Menu Bar, select **File**, **Save As** and save the worksheet as **TASK4H**.

6 From the Tool Bar, select the 🖨 **Print** icon to print a copy of the worksheet.

7 From the Menu Bar, select **File**, **Close** to close the worksheet.

Page breaks

When you produced TASK3I earlier you will have noticed that it was spread over three pages. The default settings in Excel are usually set at 1 inch top and bottom margins and 0.75 inch left and right margins on an A4 portrait sheet. Where the rows or columns extend beyond this, a page break is automatically inserted, indicated by a dashed line, and the extra rows or columns are moved on to the next page. Where the data is excessive for one page, you cannot remove these page breaks, although you *can* alter the margins or decrease the row/column size to try to fit more on to a page. However, you may wish to position the page break at a more appropriate point, e.g. if you wanted to print the data on one page and the calculations on another, you could insert a manual page break, as follows.

Inserting a page break

*   Position the mouse pointer on the cell where you wish to insert the page break and click once. The page break will be inserted *above* and to the *left* of the active cell.

*   From the Menu Bar, select:

    Insert   Page Break

    A dashed line will indicate where the pages have been split.

Removing a page break

*   Position the mouse pointer on the cell immediately *below* and to the *right* of the dashed lines of the page break and click once.

*   From the Menu Bar, select:

    Insert   Remove Page Break

    The dashed line will be removed.

Removing all the page breaks

*   Position the mouse pointer on the square in the top left-hand corner of the worksheet and click once to select the entire worksheet.

*   From the Menu Bar, select:

    Insert   Remove Page Break

    The dashed line will be removed.

Print a range of information

Sometimes, rather than printing the entire worksheet, you may wish to print a range of cells and, in this case, you must first of all select the range.

Printing a range of information

*   Select the range you wish to print.

*   From the Menu Bar, select:

    File   Print

    or, from the Tool Bar, select the 🖨 **Print** icon

    or, from the keyboard, press **Ctrl/P**.

    The Print dialogue box is displayed on screen.

*   From the Print What text box, select:

    Selection

*   Click **OK** or press **Enter** to accept the other settings.

Task 4I

1 From the Menu Bar, select **File**, **Open** and open the file **TASK3I**. Select cell **B18** and from the Menu Bar, select **Insert**, **Page Break** to insert a page break to the left of column **B** and above row **18**. From the Menu Bar, select **File**, **Print Preview** to check the appearance of your worksheet and to ensure that the **TYPE** of vehicles appears on its own on the first page. Click **Next** a couple of times to see how the other columns have been moved on to pages 2 and 3; click **Previous** to move back a page. Click **Close** when finished.

2 Select cell **G15** and key in **TASK4I**.

3 Click on cell **G2** and drag down to **G15** to highlight this range to print only the selling price details; from the Menu Bar, select **File**, **Print**; in the **Print What** text box click **Selection**; click **OK**.

4 Select cell **B18** and from the Menu Bar, select **Insert**, **Remove Page Break** to remove the page break and to leave the worksheet with its original automatic page breaks. From the Menu Bar, select **File**, **Print Preview** to check the appearance of your worksheet and to ensure that the monthly period TOTAL columns appear again on the first page. Click **Next** to see how the other columns have been moved on to the next pages; click **Previous** to move back a page. Click **Close** when finished.

5 From the Menu Bar, select **File**, **Close**; click **No** when presented with the 'Save changes in TASK3I.XLS?' dialogue box to close the worksheet without saving the changes.

Task 4J

1 From the Menu Bar, select **File**, **Open** and open the file **TASK4H**. Further projections are to be made to help the manager of the community club calculate the cost of employing an extra 23 more staff. These extra staff are to be based on the figures already available for Martin Grey.

2 To insert sufficient blank rows for these new entries, select row heading button **17** and drag to column heading button **39**; from the Menu Bar, select **Insert**, **Rows**.

3 Select cell **A16** and drag down to cell **G39** to highlight this range. From the Menu Bar, select **Edit**, **Fill**, **Down**. This will project Martin Grey's details for the potential new staff.

4 Select cell **B40** and from the Tool Bar, select the Σ **Autosum** icon; check that the formula **=SUM(B6:B39)** appears in the Formula Bar; click the ✔ **Enter** box in the Formula Bar.

5 With cell **B40** still selected, from the Tool Bar, select the 🗐 **Copy** icon; select cell **C40** and from the Tool Bar, select the 📋 **Paste** icon; check that the formula **=SUM(C6:C39)** appears in the Formula Bar; select cell **G40** and from the Tool Bar, select the 📋 **Paste** icon; check that the formula **=SUM(G6:G39)** appears in the Formula Bar.

6 Select cell **B42**; click once in the Formula Bar and amend the formula to **=AVERAGE(B6:B39)**; click the ✔ **Enter** box in the Formula Bar.

7 With cell **B42** still selected, drag across to **G42** to highlight this range; from the Menu Bar, select **Edit**, **Fill**, **Right**.

8 Select cell **B43**; click once in the Formula Bar and amend the formula to **=MAX(B6:B39)**; click the ✔ **Enter** box in the Formula Bar.

9 Select cell **B44**; click once in the Formula Bar and amend the formula to **=MIN(B6:B39)**; click the ✔ **Enter** box in the Formula Bar.

10 Select cell **B46**; click once in the Formula Bar and amend the formula to **=COUNT(B6:B39)**; click the ✔ **Enter** box in the Formula Bar.

11 Select row heading button **47**; from the Menu Bar, select **Edit**, **Delete** to delete this row, which is no longer required.

12 From the Menu Bar, select **File**, **Page Setup**; select the **Page** tab and in the **Orientation** section, select the **Landscape** button; click **OK**.

13 From the Menu Bar, select **File**, **Print Preview** to check the appearance of your worksheet. Click **Next** and click **Previous** to view each page. Click **Close** when finished.

14 As it is difficult to remember which column headings the figures on page 2 relate to, these column headings can also be shown on page 2 as follows. Once you have checked the range of the rows to be repeated (i.e. A3:G4) from the Menu Bar, select **File**, **Page Setup**; select the **Sheet** tab and in the **Print Titles** section click on the text box **Rows to Repeat at Top**: and key in the range **A3:G4**; click **OK**.

15 Select cell **A51** and enter the filename **TASK4J**.

16 From the Menu Bar, select **File**, **Print Preview** to check the appearance of your worksheet and to ensure that it corresponds with the key. Click once to zoom in and once again to zoom out. Click **Close** when finished.

17 From the Menu Bar, select **File**, **Save As** and save the worksheet using a unique filename, e.g. **TASK4J**.

18 From the Tool Bar, select the 🖨 **Print** icon to print a copy of the worksheet.

19 From the Menu Bar, select **File**, **Close** to close the worksheet; select **File**, **Exit** to exit from Excel.

Don't forget to complete the Record of Progress sheet to indicate that you have finished this unit successfully. If you feel that you would like to do further work to consolidate what you have learned so far, then try Extra Practice Task 4.

▬ | **Extra Practice Task 4** | **▼ ▲**

Imagine you work in a garden centre where there are 18 employees, based in two divisions, one at Dart and the other at Sawel. Staff are employed in two main aspects of the business: CULTIVATION, i.e. those who cultivate the plants and shrubs both indoors in greenhouses and outdoors in the nursery grounds; and CONSTRUCTION, i.e. those who construct the greenhouses and sheds which are sold to mail-order customers for their own gardens or allotments. Both these aspects are co-ordinated by the centre manager.

The data you require is given in Figure 4.14 in the form of clock cards. You must read the questions very carefully and it will probably help if you underline or highlight the key requirements before you extract the specified data.

Initially you will be required to design a worksheet which can be used in wages calculations for employees. It should display the wages for construction employees who have worked overtime at the Dart division. You will need to organise your data to show the staff names, weekly hours and overtime hours. Formulae to calculate the gross, tax, NI (national insurance) and net for each employee should be inserted. You will also be expected to provide a total for each of these calculations as well as the overall total wages bill.

1 Load Excel and in cell **A1** of the new worksheet, key in the following title:

SPERRIN SKYWAY GARDEN CENTRE

2 In cell **A2** key in the following subtitle:

Construction Employees, Dart Division

3 Study the details on the clock cards in Figure 4.14 and extract the names of the Dart division construction employees who have worked overtime. Enter these names into column **A**; enter their weekly hours into column **B**; enter their overtime into column **C**. Your worksheet should be set out similar to the one below and must include the following, although headings can be abbreviated:

Name	Weekly hours	Over- time	Gross	Tax	NI	Net

TOTAL

Ensure that

NAME appears in cell **A3**.

The **name of the first** full-time employee appears in cell **A6**.

TOTAL appears in cell **A16**.

DART	CLOCK CARD	DART	CLOCK CARD
NAME:	Anne Moore	NAME:	Joanne Fisher
GRADE:	Construction	GRADE:	Construction
WEEKLY HRS:	42	WEEKLY HRS:	42
OVERTIME:	7	OVERTIME:	0
DART	CLOCK CARD	DART	CLOCK CARD
NAME:	Peter Rushton	NAME:	Denise Birch
GRADE:	Cultivation	GRADE:	Construction
WEEKLY HRS:	42	WEEKLY HRS:	42
OVERTIME:	7	OVERTIME:	7.5
DART	CLOCK CARD	SAWEL	CLOCK CARD
NAME:	Louise Atkinson	NAME:	Kevin Matthews
GRADE:	Construction	GRADE:	Cultivation
WEEKLY HRS:	42	WEEKLY HRS:	42
OVERTIME:	7.5	OVERTIME:	7
DART	CLOCK CARD	DART	CLOCK CARD
NAME:	Sylvia Cheshire	NAME:	Richard Alford
GRADE:	Construction	GRADE:	Cultivation
WEEKLY HRS:	42	WEEKLY HRS:	42
OVERTIME:	2.5	OVERTIME:	0
SAWEL	CLOCK CARD	DART	CLOCK CARD
NAME:	Kathy Bowker	NAME:	Margery Bartram
GRADE:	Construction	GRADE:	Construction
WEEKLY HRS:	42	WEEKLY HRS:	42
OVERTIME:	9	OVERTIME:	9.5
DART	CLOCK CARD	DART	CLOCK CARD
NAME:	Mike Brown	NAME:	Jolanta Hughes
GRADE:	Construction	GRADE:	Construction
WEEKLY HRS:	42	WEEKLY HRS:	42
OVERTIME:	7.5	OVERTIME:	9
SAWEL	CLOCK CARD	DART	CLOCK CARD
NAME:	David Wild	NAME:	Keith Wiseman
GRADE:	Cultivation	GRADE:	Cultivation
WEEKLY HRS:	42	WEEKLY HRS:	42
OVERTIME:	5.5	OVERTIME:	7.5
DART	CLOCK CARD	DART	CLOCK CARD
NAME:	Michelle Blackham	NAME:	Christine Gilman
GRADE:	Construction	GRADE:	Construction
WEEKLY HRS:	42	WEEKLY HRS:	42
OVERTIME:	7	OVERTIME:	7.5
DART	CLOCK CARD	DART	CLOCK CARD
NAME:	Bill Boulton	NAME:	Bob Nangle
GRADE:	Centre Manager	GRADE:	Construction
WEEKLY HRS:	42	WEEKLY HRS:	42
OVERTIME:	0	OVERTIME:	7

Figure 4.14 Extra Practice Task 4 – clock cards

4   Once you have entered the text and data, it should look like Figure 4.15 – if not, read the questions again carefully to find where you went wrong and amend it so that it appears the same. Also ensure that

- column **A** is widened sufficiently to display the staff names as follows. Select column **A** heading button; from the Menu Bar, select **Format**, **Column**, **Width**; key in **16**; click **OK**; click anywhere to **deselect**.

- the text in the first column is left aligned as follows. Select column **A** heading button to highlight the entire column and from the Tool Bar, select ▤ **Align Left**.

- the other column headings are right aligned as follows. Position the mouse pointer on the cell containing **WEEKLY**; click and drag down to highlight a range to include the row below containing **HOURS**, whilst also dragging across to include the other columns as far as **NET**; from the Tool Bar, select ▤ **Align Right**.

- the weekly and overtime hours are displayed to **one** decimal place as follows. Select the column heading buttons of the columns containing **WEEKLY HOURS** and **OVERTIME** to highlight both columns. From the Menu Bar, select **Format**, **Cells**, **Number**. From **Category** select **Number** and in the **Decimal Places** spin box select **1**; click **OK**.

- any monetary amounts are displayed to **two** decimal places as follows. Select the column heading buttons of the columns containing **GROSS**, **TAX**, **NI**, **NET** to highlight these columns. From the Menu Bar, select **Format**, **Cells**, **Number**. From **Category** select **Number** and in the **Decimal Places** spin box select **2** if it is not already displayed; click **OK**.

	A	B	C	D	E	F	G
1	SPERRIN SKYWAY GARDEN CENTRE						
2	Construction Employees, Dart Division						
3	NAME	WEEKLY	OVER-	GROSS	TAX	NI	NET
4		HOURS	TIME				
5							
6	Anne Moore	42.0	7.0				
7	Louise Atkinson	42.0	7.5				
8	Sylvia Cheshire	42.0	2.5				
9	Mike Brown	42.0	7.5				
10	Michelle Blackham	42.0	7.0				
11	Denise Birch	42.0	7.5				
12	Margery Bartram	42.0	9.5				
13	Jolanta Hughes	42.0	9.0				
14	Christine Gilman	42.0	7.5				
15	Bob Nangle	42.0	7.0				
16	TOTAL						

Figure 4.15 Extra Practice Task 4 – worksheet

5   Staff are paid £10.25 per hour and £12.50 per overtime hour. Using the appropriate formula, generate the **GROSS** (WEEKLY HOURS multiplied by 10.25) + (OVERTIME multiplied by 12.5) for the first employee. Replicate this formula for each of the other employees as follows. Select cell **D6** and key in the formula **=(B6*10.25)+(C6*12.50)** ensuring that it appears exactly like this in the Formula Bar; click the ✔ **Enter** box in the Formula Bar. With cell **D6** still selected click and drag to **D15** to highlight this range; from the Menu Bar, select **Edit**, **Fill**, **Down**.

6 The gross income is to be taxed at a basic rate of 25%. Using the appropriate formula, generate the **TAX** (GROSS multiplied by 25%) for the first employee. Replicate this formula for each of the other employees as follows. Select cell **E6**; key in **=** and then select cell **D6** (using either the mouse to point and click once or the ← left cursor arrow key); key in ***25%** and ensure that the formula **=D6*25%** appears exactly like this in the Formula Bar; click the ✓ **Enter** box in the Formula Bar. With cell **E6** still selected click and drag to **E15** to highlight this range; from the Menu Bar, select **Edit**, **Fill**, **Down**.

7 The NI is to be calculated at a rate of 7%. Using the appropriate formula, generate the **NI** (GROSS multiplied by 7%) for the first employee. Replicate this formula for each of the other employees as follows. Select cell **F6** and key in the formula **=D6*7%** ensuring that it appears exactly like this in the Formula Bar; click the ✓ **Enter** box in the Formula Bar. With cell **F6** still selected click and drag to **F15** to highlight this range; from the Menu Bar, select **Edit**, **Fill**, **Down**.

8 Using the appropriate formula, generate the **NET** (GROSS minus TAX minus NI) for the first employee. Replicate this formula for each of the other employees as follows. Select cell **G6**; key in **=** and then select cell **D6**; key in **–** and then select cell **E6**; key in **–** and then select cell **F6**; ensure that the formula **=D6-E6-F6** appears exactly like this in the Formula Bar; click the ✓ **Enter** box in the Formula Bar. With cell **G6** still selected click and drag to **G15** to highlight this range; from the Menu Bar, select **Edit**, **Fill**, **Down**.

9 On the TOTAL row, using the appropriate formulae, generate **TOTALS** for the columns **WEEKLY HOURS**, **OVERTIME** and **NET** *only* as follows. Select cell **B16** and from the Tool Bar, select the Σ **Autosum** icon; check that the formula **=SUM(B6:B15)** appears in the Formula Bar; click the ✓ **Enter** box in the Formula Bar. With cell **B16** still selected, from the Tool Bar, select the 📋 **Copy** icon; select cell **C16** and from the Tool Bar, select the 📋 **Paste** icon; select cell **G16** and from the Tool Bar, select the 📋 **Paste** icon; with cell **G16** still selected from the Tool Bar, select .00/+.0 **Increase Decimal** to make this cell consistent with the others.

10 Select cell **A25** and enter your name; select cell **A26** and enter the filename **EPTASK4A**.

11 From the Menu Bar, select **File**, **Print Preview** to check the appearance of your worksheet and to ensure that it corresponds with the key. Click once to zoom in and once again to zoom out. Click **Close** when finished.

12 From the Menu Bar, select **File**, **Save**; ensure that the **Save in** text box displays Drive **A** and in the **File name** text box key in **EPTASK4A**; click **Save** to save the worksheet using a unique filename.

13 From the Tool Bar, select the 🖶 **Print** icon to print a copy of the worksheet.

14 Joanne Fisher's overtime hours were entered incorrectly on her clock card. She worked **10** overtime hours. Extend the worksheet by inserting a new row above **Anne Moore** and adding the new details as follows. Select row **6** heading button; from the Menu Bar, select **Insert**, **Rows**; select cell **A6** and key in Joanne Fisher (NB once you key in the first letter, it offers a match from the other cells, i.e. Jolanta Hughes); select cell **B6** and key in **42.0**; select cell **C6** and key in **10**.

15 Replicate the necessary formulae and ensure that the display is consistent as follows. Select cell **D7** and click and drag across to **G7** and upwards to extend the range to include the new row, i.e. from **D6** to **G6**; from the Menu Bar, select

Edit, **Fill**, **Up**. The formulae will be copied up and as you formatted the entire columns earlier to two decimal places the results should be consistent with the rest of the worksheet.

16 Correct any erroneous formulae as follows. Select cell **B17** and note from the Formula Bar that the range does not include the new row 6; click once between the letter **B** and the figure **7** in the Formula Bar and amend the formula to **=SUM(B6:B16)**; click the ✔️ **Enter** box in the Formula Bar; select cell **C17**; click once in the Formula Bar and amend the formula to **=SUM(C6:C16)**; click the ✔️ **Enter** box in the Formula Bar; select cell **G17**; click once in the Formula Bar and amend the formula to **=SUM(G6:G16)**; click the ✔️ **Enter** box in the Formula Bar. (Alternatively, you could have copied the new formula from B17 and pasted it to **C17** and **G17**.) With cell **G17** still selected from the Tool Bar, select 📊 **Increase Decimal** to make this cell consistent with the others.

17 In **A19** key in **AVERAGE**; in **A20** key in **HIGHEST**; in **A21** key in **LOWEST**; in **A22** key in **NO OF EMPLOYEES**; place the mouse pointer between column **A** and column **B** heading buttons until it becomes a double-headed arrow and then drag to the right to widen column **A** to display these entries fully.

18 Use the **AVERAGE** function to calculate the average weekly hours as follows. Select cell **B19**; key in **=AVERAGE(** and enter the range by either keying in **B6:B16** or by pointing to B6 and clicking and dragging to highlight the range to **B16**; key in **)** and ensure the formula **=AVERAGE(B6:B16)** is displayed in the Formula Bar; click the ✔️ **Enter** box in the Formula Bar.

19 Replicate this formula across the other columns as follows. With cell **B19** still selected, click and drag across to **G19**; from the Menu Bar, select **Edit**, **Fill**, **Right**.

20 With the range **B19–G19** still selected, from the Menu Bar choose **Format**, **Cells**, **Number**, from **Category** select **Number**, from **Decimal Places** select **0**; click **OK**.

21 Use the **MAX** function to calculate the highest number of overtime hours as follows. Select cell **C20**; key in **=MAX(** and enter the range **C6:C16**; key in **)** and ensure the formula **=MAX(C6:C16)** is displayed in the Formula Bar; click the ✔️ **Enter** box in the Formula Bar.

22 Use the **MIN** function to calculate the lowest number of overtime hours as follows. Select cell **C21**; key in **=MIN(** and enter the range **C6:C16**; key in **)** and ensure the formula **=MIN(C6:C16)** is displayed in the Formula Bar; click the ✔️ **Enter** box in the Formula Bar.

23 Use the **COUNT** function to calculate the number of employees as follows. Select cell **B22**; key in **=** and from the Tool Bar, select the 🔧 **Function Wizard** icon; from **Function Category** select **Most Recently Used**; from **Function Name**, select **COUNT**; click **Next>** and in **value1** text box key in **B6:B16** and click **Finish**; ensure the formula **=COUNT(B6:B16)** is displayed in the Formula Bar; click the ✔️ **Enter** box in the Formula Bar.

24 The centre manager of the garden centre may require all these staff to work a minimum of seven hours overtime during the next few weeks. In order to make a projection on the effect this might have, amend as follows. Select cell **C9** and increase Sylvia Cheshire's overtime hours from 2.5 to **7**; select cell **A24** and key in **PROJECTION**; select cell **B24** and key in the new **TOTAL** figure **3955**.4 for **NET**.

25 As this increase is only a projection, return the worksheet to its original values as follows. Select cell **C9**; key in **2.5** and note the effect this has on the TOTAL figure for NET.

26 Select cell **A27** and amend the filename to **EPTASK4B**.

27 From the Menu Bar, select **File**, **Print Preview** to check the appearance of your worksheet and to ensure that it corresponds with the key. Click once to zoom in and once again to zoom out. Click **Close** when finished.

28 From the Menu Bar, select **File**, **Save As** and save the worksheet to the disk in Drive A, using a unique filename, e.g. **EPTASK4B**.

29 From the Tool Bar, select the 🖨 **Print** icon to print a copy of the worksheet.

30 From the Menu Bar, select **File**, **Page Setup**; click the **Header/Footer** tab; select the **Custom Header …** button. Click once inside the **Left Section** text box and key in **SPERRIN SKYWAY**; select this text and click the **Font** icon to display the Font dialogue box; from **Font Style** select **Bold Italic** and from **Size** select **12**; click **OK**; in the **Centre Section** text box select (if necessary) the default code **&[Tab]** and press the **Delete** key on the keyboard; in the **Right Section** text box key in **GARDEN CENTRE ACCOUNTS**; click **OK**. This will return you to the **Header/Footer** tab window.

31 Select the **Custom Footer …** button to create your own footer. In the **Left Section** text box key in **Prepared by (YOUR NAME)**, **Date:** and press the **Space Bar** on the keyboard; click the **Date** icon to insert the current date code **&[Date]**; in the **Centre Section** text box select (if necessary) the default code **&[Page]** and press the **Delete** key on the keyboard; in the **Right Section** text box key in **Page** and press the **Space Bar** on the keyboard; click the **Page** icon to insert the current page number; click **OK**.

32 Select the **Print Preview** button to see how your worksheet now looks and to check this with the key; select **Close** when finished.

33 Select cell **A27** and amend the filename to **EPTASK4C**.

34 From the Menu Bar, select **File**, **Save As** and save the worksheet as **EPTASK4C**.

35 From the Tool Bar, select the 🖨 **Print** icon to print a copy of the worksheet.

36 Further projections are to be made to help the centre manager of the garden centre calculate the cost of employing an extra 23 more staff. These extra staff are to be based on the figures already available for Bob Nangle. To insert sufficient blank rows for these new entries, select row heading button **17** and drag to column heading button **39**; from the Menu Bar, select **Insert**, **Rows**.

37 Select cell **A16** and drag down to cell **G39** to highlight this range. From the Menu Bar, select **Edit**, **Fill**, **Down**. This will project Bob Nangle's details for the potential new staff.

38 Select cell **B40** and from the Tool Bar, select the Σ **Autosum** icon; check that the formula **=SUM(B6:B39)** appears in the Formula Bar; click the ✔ **Enter** box in the Formula Bar.

39 With cell **B40** still selected, from the Tool Bar, select the 📋 **Copy** icon; select cell **C40** and from the Tool Bar, select the 📋 **Paste** icon; check that the formula **=SUM(C6:C39)** appears in the Formula Bar; select cell **G40** and from the Tool Bar, select the 📋 **Paste** icon; check that the formula **=SUM(G6:G39)** appears in the Formula Bar, with cell **G40** still selected from the Tool Bar, select ⁺⁰⁄₀₀ **Increase Decimal** to make this cell consistent with the others.

40 Select cell **B42**; click once in the Formula Bar and amend the formula to **=AVERAGE(B6:B39)**; click the ✔ **Enter** box in the Formula Bar.

41 With cell **B42** still selected, drag across to **G42** to highlight this range; from the Menu Bar, select **Edit**, **Fill**, **Right**.

42 Select cell **C43**; click once in the Formula Bar and amend the formula to **=MAX(C6:C39)**; click the ✔ **Enter** box in the Formula Bar.

43 Select cell **C44**; click once in the Formula Bar and amend the formula to **=MIN(C6:C39)**; click the ✔ **Enter** box in the Formula Bar.

44 Select cell **B45**; click once in the Formula Bar and amend the formula to **=COUNT(B6:B39)**; click the ✔ **Enter** box in the Formula Bar.

45 Select row heading button **47**; from the Menu Bar, select **Edit**, **Delete** to delete this row, which is no longer required; deselect.

46 From the Menu Bar, select **File**, **Page Setup**, select the **Page** tab and in the **Orientation** section, select the **Landscape** radio button; click **OK**.

47 From the Menu Bar, select **File**, **Print Preview** to check the appearance of your worksheet. Click **Next** and click **Previous** to view each page. Click **Close** when finished.

48 As it is difficult to remember which column headings the figures on page 2 relate to, these column headings can also be shown on page 2 as follows. Once you have checked the range of the rows to be repeated (i.e. **A3:G4**) from the Menu Bar, select **File**, **Page Setup**; select the **Sheet** tab and in the **Print Titles** section click on the text box **Rows to Repeat at Top:** and key in the range **A3:G4**; click **OK**.

49 Select cell **A49** and enter the filename **EPTASK4D**.

50 From the Menu Bar, select **File**, **Print Preview** to check the appearance of your worksheet and to ensure that it corresponds with the key. Click once to zoom in and once again to zoom out. Click **Close** when finished.

51 From the Menu Bar, select **File**, **Save As** and save the worksheet using a unique filename, e.g. **EPTASK4D**.

52 From the Tool Bar, select the 🖨 **Print** icon to print a copy of the worksheet.

53 From the Menu Bar, select **File**, **Close** to close the worksheet; select **File**, **Exit** to exit from Excel.

Don't forget to complete the Record of Progress sheet to indicate that you have finished this unit successfully.

Imagine you work in an organisation where there are 18 employees, based in two divisions, one at Donard and the other at Ards. Staff are employed in two main aspects of the business: retail outlet and mail order, both of which are co-ordinated by the Division Manager.

The data you require is given in Figure 4.16 in the form of clock cards. You must read the questions very carefully and it will probably help if you underline or highlight the key requirements before you extract the specified data.

Initially you will be required to design a worksheet which can be used in wages calculations for employees. It should display the wages for mail-order employees who have worked overtime at the Donard division. You will need to organise your data to show the staff names, weekly hours and overtime hours. Formulae to calculate the gross, tax, NI (National Insurance) and net for each employee should be inserted. You will also be expected to provide a total for each of these calculations as well as the overall total wages bill.

1   Load Excel and in cell **A1** of the new worksheet, key in the following title:

THE DESIGNER COLLECTION

2   In cell **A2** key in the following subtitle:

Mail Order Employees, Donard Division

3   Study the details on the clock cards in Figure 4.16 and extract the names of the Donard division mail-order employees who have worked overtime. Enter these names into column **A**; enter their weekly hours into column **B**; enter their overtime into column **C**. Your worksheet should be set out similarly to the one below and must include the following, although headings can be abbreviated:

NAME	WEEKLY HOURS	OVER-TIME	GROSS	TAX	NI	NET

TOTAL

Ensure that:
• **NAME** appears in cell **A3**.
• The **name** of the first full-time employee appears in cell **A6**.
• **TOTAL** appears in cell **A16**.

4   Once you have entered the text and data, it should look like Figure 4.17 – if not, read the questions again carefully to find where you went wrong and amend it so that it appears the same. Please also ensure that

• column **A** is widened sufficiently to display the staff names, using the Menu Bar;
• the text in the first column is left aligned, using the Tool Bar;
• the other column headings are right aligned, using the Tool Bar;
• the weekly and overtime hours are displayed to **one** decimal place, using the Menu Bar; and
• any monetary amounts are displayed to **two** decimal places, using the Menu Bar.

5   Staff are paid £6.25 per hour and £7.81 per overtime hour. Enter an appropriate formula to calculate the **GROSS** (WEEKLY HOURS multiplied by 6.25) + (OVERTIME multiplied by 7.81) for the first employee. Replicate this formula for each of the other employees using the **Fill** command from the Menu Bar.

DONARD	CLOCK CARD		DONARD	CLOCK CARD
NAME:	Margaret Smyth		**NAME:**	Mary Bradley
GRADE:	MAIL ORDER		**GRADE:**	MAIL ORDER
WEEKLY HRS:	42		**WEEKLY HRS:**	42
OVERTIME:	8		**OVERTIME:**	0
DONARD	CLOCK CARD		DONARD	CLOCK CARD
NAME:	Martin Mason		**NAME:**	Julie Broady
GRADE:	RETAIL OUTLET		**GRADE:**	MAIL ORDER
WEEKLY HRS:	42		**WEEKLY HRS:**	42
OVERTIME:	8		**OVERTIME:**	8.5
DONARD	CLOCK CARD		ARDS	CLOCK CARD
NAME:	Rose Cullen		**NAME:**	David Bell
GRADE:	MAIL ORDER		**GRADE:**	RETAIL OUTLET
WEEKLY HRS:	42		**WEEKLY HRS:**	42
OVERTIME:	8.5		**OVERTIME:**	12
DONARD	CLOCK CARD		DONARD	CLOCK CARD
NAME:	Kathy Crowe		**NAME:**	Neville Stanway
GRADE:	MAIL ORDER		**GRADE:**	RETAIL OUTLET
WEEKLY HRS:	42		**WEEKLY HRS:**	42
OVERTIME:	4.5		**OVERTIME:**	0
ARDS	CLOCK CARD		DONARD	CLOCK CARD
NAME:	Jayne Taylor		**NAME:**	Diane Henderson
GRADE:	MAIL ORDER		**GRADE:**	MAIL ORDER
WEEKLY HRS:	42		**WEEKLY HRS:**	42
OVERTIME:	10		**OVERTIME:**	8
DONARD	CLOCK CARD		DONARD	CLOCK CARD
NAME:	John Masters		**NAME:**	Anna Gee
GRADE:	MAIL ORDER		**GRADE:**	MAIL ORDER
WEEKLY HRS:	42		**WEEKLY HRS:**	42
OVERTIME:	12		**OVERTIME:**	10
ARDS	CLOCK CARD		DONARD	CLOCK CARD
NAME:	Charlie Phillips		**NAME:**	Jim Johnston
GRADE:	RETAIL OUTLET		**GRADE:**	RETAIL OUTLET
WEEKLY HRS:	42		**WEEKLY HRS:**	42
OVERTIME:	3		**OVERTIME:**	6
DONARD	CLOCK CARD		DONARD	CLOCK CARD
NAME:	Jean Madden		**NAME:**	Helen Stevens
GRADE:	MAIL ORDER		**GRADE:**	MAIL ORDER
WEEKLY HRS:	42		**WEEKLY HRS:**	42
OVERTIME:	8		**OVERTIME:**	8.5
DONARD	CLOCK CARD		DONARD	CLOCK CARD
NAME:	Graham Murray		**NAME:**	Jim Mather
GRADE:	Division Manager		**GRADE:**	MAIL ORDER
WEEKLY HRS:	42		**WEEKLY HRS:**	42
OVERTIME:	0		**OVERTIME:**	8

Figure 4.16 YOYO4 clock cards

	A	B	C	D	E	F	G	
1	THE DESIGNER COLLECTION							
2	Mail Order Employees, Donard Division							
3	NAME	WEEKLY	OVER-	GROSS	TAX	NI	NET	
4		HOURS	TIME					
5								
6	Margaret Smyth	42.0	8.0					
7	Rose Cullen	42.0	8.5					
8	Kathy Crowe	42.0	4.5					
9	John Masters	42.0	12.0					
10	Jean Madden	42.0	8.0					
11	Julie Broady	42.0	8.5					
12	Diane Henderson	42.0	8.0					
13	Anna Gee	42.0	10.0					
14	Helen Stevens	42.0	8.5					
15	Jim Mather	42.0	8.0					
16	TOTAL							

Figure 4.17 YOYO4 worksheet

6 The gross income is to be taxed at a basic rate of 25%. Enter an appropriate formula to calculate the **TAX** (GROSS multiplied by 25%) for the first employee. Replicate this formula for each of the other employees using the **Fill** command from the Menu Bar.

7 The NI is to be calculated at a rate of 7%. Enter an appropriate formula to calculate the **NI** (GROSS multiplied by 7%) for the first employee. Replicate this formula for each of the other employees using the **Fill** command from the Menu Bar.

8 Enter an appropriate formula to calculate the **NET** (GROSS minus TAX minus NI) for the first employee. Replicate this formula for each of the other employees using the **Fill** command from the Menu Bar.

9 On the **TOTAL** row, enter appropriate formulae to calculate totals for the columns WEEKLY HOURS, OVERTIME and NET **only** using **Autosum** from the Tool Bar. Ensure that the display in cell **G16** is consistent with the rest of column **G**.

10 Select cell **A25** and enter your name; select cell **A26** and enter the filename **YOYO4A**.

11 Display **Print Preview** to check the appearance of your worksheet and to ensure that it corresponds with the key.

12 Save the worksheet using a unique filename, i.e. **YOYO4A**.

13 Print a copy of the worksheet.

14 Mary Bradley's overtime hours were entered incorrectly on her clock card. She worked **10** overtime hours and therefore needs to be included in the worksheet. Extend the worksheet by inserting a new row above **Margaret Smyth** and add the new details as follows: in cell **A6** key in **Mary Bradley**; in cell **B6** key in **42.0**; in cell **C6** key in **10**.

15 Replicate the necessary formulae in row **6** and ensure that the display is consistent. Since you formatted the entire columns earlier to two decimal places the results should be consistent with the rest of the worksheet.

16 Correct any erroneous formulae (check cells **B17**, **C17**, **G17**). Ensure that the data in cell **G17** is consistent with the rest of column G.

17 In **A19** key in **AVERAGE**; in **A20** key in **HIGHEST**; in **A21** key in **LOWEST**; in **A22** key in **NO OF EMPLOYEES**; ensure that column **A** is widened sufficiently to display these entries fully.

18 In cell **B19** enter a formula, using the **AVERAGE** function, to calculate the average weekly hours.

19 Replicate this formula across from cell **B19** to **G19**.

20 Format the **AVERAGE** figures for integer (no decimal places).

21 In cell **C20** enter a formula, using the **MAX** function, to calculate the highest number of overtime hours.

22 In cell **C21** enter a formula, using the **MIN** function, to calculate the lowest number of overtime hours.

23 In cell **B22** enter a formula, using the **COUNT** function, to calculate the number of employees – try using the **Function Wizard** from the Tool Bar.

24 The Division Manager of the organisation may require all staff (including Kathy Crowe) to work a minimum of 8 hours overtime during the next few weeks. In order to make a projection on the effect this might have, please increase Kathy Crowe's overtime hours from 4.5 to **8**; select cell **A24** and key in **PROJECTION**; select cell **B24** and key in the new **TOTAL** figure for **NET** (**2481.3**).

25 As this increase is only a projection, return the worksheet to its original values and note the effect this has on the TOTAL figure for NET.

26 Amend the filename on the worksheet to **YOYO4B**.

27 Display **Print Preview** to check the appearance of your worksheet and to ensure it corresponds with the key.

28 Save the worksheet to the disk in Drive A, using a unique filename, e.g. **YOYO4B**.

29 Print a copy of the worksheet.

30 From the **Print Preview** screen, display the **Custom Header ...** dialogue box. Click once inside the **Left Section** text box and key in **THE DESIGNER COLLECTION**; select this text and display the data in bold italic, font size 12; in the **Centre Section** text box remove (if necessary) the default code **&[Tab]**; in the **Right Section** text box key in **ACCOUNTS**; return to the **Header/Footer** tab window .

31 Display the **Custom Footer ...** dialogue box. In the **Left Section** text box key in **Prepared by YOUR NAME**, **Date:** and insert the correct date code; in the **Centre Section** text box delete (if necessary) the default page code; in the **Right Section** text box key in **Page** and insert the current page number code.

32 Select **Print Preview** to see how your worksheet now looks and to check this with the key.

33 Amend the filename on the worksheet to **YOYO4C**.

34 Save the worksheet as **YOYO4C**.

35 Print a copy of the worksheet.

36 Further projections are to be made to help the Division Manager of the organisation calculate the cost of employing 23 extra staff. These extra staff are to be based on the figures already available for Jim Mather. Using the Menu Bar, insert sufficient blank rows for these 23 new entries, from row **17** to row **39**.

37 Use Jim Mather's details in row **16** to project the figures down to row **39** for the potential new staff.

38 In the **TOTAL** cell for **WEEKLY HOURS** amend the formula to include the new rows.

39 Copy this formula to the **TOTAL** cell for **OVERTIME** and the **TOTAL** cell for **NET**. Ensure that each **TOTAL** is displayed consistently with the rest of the data in the column.

40 In the **AVERAGE** cell for **WEEKLY HOURS** amend the formula to include the 23 new rows.

41 Copy this formula across for the rest of the data in the **AVERAGE** row.

42 In the **HIGHEST** cell for **OVERTIME** amend the formula to include the 23 new rows.

43 In the **LOWEST** cell for **OVERTIME** amend the formula to include the 23 new rows.

44 In the **NO OF EMPLOYEES** cell for **WEEKLY HOURS** amend the formula to include the 23 new rows.

45 Delete the row containing **PROJECTION**, which is no longer required.

46 Select **Page Setup** to change the **Orientation** to **Landscape**.

47 Display **Print Preview** to check the appearance of your worksheet.

48 As it is difficult to remember which column headings the figures on page 2 relate to, these column headings should also be shown on page 2. Check the range of the rows to be repeated and select **Page Setup** to enter the range of rows to repeat at the top.

49 Amend the filename on the worksheet to **YOYO4D**.

50 Display **Print Preview** to check the appearance of your worksheet and to ensure it corresponds with the key.

51 Save the worksheet using a unique filename, e.g. **YOYO4D**.

52 Print a copy of the worksheet.

53 Close the worksheet and exit from Excel.

Don't forget to complete the Record of Progress sheet to indicate that you have finished this unit successfully.

5 worksheet development and testing

By the end of this unit you should be able to:

- *update and amend an existing worksheet*
- *obtain data from other worksheets by linking worksheets*
- *use absolute, relative and mixed cell reference addresses*
- *assign names to cells and ranges of cells*
- *protect worksheets*

Update and amend an existing worksheet

By now you should have mastered the basics of worksheet creation, amendment and manipulation, which are essential requirements for the RSA Stage II Spreadsheets examination. In this examination, and indeed at work, you will be expected to load and update fairly large (approximately 300 cells of supplied data) worksheets. This must be done with 100% accuracy of number and formula input, although there is a small error margin for text and labels of three data entry errors. Clearly, then, it is of paramount importance that you constantly check and proofread your work to ensure that your figures are 100% accurate and that you have carried out the exact requirements of the task. At the end of the examination, it is vital that you go back to the beginning of the examination paper and reread each individual question, checking that every instruction has been carried out and can be evidenced by your printouts.

In this unit you will revise updating and amending existing worksheets and then you will be introduced to a range of ways of testing and checking your data to ensure its integrity.

Before you start TASK 5A make sure that you have a file on your floppy disk (which is called TASK4J) containing the worksheet which you will be required to amend, update and display.

Task 5A

1 Load Excel and open the file **TASK4J**.

2 It has been noticed that Angela Black's time sheet was given for Week 33 by mistake. Her details should have been recorded in Week 32 instead, so the worksheet needs to be extended to include this. Select row **12** heading button and from the Menu Bar, select **Insert**, **Rows** to add a row between Kevin Barrat and Mike Green; select cell **A12** and enter the following:

NAME	WEEKLY HOURS	OVERTIME
Angela Black	**40**	**0**

Select cell **B41** and ensure that the formulae to generate the **TOTAL WEEKLY HOURS** includes this row.

Extend the formulae for **GROSS**, **TAX**, **NI** and **NET** to include the new row as follows. Select **D11** and drag down to **G12** to highlight this range; from the Menu Bar, select **Edit**, **Fill**, **Down**.

3 Another omission has been made – details for Julie White should also have been recorded in Week 32, so the worksheet needs to be extended to include this. Select row **6** heading button and from the Menu Bar, select **Insert**, **Rows** to add a row above Keith Daley; select cell **A6** and enter the following:

NAME	WEEKLY HOURS	OVERTIME
Julie White	**42**	**12.5**

Select cell **B42** and ensure that the formula to generate the **TOTAL WEEKLY HOURS** includes this row as follows. Click once in the Formula Bar and amend the formula **=SUM(B6:B41)**; click ✔ **Enter** box in the Formula Bar; with cell **B42** still selected, from the Tool Bar, select the 📋 **Copy** icon; select cell **C42** and from the Tool Bar, select the 📋 **Paste** icon; check that the formula **=SUM(C6:C41)** appears in the Formula Bar; select cell **G42** and from the Tool Bar, select the 📋 **Paste** icon; check that the formula **=SUM(G6:G41)** appears in the Formula Bar.

Extend the formulae for **GROSS**, **TAX**, **NI** and **NET** to include the new row as follows. Select **D7** and drag up to **G6**; from the Menu Bar, select **Edit**, **Fill**, **Up**.

4 It has been realised that the details for **Bob Dunn** were entered for Week 32 by mistake, as he did not actually commence work at the community club until Week 33. The worksheet needs to be reduced to reflect this. Delete the whole row containing this information as follows. Select row **17** heading button; from the Menu Bar, select **Edit**, **Delete**. Select cell **B41** to check that the worksheet has recalculated automatically to take account of this deletion.

5 Other errors have been discovered on the worksheet. Make the following amendments to the data:

- The **WEEKLY HOURS** for **Keith Daley** should be **42**, not 40.
- The **OVERTIME** for **Jake Johnston** should be **12.5**, not 7.5.
- **Kevin Barrat** has been spelt incorrectly and should be **Kevin Barratt**.
- **Paul Gibson** is not the complete name and should be **Paul Gibson-Greene**.
- The **WEEKLY HOURS** for **Vera Brown** should be **42**, not 40.
- **Adrian Lang** has been spelt incorrectly and should be **Adrian Long**.

Check that the amendments you have made are correct as total accuracy is required.

6 Within the worksheet, projected figures have been used for the potential employment of a number of new staff. The manager would prefer to see the actual cost of wages for Week 32 separated from the estimated cost were these new staff to be employed. This will require you to divide the worksheet into two sections and to insert new rows as follows:

Select row 6 heading button; from the Menu Bar, select **Insert**, **Rows** to insert two rows; select cell **A6** and key in **CURRENT EMPLOYEES**; select row **19** heading button and drag to row **20** heading button; from the Menu Bar, select **Insert**, **Rows**; select cell **A20** and key in **POTENTIAL EMPLOYEES**.

Change the column width of the first column from its current setting so that the new information can be displayed in full, leaving at least two character spaces at the end of the longest label as follows. Position the mouse pointer between column **A** and **B** heading buttons until it changes to a double-headed arrow; click and drag to the right until column **A** extends to at least two character spaces beyond the phrase **POTENTIAL EMPLOYEES**.

Check that the formulae used to calculated the totals are correct by selecting cells **B44**, **C44** and **G44** and ensuring the rows **7–43** are included.

7 It has been decided that the summary information on the worksheet would be more useful to the manager if it related to **NET** figures rather than **HOURS**. Delete the cell contents as follows: select cell **B46** and drag to cell **G50** to highlight this range; from the Menu Bar, select **Edit**, **Clear**, **All**; select cell **A46** and amend the entry to **AVERAGE WEEKLY WAGE**; select cell **A47** and amend the entry to **HIGHEST WEEKLY WAGE**; select cell **A48** and amend the entry to **LOWEST WEEKLY WAGE**.

- Use the **AVERAGE** function to calculate the average net wages for a member of staff and enter this in the second column alongside the label **AVERAGE WEEKLY WAGE** as follows. Select **B46** and key in **=AVERAGE(G7:G43)**; press ↵ (**Enter**).

- Use the **MAXIMUM** function to calculate the maximum net wages for a member of staff and enter this in the second column alongside the label **HIGHEST WEEKLY WAGE** as follows. Select **B47** and key in **=MAX(G7:G43)**; press ↵ (**Enter**).

- Use the **MINIMUM** function to calculate the minimum net wages for a member of staff and enter this in the second column alongside the label **LOWEST WEEKLY WAGE** as follows. Select **B48** and key in **=MIN(G7:G43)**; press ↵ (**Enter**).

- Use the **COUNT** function to calculate the number of staff employed and enter this in the second column alongside the label **NO OF EMPLOYEES** as follows. Select **B50** and key in **=COUNT(G7:G43)**; press ↵ (**Enter**).

8 The **AVERAGE WEEKLY WAGE** should be displayed in integer format (no decimal places) as follows. Select cell **B46**; from the Menu Bar, select **Format**, **Cells**, **Number**; from **Category**, select **Number**; from **Decimal Places**, select **0**; click **OK**.

9 The **HIGHEST** and **LOWEST WEEKLY WAGE** should be displayed in currency format to two decimal places as follows. Select cell **B47** and drag to include cell **B48**; from the Menu Bar, select **Format**, **Cells**, **Number**; from **Category**, select **Currency**; from **Decimal Places**, select 2; from **Symbol** select **£ English (British)**; click **OK**.

10 Insert three new rows after the summary information as follows. Select row **52** heading button and drag to row **55** heading button; from the Menu Bar, select **Insert**, **Rows**; select cell **A52** and key in **CURRENT EMPLOYEES**; select cell **A53** and key in **GROSS WEEKLY WAGES**; select cell **B53** and key in **=SUM(D7:D18)**; select cell **A54** and key in **GROSS MONTHLY WAGES**; select cell **B54** and key in **=B53*4** to calculate the monthly cost (based on four weeks for simplicity).

11 Select cell **A53** and amend the filename to **TASK5A**.

12 From the Menu Bar, select **File**, **Print Preview** to check the appearance of your worksheet and to ensure that it corresponds with the key. Click once to zoom in and once again to zoom out. Click **Close** when finished.

13 From the Menu Bar, select **File**, **Save As** and save the worksheet as **TASK5A**.

14 From the Tool Bar, select the 🖶 **Print** icon to print a copy of the worksheet.

15 Show the formulae (cell contents) and ensure that the printout will display the entire width of each formula used as follows. From the Menu Bar, select **Tools**, **Options** and click the **View** tab; from the **Window Options** column click on the checkbox beside **Formulae** to display √ and click **OK**. Your worksheet will now be shown with all the formulae displayed and the columns will be widened automatically to accommodate this. Try to decrease the width of the worksheet as follows. Place the mouse pointer between column **A** and **B** heading buttons until it changes to a double-headed arrow; click and drag to the left so that the column is sufficiently wide to display the longest label, i.e. **AVERAGE WEEKLY WAGE**; continue to alter the other columns widths in the same way so that the worksheet fits on to one page and ensuring that the formulae are fully displayed.

16 Select cell **A57** and amend the filename to **TASK5AF**.

17 From the Menu Bar, select **File**, **Print Preview** to check the appearance of your worksheet and to ensure that it corresponds with the key. Click once to zoom in and once again to zoom out. Click **Close** when finished.

18 From the Menu Bar, select **File**, **Save As** and save the worksheet as **TASK5AF**.

19 Print a copy of the summary formulae only, as follows. Select cell **A44** and drag to cell **G57** to highlight this range; from the Menu Bar, select **File**, **Print**; in the **Print What** box click on the **Selection** button; click **OK**.

20 From the Menu Bar, select **File**, **Close** to close the file.

Link worksheets

Linking worksheets can be done by referring to a specific cell reference in one worksheet file and linking it to a specific cell reference in another worksheet file. This means that when you make a change to a cell in one worksheet it will automatically update the cell in the other worksheet. In the case study of the community club, for instance, you could link the cell containing the overall total wages for the instructors in the wages worksheet file to a cell for wages costs in perhaps an income and expenditure worksheet file. This would ensure that any alteration to the instructors' wages would also be reflected in the income and expenditure account.

It is good business practice not to let your worksheet get so large and cumbersome that a manager might have difficulty in comprehending the sheer volume of information provided. It is helpful, therefore, to create several smaller but related worksheets and perhaps to produce a summary worksheet which links and summarises key data such as overall totals.

Linking worksheets

- Ensure that all the required worksheet files are opened, e.g. **TASK5A**, **TASK5B**. One will be placed on top of the other, the names of which will be displayed in a drop-down list if you click on **Window** in the Menu Bar.

- On the worksheet where you wish to establish the link, e.g. **TASK5B**, select the cell that is to be linked, e.g. **C25**.

- Key in the **=** sign.

- From the Menu Bar, select **Windows** and from the drop-down list, click once on the required worksheet filename, e.g. **TASK5A**.

- On this worksheet, e.g. **TASK5A**, select the cell containing the data or formulae that you wish to be linked, e.g. **B54**.

- Click the ✔ **Enter** box in the Formula Bar or press **Enter**. The cell reference of the linked cell, preceded by the name of the workbook and the worksheet, will be displayed in the Formula Bar, e.g. **[TASK5A]Sheet1!$B$54**.

In future, each time you open a worksheet containing a linked cell (or cells), it will automatically retrieve the contents of the cell (or cells) from the linked worksheet without you having to open this worksheet file. A dialogue box similar to the one in Figure 5.1 will be displayed and you should click **Yes** to re-establish the links.

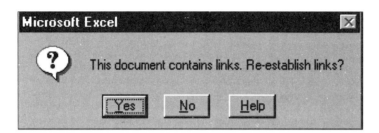

Figure 5.1 Re-establishing Links dialogue box

You can of course open this worksheet file if required by selecting from the Menu Bar **Edit**, **Links …** A dialogue box similar to the one in Figure 5.2 will be displayed, listing all the workbook and worksheet filenames that are linked to the current worksheet. In the example in Figure 5.2 the file linked to the one on screen is shown as the source file, i.e. Task5A.xls.

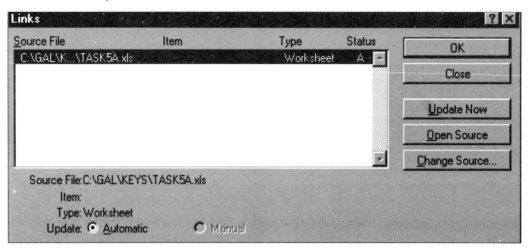

Figure 5.2 Links dialogue box

Select the worksheet that you wish to open and click once on the **Open Source** button.

Task 5B

To enable the manager to estimate what the cash flow might be over a six-month period, you are required to plan a simple worksheet to show the predicted receipts and payments from **JAN** to **JUL**. The first section should include the **INCOME** from

SUBSCRIPTIONS
FEES
BAR SALES

The second section should include **EXPENDITURE** for

WAGES – INSTRUCTORS
WAGES – OTHERS
OVERHEADS
BAR SUPPLIES

You will need to extract the information from the test data financial statistics below and you will have to link this worksheet with the worksheet from **TASK 5A**:

Test data: financial statistics

- Monthly income from subscriptions is £15,080.
- Monthly income from fees from non-members is £6,940.
- Weekly bar sales amount to £5,950.
- Weekly bar supplies cost £2,957.
- Wages: Instructors – monthly figure to be taken from the worksheet on wages.
    Other – £4,200 per month.

- Overheads amount to £1,200 per week.

1   Open **TASK5A** as you will now be required to link data from this worksheet with a new worksheet. With **TASK5A** open on screen, from the Tool Bar click once on 🗋 **New workbook** to open a new workbook on to your screen. (TASK5A is still there underneath this new workbook as you will need to refer to it later in this task.)

2   Select cell **A1** and enter the title **SPERRIN VIEW COMMUNITY CLUB INCOME AND EXPENDITURE ACCOUNT**.

3   Select cell **B3** and enter the heading **JAN**; click the ✔ **Enter** box in the Formula Bar; position the mouse pointer at the bottom right edge of cell **B3** until it changes to a ✛ (cross); click and drag to cell **G3** to fill the cells with the months **FEB, MAR, APR, MAY, JUN**.

4   Select cell **A4** and key in **INCOME**; select cell **A5** and key in **SUBSCRIPTIONS**; select cell **A6** and key in **FEES**; select cell **A7** and key in **BAR SALES**; select cell **A8** and key in **TOTAL INCOME**.

5   Select cell **A10** and key in **EXPENDITURE**; select cell **A11** and key in **WAGES – INSTRUCTORS**; select **A12** and key in **WAGES – OTHER**; select cell **A13** and key in **OVERHEADS**; select cell **A14** and key in **BAR SUPPLIES**; select cell **A15** and key in **TOTAL EXPENDITURE**.

6   Select cell **A17** and key in **STATISTICAL ANALYSIS**; place the mouse pointer between column **A** and **B** heading buttons until it changes to a double-headed arrow and click and drag to the right so that the column is sufficiently widened; select cell **B17** and key in **WEEKLY**; select cell **C17** and key in **MONTHLY**; select cell **A4** and drag down to cell **A15** to highlight this range; from the Tool Bar, select 📋 **Copy**; select cell **A18** and from the Tool Bar, select 📋 **Paste** to place a copy of the row headings from row **18** to **29**.

7   Refer to the **FINANCIAL STATISTICS** and enter the test data that has been

provided as follows. Select cell **C19** and enter **15080** (the monthly income from subscriptions); select cell **C20** and enter **6940** (the monthly income from fees from non-members); select cell **B21** and enter **5950** (the weekly bar sales); select cell **B28** and enter **2957** (the weekly bar supplies); select cell **C25** and link this cell to the worksheet on wages to generate the instructors' wages amount as follows: key in **=** and from the Menu Bar, select <u>**Window**</u> and from the filenames at the bottom of the drop-down options click once on the filename **TASK5A** to bring this file to the front; on the worksheet **TASK5A**, select **GROSS MOTHLY WAGES** in cell **B54** and click the ✔ **Enter** box in the formula bar. This returns you to cell **C25** in your other worksheet and links this cell with the **GROSS MONTHLY WAGES** figure in **TASK5A**. Select cell **C25** and note the link details in the Formula Bar, i.e. **=[TASK5A]Sheet1!$B$54**.

8   Select cell **C26** and key in **4200** (other expenditure per month); select cell **B27** and key in **1200** (overheads per week).

9   Select **A31** and key in **YOUR NAME**; select cell **A32** and key in **TASK5B**.

10 From the Menu Bar, select <u>**File**</u>, **Print Pre<u>v</u>iew** to check the appearance of your worksheet and to ensure that it corresponds with the key. Click once to zoom in and once again to zoom out. Click <u>**Close**</u> when finished.

11 From the Menu Bar, select <u>**File**</u>, **Save <u>A</u>s** and save the worksheet as **TASK5B**.

12 From the Tool Bar, select the 🖨 **Print** icon to print a copy of the worksheet.

Absolute, relative and mixed cell references

Until now, when you have input formulae Excel, by default, has used *relative* cell references. As a result, when you have copied a formula from one cell to another, the cell references have changed to reflect the formula's new location. This is because the formula is carried out in relation to the position of a cell or range of cells. Suppose you input a formula, such as the *sum* of a range of rows in column **A**; then copy this to column **B**; it will carry out the same function relative to the range of rows in column **B**.

However, there may be times when you want a formula to refer to one specific cell in the worksheet. To do this you need to use an *absolute* cell reference so Excel will refer to one specific cell even when you copy or move the formula to another location. The $ symbol is used to indicate an absolute cell reference, e.g. **$C$19** which means that any formula containing this reference will always refer to cell **C19** regardless of where the formula is copied or moved to in the worksheet.

Sometimes you may want a formula to refer only to one specific row or column in the worksheet. To do this you can use a *mixed* cell reference, so Excel will refer to the values in a specific row (absolute), but the values in the columns will change (relative) or conversely refer to the values in a specific column, but the values in the row will change.

Using absolute, relative and mixed cell references

•   Select the cell where the formula containing the absolute cell reference is to appear.

•   Key in the formula and key in the cell reference, preceded by the **$** symbol

or

- key in the formula, point to the cell reference and press the function key **F4**. Repeatedly pressing F4 will toggle you through the different types of cell referencing, as shown in the examples below:

C19 (a *relative* cell reference)   A formula containing this will use different cell references relative to its position when it is copied or moved, so as to reflect the formula's new location in the worksheet.

$C$19 (an *absolute* cell reference)   A formula containing this will always use this specific cell when it is copied or moved, regardless of its location in the worksheet.

C$19 (a *mixed* cell reference)   A formula containing this will use different columns relative to its position but will always use this specific row, when it is copied or moved.

$C19 (a *mixed* cell reference)   A formula containing this will always use this specific column but will use different rows relative to its position, when it is copied or moved.

	Task 5C	▼ ▲

1   With **TASK5B** still on screen you will now need to extract the data from the statistical analysis section to produce the predictions for the income and expenditure account. Since there will be several times when we wish a formula to refer to one specific cell in the statistical analysis section, we need to use absolute cell references for the monthly figures as follows:

Select cell **B5** and key in **=$C$19** and click the ✓ **Enter** box in the Formula Bar; position the mouse pointer at the bottom right edge of cell **B5** until it changes to a ⊕ (cross); click and drag to cell **G5** to replicate this formula across to the other cells.

Select cell **B6** and key in **=$C$20** and click the ✓ **Enter** box in the Formula Bar; position the mouse pointer at the bottom right edge of cell **B6** until it changes to a ⊕ (cross); click and drag to cell **G6** to replicate this formula across to the other cells.

Select cell **B11** and key in **=$C$25** and click the ✓ **Enter** box in the Formula Bar; position the mouse pointer at the bottom right edge of cell **B11** until it changes to a ⊕ (cross); click and drag to cell **G11** to replicate this formula across to the other cells.

Select **B12** and key in **=$C$26** and click the ✓ **Enter** box in the Formula Bar; position the mouse pointer at the bottom right edge of cell **B12** until it changes to a ⊕ (cross); click and drag to cell **G12** to replicate this formula across to the other cells.

2   To enable you to perform a cross-check on the test data later you can, at this stage, set up the formulae that will calculate the totals, as follows:

Select cell **B8**; from the Tool Bar, click **Autosum** and ensure that the formula **=SUM(B5:B7)** appears in the Formula Bar; click the ✓ **Enter** box in the Formula Bar; position the mouse pointer at the bottom right edge of cell **B8** until it changes to a ⊕ (cross); click and drag to cell **G8** to replicate this formula across to the other cells.

Select cell **B15**; from the Tool Bar, click **Σ** **Autosum** and sure that the formula **=SUM(B11:B14)** appears in the Formula Bar; click the ✓ **Enter** box in the Formula Bar; position the mouse pointer at the bottom right edge of cell **B15** until it changes to a ⊕ (cross); click and drag to cell **G15** to replicate this formula across to the other cells.

Select cell **C22**; from the Tool Bar, click **Σ Autosum** and ensure that the formula **=SUM(C19:C21)** appears in the Formula Bar; click the **✔ Enter** box in the Formula Bar.

Select cell **C29**; from the Tool Bar, click **Σ Autosum** and ensure that the formula **=SUM(C25:C28)** appears in the Formula Bar; click the **✔ Enter** box in the Formula Bar.

3 Since it would also be useful to display the potential profit or loss, insert two blank rows for this calculation as follows. Select row **17** heading button and drag to row **18** heading button to highlight these two rows; from the Menu Bar, select **Insert, Rows**; select cell **A17** and key in **PROFIT/LOSS**; select cell **B17** and key in **=B8-B15** (total income minus total expenditure); click the **✔ Enter** box in the Formula Bar; position the mouse pointer at the bottom right edge of cell **B17** until it changes to a ✛ (cross); click and drag to cell **G17** to replicate this formula across to the other cells. The figures will not be completely accurate at this stage since not all the data has been input yet.

4 Also to help you cross-check your data later you can input formula for the monthly profit or loss in the statistical analysis as follows. Select row **33** heading button and drag to row **34** heading button to highlight these two rows; from the Menu Bar, select **Insert, Rows**; select cell **A33** and key in **PROFIT/LOSS**; select cell **C33** and key in **=C24-C31** (total income minus total expenditure); click the **✔ Enter** box in the Formula Bar.

5 Select cell **A36** and amend the filename to **TASK5C**.

6 From the Menu Bar, select **File, Print Preview** to check the appearance of your worksheet and to ensure that it corresponds with the key. Click once to zoom in and once again to zoom out. Click **Close** when finished.

7 From the Menu Bar, select **File, Save As** and save the worksheet as **TASK5C**.

8 From the Tool Bar, select the **Print** icon to print a copy of the worksheet.

Named cells and ranges

If you found using absolute cell references slightly cumbersome you might find it easier to *name* a particular cell or range of cells. Since a name is an absolute reference, by default, it is not affected by copying or moving the formula(e) to other locations in the worksheet. You can of course change the default to make a named cell or cell range relative if required.

Naming a cell or range of cells has many advantages:

• A name is more meaningful than a cell reference.
• It is shorter, easier to read and to remember.
• It can be used in a formula, making it easier to write and may reduce the chance of errors.
• In complex worksheets it avoids having to scroll across large areas to point to a cell or cell range.
• It can be selected from a list and saves time searching for a cell or cell range.
• It can be referred to in all the sheets in a workbook.

A cell or cell range can be named by using the **Name** box (located beneath the font box) as shown in Figure 5.3, which is the quickest method. It can also be named by using the **Insert, Name, Define** command which is also required if you need to delete a name or modify the cell or cell range references.

Naming a cell or cell range – using the Name box

- Select the cell or cell range that you wish to name, e.g. **B23**.

- From the Formula Bar, click on ![down arrow] in the **Name** box. A drop-down list will be displayed (Figure 5.3).

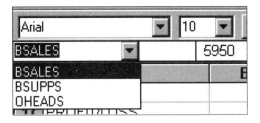

Figure 5.3 Name box drop-down list

- Key in the name, e.g. **BSALES**:

  The name must start with a letter, a backslash or an underscore.
  A name cannot start with a number but numbers can be used within the name.
  A name can have upper or lower-case letters.
  A name cannot contain any spaces – use an underscore to represent a space.

- Press **Enter**. The name will now appear in the Name box drop-down list and each time you select the cell or cell range its name will be displayed in the Name box in the Formula Bar.

  If you enter a name that has already been used for another cell or cell range, the newly named cell or cell range will replace this.

Naming and deleting a cell or cell range – using the Insert, Name, Define command

- Select the cell or cell range that you wish to name, e.g. **C21**.

- From the Menu Bar, select:

  Insert   **Name**   **Define**

  A Define Name dialogue box similar to the one in Figure 5.4 will be displayed.

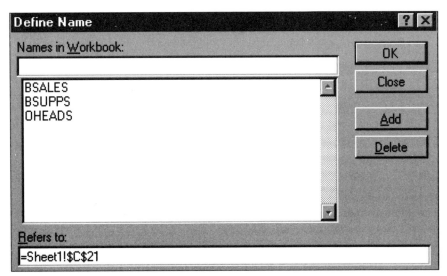

Figure 5.4 Define Name dialogue box

- In the **Refers to:** text box check that the correct cell or cell range is specified; if not, highlight the contents and key in the range.

- In the **Names in Workbook** text box key in the name, e.g. **BSALES**. The name from an adjacent cell may already be displayed in this text box which will be overwritten by your entry.

- Click the **Add** button.

  To delete a name:

  If you wish to delete a name, select it from the list and click the **Delete** button.

  To create other names:

  If you wish to create other names, repeat the above three steps.

- Click **OK**.

Task 5D

1   With **TASK5C** still on screen you will now complete the input of the monthly figures, this time using named cells, as follows:

Select cell **B23**; from the Formula Bar, click on ▼ in the **Name** box and key in **BSALES**; press **Enter**.

Select cell **B29**; from the Formula Bar, click on the ▼ in the **Name** box and key in **OHEADS**; press **Enter**.

Select cell **B30**; from the Formula Bar, click on the ▼ in the **Name** box and key in **BSUPPS**; press **Enter**.

2   The weekly figures in the named cells now need to be converted into monthly figures, as follows and to keep things simple we will assume that there are four weeks in every month:

Select cell **B7** and key in **=BSALES*4**; click the ✓ **Enter** box in the Formula Bar; position the mouse pointer at the bottom right edge of cell **B7** until it changes to a ⊹ (cross); click and drag to cell **G7** to replicate this formula across to the other cells.

Select cell **B13** and key in **=OHEADS*4**; click the ✓ **Enter** box in the Formula Bar; position the mouse pointer at the bottom right edge of cell **B13** until it changes to a ⊹ (cross); click and drag to cell **G13** to replicate this formula across to the other cells.

Select **B14** and key in **=BSUPPS*4**; click the ✓ **Enter** box in the Formula Bar; position the mouse pointer at the bottom right edge of cell **B14** until it changes to a ⊹ (cross); click and drag to cell **G14** to replicate this formula across to the other cells.

Select cell **C23** and key in **=BSALES*4**; click the ✓ **Enter** box in the Formula Bar.

Select cell **C29** and key in **=OHEADS*4**; click the ✓ **Enter** box in the Formula Bar.

Select cell **C30** and key in **=BSUPPS*4**; click the ✓ **Enter** box in the Formula Bar.

3   Cross-check your work to see if the results are the same as follows. Select cell **B8** and compare it with **C24**; select cell **B15** and compare it with **C31**; select **B17** and compare it with **C33**.

4   It would also be useful for the community club manager if the totals for the row headings were available, as follows:

Select cell **H3** and key in **TOTAL**; select cell **H5** and from the Tool Bar, click Σ **Autosum** and ensure that **=SUM(B5:G5)** is displayed in the Formula Bar; click the ✔ **Enter** box in the Formula Bar; position the mouse pointer at the bottom right edge of cell **H5** until it changes to a ✛ (cross); click and drag down to cell **H8** to replicate this formula down to the other cells.

Select cell **H11** and from the Tool Bar, click Σ **Autosum** and ensure that **=SUM(B11:G11)** is displayed in the Formula Bar; click the ✔ **Enter** box in the Formula Bar; position the mouse pointer at the bottom right edge of cell **H11** until it changes to a ✛ (cross); click and drag down to cell **H15** to replicate this formula down to the other cells.

5 To enable the community club manager to see the annual total, extend the worksheet, as follows:

Select cell **I3** and key in **TOTALPA**; select cell **I5** and key in **=H5*2** to calculate the total pa (which is **TOTAL*2**); click the ✔ **Enter** box in the Formula Bar; position the mouse pointer at the bottom right edge of cell **I5** until it changes to a ✛ (cross); click and drag down to cell **I8** to replicate this formula down to the other cells.

Select cell **I11** and key in **=H11*2**; click the ✔ **Enter** box in the Formula Bar; position the mouse pointer at the bottom right edge of cell **I11** until it changes to a ✛ (cross); click and drag down to cell **I15** to replicate this formula down to the other cells.

6 Replicate the formulae for the **PROFIT/LOSS** to include the two new columns as follows. Select cell **G17**; position the mouse pointer at the bottom right edge of cell **G17** until it changes to a ✛ (cross); click and drag across to cell **I17** to copy the formula across.

7 Format the cells containing the key total figures, for currency, as follows:

Select cell **I8** and from the Menu Bar, select **Format**, **Cells**; select the **Number** tab and from **Category** select **Currency**; from **Decimal Places** select **0**; from **Symbol** select **£ English (British)**; click **OK**.

Select cell **I15** and from the Menu Bar, select **Edit**, **Repeat Format Cells**.

Select cell **I17** and from the Menu Bar, select **Edit**, **Repeat Format Cells**.

8 Select cell **A36** and amend the filename to **TASK5D**.

9 From the Menu Bar, select **File**, **Print Preview** to check the appearance of your worksheet. As it extends to two A4 pages, it is probable best to display it in landscape format as follows. From the current **Print Preview** screen, select the **Set Up** button and in the **Page Setup** dialogue box click once on the **Landscape** button and click **OK**. Ensure that your worksheet corresponds with the key. Click once to zoom in and once again to zoom out. Click **Close** when finished.

10 From the Menu Bar, select **File**, **Save As** and save the worksheet as **TASK5D**.

11 From the Tool Bar, select the 🖨 **Print** icon to print a copy of the worksheet.

Protect the worksheet

Once complex worksheets have been produced it is important that essential data or formulae are not changed. To prevent this Excel offers various options for protecting cells, worksheets and workbooks which range from preventing others opening and looking at workbooks to preventing them amending, deleting or overwriting data or formulae.

Often you will need to protect certain cells from being overwritten, such as those containing formulae, whilst leaving others unlocked so that changes in data can be input.

By default, Excel locks all cells in a worksheet. However, the worksheet first needs to be protected before this locking will take effect. So to protect a cell or cell range, you must first unlock the cells and then protect the worksheet.

Protecting the worksheet
- Highlight the cell or cell range that you want to remain unlocked.

- From the Menu Bar, select:

Format   Cells

A Format Cells dialogue box, similar to the one in Figure 5.5 will be displayed.

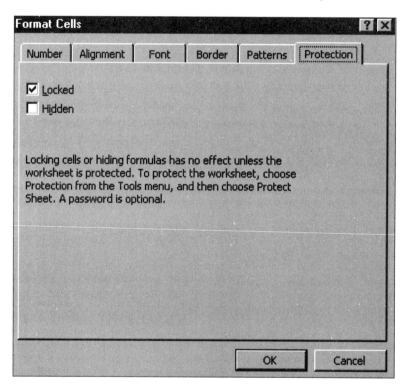

Figure 5.5   Format Cells dialogue box

- From the **Format Cells** dialogue box select the **Protection** tab.

- Click once on the **Locked** checkbox to remove the √ so that the locking is switched off.

- Click **OK**.

- From the Menu Bar, select:

Tools   Protection   Protect Sheet ...

Figure 5.6 Password Optional text box

A Password Optional text box similar to the one in Figure 5.6 is displayed.

NB If you decide to key in a password you should make a note of it with specific reference to the worksheet since if you later cannot remember it, you will be unable to access it!

• Ignore the **Password optional** text box which is offered and click **OK** to apply the protection of the sheet without an password.

To turn off the protection:

• From the Menu Bar, select:

Tools   **Protection**   **Unprotect Sheet ...**

Key in a password if one has been used.

Task 5E

1 With **TASK5D** still on screen, show the formulae (cell contents) and ensure that the printout will display the entire width of each formula used as follows. From the Menu Bar, select **Tools, Options** and click the **View** tab; from the **Window Options** column click on the checkbox beside **Formulae** to display √ and click **OK**. Your worksheet will now be shown with all the formulae displayed and the columns will be automatically widened to accommodate this. Try to decrease the width of the worksheet as follows. Place the mouse pointer between column **A** and **B** heading buttons until it changes to a double-headed arrow; click and drag to the left so that the column is sufficiently wide to display the longest label, i.e. **STATISTICAL ANALYSIS**; continue to alter the other columns widths in the same way so that the worksheet, including the formulae, is displayed to best effect.

2 You are now required to protect the contents of the column of cells containing the annual totals as follows. Select cell **A1** and drag down to cell **H36** to highlight the range of cells you want to remain unlocked; from the Menu Bar, select **Format, Cells**; from the **Format Cells** dialogue box select the **Protection** tab; click once on the **Locked** checkbox to remove the √ so that the locking is switched off; click **OK**; from the Menu Bar, select **Tools, Protection, Protect Sheet ...**; ignore the **Password optional** text box which is offered and click **OK** to apply the protection of the sheet without a password.

3 Select cell **A36** and amend the filename to **TASK5E**. Excel will allow you to change this cell as it is within the area **(A1:H36)** that has been unlocked. Click on cell **I36** and try keying in your name – you will find that an information box will inform you that the cell is protected (Figure 5.7); click **OK**. As this is outside the unlocked area, it has been protected.

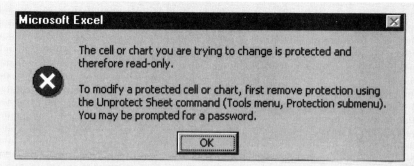

Figure 5.7 Cell protection information box

4 From the Menu Bar, select **File**, **Save As** and save the worksheet as **TASK5E**.

5 From the Menu Bar, select **File**, **Print Preview** to check the appearance of your worksheet. Click once to zoom in and once again to zoom out. Click **Close** when finished.

6 Since only the first three columns of the income and expenditure account need to be printed, select the range as follows. Select cell **A1** and drag down to cell **C36** to highlight this range; from the Menu Bar, select **File**, **Print**; in the **Print What** text box, select **Selection**; click **OK**.

7 From the Menu Bar, select **File**, **Close** to close the file.

8 You will find that **TASK5A** is revealed as it was still open underneath. From the Menu Bar, select **File**, **Close** to close the worksheet; select **File**, **Exit** to exit from Excel.

Don't forget to complete the Record of Progress sheet to indicate that you have finished this unit successfully. If you feel that you would like to do further work to consolidate what you have learned so far, then try Extra Practice Task 5A and B.

Extra Practice Task 5A

1 Load Excel and open the file **EPTASK4D**.

2 It has been noticed that Kathy Bowker's clockcard indicated that she worked in the Sawel division, by mistake. Her employment is actually with the Dart division, so the worksheet needs to be extended to include this. Select row **12** heading button and from the Menu Bar, select **Insert**, **Rows** to add a row between Michelle Blackham and Denise Birch; select cell **A12** and enter the following:

NAME	WEEKLY HOURS	OVERTIME
Kathy Bowker	42	9

Select cell **B41** and ensure that the formula to generate the **TOTAL WEEKLY HOURS** includes this row.

Extend the formulae for **GROSS**, **TAX**, **NI** and **NET** to include the new row as follows. Select **D11** and highlight the range down to **G12**; from the Menu Bar, select **Edit**, **Fill**, **Down**.

3 Another omission has been made – details for Gregory Smith should also have been recorded in the Dart division, so the worksheet needs to be extended to include this. Select row **6** heading button and from the Menu Bar, select **Insert**, **Rows** to add a row above Joanne Fisher; select cell **A6** and enter the following:

NAME	WEEKLY HOURS	OVERTIME
Gregory Smith	42	12.5

Select cell **B42** and ensure that the formula to generate the **TOTAL WEEKLY HOURS** includes this row as follows. Click once in the Formula Bar and amend the formula to **=SUM(B6:B41)**; click the ✅ **Enter** box in the Formula Bar; with cell **B42** still selected, from the Tool Bar, select the 📋 **Copy** icon; select cell **C42** and from the Tool Bar, select the 📋 **Paste** icon; check that the formula **=SUM(C6:C41)** appears in the Formula Bar; select cell **G42** and from the Tool Bar, select the 📋 **Paste** icon; check that the formula **=SUM(G6:G41)** appears in the Formula Bar.

Extend the formulae for **GROSS**, **TAX**, **NI** and **NET** to include the new row as follows. Select **D7** and highlight the range up to **G6**; from the Menu Bar, select **Edit**, **Fill**, **Up**.

4   It has been realised that the details for **Christine Gilman** were entered for the Dart division by mistake, as she actually works for the Sawel division. The worksheet needs to be reduced to reflect this. Delete the whole row containing this information as follows. Select row **17** heading button; from the Menu Bar, select **Edit**, **Delete**. Select cell **B41** to check that the worksheet has recalculated automatically to take account of this deletion.

5   Other errors have been discovered on the worksheet. Make the following amendments to the data:

   • The **WEEKLY HOURS** for **Joanne Fisher** should be **40**, not 42.
   • The **OVERTIME** for **Jolanta Hughes** should be **10**, not 9.
   • **Mike Brown** has been spelt incorrectly and should be **Mike Browne**.
   • **Anne Moore** is not the complete name and should be **Anne-Marie Moore**.
   • The **WEEKLY HOURS** for **Margery Bartram** should be **40**, not 42.
   • **Louise Atkinson** has been spelt incorrectly and should be **Louisa Atkinson**.

Check that the amendments you have made are correct as total accuracy is required.

6   Within the worksheet, projected figures have been used for the potential employment of a number of new staff. The manager would prefer to see the actual cost of wages for Week 32 separated from the estimated cost were these new staff to be employed. This will require you to divide the worksheet into two sections and to insert new rows as follows:

Select row **6** heading button; from the Menu Bar, select **Insert**, **Rows**; select cell **A6** and key in **CURRENT EMPLOYEES**; select row **19** heading button and drag to row **20** heading button; from the Menu Bar, select **Insert**, **Rows**; select cell **A20** and key in **POTENTIAL EMPLOYEES**.

Change the column width of the first column from its current setting so that the new information can be displayed in full, leaving at least two character spaces at the end of the longest label, as follows. Position the mouse pointer between column **A** and **B** heading buttons until it changes to a double-headed arrow; click and drag to the right until column **A** extends to at least two character spaces beyond the phrase **POTENTIAL EMPLOYEES**.

Check that the formulae used to calculated the totals are correct by selecting cells **B44**, **C44** and **G44** and ensuring that rows **7–43** are included.

7   It has been decided that the summary information on the worksheet would be more useful to the manager if it related to **NET** figures rather than **HOURS**. Delete the cell contents as follows. Select cell **B46** and highlight the range down and across to cell **G49** to highlight this range; from the Menu Bar, select **Edit**, **Clear**, **All**; select cell **A46** and amend the entry to **AVERAGE WEEKLY WAGE**; select cell **A47** and amend the entry to **HIGHEST WEEKLY WAGE**; select cell **A48** and amend the entry to **LOWEST WEEKLY WAGE**.

- Use the **AVERAGE** function to calculate the average net wages for a member of staff and enter this in the second column alongside the label **AVERAGE WEEKLY WAGE** as follows. Select **B46** and key in **=AVERAGE(G7:G43)**; press **Enter**.

- Use the **MAXIMUM** function to calculate the maximum net wages for a member of staff and enter this in the second column alongside the label **HIGHEST WEEKLY WAGE** as follows. Select **B47** and key in **=MAX(G7:G43)**; press **Enter**.

- Use the **MINIMUM** function to calculate the minimum net wages for a member of staff and enter this in the second column alongside the label **LOWEST WEEKLY WAGE** as follows. Select **B48** and key in **=MIN(G7:G43)**; press **Enter**.

- Use the **COUNT** function to calculate the number of staff employed and enter this in the second column alongside the label **NO OF EMPLOYEES** as follows. Select **B49** and key in **=COUNT(G7:G43)**; press **Enter**.

8   The **AVERAGE WEEKLY WAGE** should be displayed in integer format (no decimal places) as follows. Select cell **B46**; from the Menu Bar, select **Format, Cells, Number**; from **Category** select **Number**; from **Decimal Places** select **0**; click **OK**.

9   The **HIGHEST** and **LOWEST WEEKLY WAGE** should be displayed in currency format to two decimal places as follows. Select cell **B47** and drag to include cell **B48**; from the Menu Bar, select **Format, Cells, Number**; from **Category** select **Currency**; from **Decimal Places** select **2**; from **Symbol** select **£ English (British)**; click **OK**.

10 Insert four new rows after the summary information as follows. Select row **52** heading button and drag to row **55** heading button; from the Menu Bar, select **Insert, Rows**; select cell **A52** and key in **CURRENT EMPLOYEES**; select cell **A53** and key in **GROSS WEEKLY WAGES**; select cell **B53** and key in **=SUM(D7:D18)** and press **Enter**; select cell **A54** and key in **GROSS MONTHLY WAGES**; select cell **B54** and key in **=B53*4** to calculate the gross monthly wages (based on the assumption that there are four weeks in a month) and press ↵ (**Enter**).

11 Select cell **A57** and amend the filename to **EPTASK5A**.

12 From the Menu Bar, select **File, Print Preview** to check the appearance of your worksheet and to ensure that it corresponds with the key. Click once to zoom in and once again to zoom out. Click **Close** when finished.

13 From the Menu Bar, select **File, Save As** and save the worksheet as **EPTASK5A**.

14 From the Tool Bar, select the 🖨 **Print** icon to print a copy of the worksheet.

15 Show the formulae (cell contents) and ensure that the printout will display the entire width of each formula used as follows. From the Menu Bar, select **Tools, Options** and click the **View** tab; from the **Window Options** column click on the checkbox beside **Formulae** to display √ and click **OK**. Your worksheet will now be shown with all the formulae displayed and the columns will be automatically widened to accommodate this. Try to decrease the width of the worksheet as follows. Place the mouse pointer between column **A** and **B** heading buttons until it changes to a double-headed arrow; click and drag to the left so that the column is sufficiently wide to display the longest label, i.e. **AVERAGE WEEKLY WAGE**; continue to alter the other columns widths in the same way so that the worksheet fits on to one page and ensuring that the formulae are fully displayed.

16 Select cell **A57** and amend the filename to **EPTASK5AF**.

17 From the Menu Bar, select **File**, **Print Preview** to check the appearance of your worksheet and to ensure that it corresponds with the key. Click once to zoom in and once again to zoom out. Click **Close** when finished.

18 From the Menu Bar, select **File**, **Save As** and save the worksheet as **EPTASK5AF**.

19 Print a copy of the summary formulae only, as follows. Select cell **A44** and drag to cell **G57** to highlight this range; from the Menu Bar, select **File**, **Print**; in the **Print What** box click on the **Selection** button; click **OK**.

Extra Practice Task 5B

To enable the manager to estimate what the cash flow might be over a six-month period, you are required to plan a simple worksheet to show the predicted receipts and payments from **JAN** to **JUL**. The first section should include the **INCOME** from

SALES – MAIL ORDER
CASH SALES – OTHER
CREDIT SALES – OTHER

The second section should include **EXPENSES** for

WAGES – CONSTRUCTION
WAGES – CULTIVATION
OVERHEADS
MATERIALS

You will need to extract the information from the test data financial statistics below and you will have to link this worksheet with the worksheet from **EPTASK5A**:

Test data: financial statistics

- Monthly income from SALES – MAIL ORDER IS £45,000.
- Monthly income from CASH SALES – OTHER is £5,000.
- Monthly income from CREDIT SALES – OTHER is £10,000.
- Monthly WAGES – CONSTRUCTION to be taken from the worksheet on wages.
- Monthly WAGES – CULTIVATION is £3,600.
- Overheads amount to £900 per week.
- Materials are estimated at 25% of all sales.

1 Open **EPTASK5A** as you will now be required to link data from this worksheet with a new worksheet. With **EPTASK5A** open on screen, from the Tool Bar, click once on **New workbook** to open a new workbook on to your screen. (EPTASK5A is still there underneath this new workbook as you will need to refer to it later in this task.)

2 Select cell **A1** and enter the title **SPERRIN SKYWAY GARDEN CENTRE CASH FORECAST**.

3 Select cell **B3** and enter the heading **JAN**; click the ✔ **Enter** box in the Formula Bar; position the mouse pointer at the bottom right edge of cell **B3** until it changes to a ✛ (cross); click and drag to cell **G3** to fill the cells with the months **FEB**, **MAR**, **APR**, **MAY**, **JUN**.

4 Select **A4** and key in **INCOME**; select cell **A5** and key in **SALES – MAIL ORDER**; select cell **A6** and key in **CASH SALES – OTHER**; select cell **A7** and key in **CREDIT SALES – OTHER**; select cell **A8** and key in **TOTAL INCOME**.

5 Select cell **A10** and key in **EXPENSES**; select cell **A11** and key in **WAGES – CONSTRUCTION**; select cell **A12** and key in **WAGES – CULTIVATION**; select cell **A13** and key in **OVERHEADS**; select cell **A14** and key in **MATERIALS**; select cell **A15** and key in **TOTAL EXPENSES**.

6 Select cell **A17** and key in **STATISTICAL ANALYSIS**; place the mouse pointer between column A and B heading buttons until it changes to a double-headed arrow and click and drag to the right so that the column is sufficiently widened. Select cell **B17** and key in **WEEKLY**; select cell **C17** and key in **MONTHLY**; select cell **A4** and drag down to cell **A15** to highlight this range; from the Tool Bar, select 📋 **Copy**; select cell **A18** and from the Tool Bar, select 📋 **Paste** to place a copy of the row headings from row **18** to **29**.

7 Refer to the **FINANCIAL STATISTICS** and enter the test data that has been provided as follows. Select cell **C19** and enter **45000**; select cell **C20** and enter **5000**; select cell **C21** and enter **10000**; select cell **C25** which is to be linked to the worksheet on wages to generate the construction wages amount; key in **=** and from the Menu Bar, select **Window** and from the filenames at the bottom of the drop-down options click once on the filename **EPTASK5A** to bring this file to the front; on the worksheet **EPTASK5A**, select **GROSS MONTHLY WAGES** in cell **B54** and click the ✔ **Enter** box in the formula bar. This returns you to cell **C25** in your other worksheet and links this cell with the **GROSS MONTHLY WAGES** figure in **EPTASK5A**. Select cell **C25** and note the link details in the Formula Bar, i.e. **=[EPTASK5A]Sheet1!$B$54**.

8 Select cell **C26** and key in **3600**; select cell **B27** and key in **900**; select cell **B28** and enter **=B8*25%**.

9 Select cell **A31** and key in **YOUR NAME**; select cell **A32** and key in **EPTASK5B**.

10 From the Menu Bar, select **File**, **Print Preview** to check the appearance of your worksheet and to ensure that it corresponds with the key. Click once to zoom in and once again to zoom out. Click **Close** when finished.

11 From the Menu Bar, select **File**, **Save As** and save the worksheet as **EPTASK5B**.

12 From the Tool Bar, select the 🖨 **Print** icon to print a copy of the worksheet.

13 You are now required to extract the data from the statistical analysis to produce the predictions for the cash forecast. We will use absolute cell references for the monthly figures as follows:

Select cell **B5** and key in **=$C$19** and click the ✔ **Enter** box in the Formula Bar; position the mouse pointer at the bottom right edge of cell **B5** until it changes to a ✚ (cross); click and drag to cell **G5** to replicate this formula across to the other cells.

Select cell **B6** and key in **=$C$20** and click the ✔ **Enter** box in the Formula Bar; position the mouse pointer at the bottom right edge of cell **B6** until it changes to a ✚ (cross); click and drag to cell **G6** to replicate this formula across to the other cells.

Select cell **B7** and key in **=$C$21** and click the ✔ **Enter** box in the Formula Bar; position the mouse pointer at the bottom right edge of cell **B7** until it changes to a ✚ (cross); click and drag to cell **G7** to replicate this formula across to the other cells.

Select cell **B11** and key in **=$C$25** and click the ✔ **Enter** box in the Formula Bar; position the mouse pointer at the bottom right edge of cell **B11** until it changes to a ⊹ (cross); click and drag to cell **G11** to replicate this formula across to the other cells.

Select cell **B12** and key in **=$C$26** and click the ✔ **Enter** box in the Formula Bar; position the mouse pointer at the bottom right edge of cell **B12** until it changes to a ⊹ (cross); click and drag to cell **G12** to replicate this formula across to the other cells.

14 To enable you to perform a cross-check on the test data later you can, at this stage, set up the formulae that will calculate the totals, as follows:

Select cell **B14** and key in **=$C$28** and click the ✔ **Enter** box in the Formula Bar; position the mouse pointer at the bottom right edge of cell **B14** until it changes to a ⊹ (cross); click and drag to cell **G14** to replicate this formula across to the other cells.

Select cell **B8**; from the Tool Bar, click Σ **Autosum** and ensure that the formula **=SUM(B5:B7)** appears in the Formula Bar (you may have to edit the formula that is displayed since the data for overheads has not yet been inserted); click the ✔ **Enter** box in the Formula Bar; position the mouse pointer at the bottom right edge of cell **B8** until it changes to a ⊹ (cross); click and drag to cell **G8** to replicate this formula across to the other cells.

Select cell **B15**; from the Tool Bar, click Σ **Autosum** and ensure that the formula **=SUM(B11:B14)** appears in the Formula Bar; click the ✔ **Enter** box in the Formula Bar; position the mouse pointer at the bottom right edge of cell **B15** until it changes to a ⊹ (cross); click and drag to cell **G15** to replicate this formula across to the other cells.

Select cell **C22**; from the Tool Bar, click Σ **Autosum** and ensure that the formula **=SUM(C19:C21)** appears in the Formula Bar; click the ✔ **Enter** box in the Formula Bar.

Select cell **C29**; from the Tool Bar, click Σ **Autosum** and ensure that the formula **=SUM(C25:C28)** appears in the Formula Bar (you may have to edit the formula that is displayed since the data for overheads has not yet been inserted); click the ✔ **Enter** box in the Formula Bar.

15 Since it would also be useful to display the potential profit or loss, insert two blank rows for this calculations as follows. Select row **17** heading button and drag to row **18** heading button to highlight these two rows; from the Menu Bar, select **Insert**, **Rows**; select cell **A17** and key in **PROFIT/LOSS**; select cell **B17** and key in **=B8-B15**; click the ✔ **Enter** box in the Formula Bar; position the mouse pointer at the bottom right edge of cell **B17** until it changes to a ⊹ (cross); click and drag to cell **G17** to replicate this formula across to the other cells. The figures will not be completely accurate at this stage since not all the data has been input yet.

16 To help you also cross-check your data later you can input a formula for the monthly profit or loss in the statistical analysis as follows. Select row **33** heading button and drag to row **34** heading button to highlight these two rows; from the Menu Bar, select **Insert**, **Rows**; select cell **A33** and key in **PROFIT/LOSS**; select cell **C33** and key in **=C24-C31**; click the ✔ **Enter** box in the Formula Bar.

17 Select cell **A36** and amend the filename to **EPTASK5C**.

18 From the Menu Bar, select **File**, **Print Preview** to check the appearance of your worksheet and to ensure that it corresponds with the key. Click once to zoom in and once again to zoom out. Click **Close** when finished.

19 From the Menu Bar, select **File**, **Save As** and save the worksheet as **EPTASK5C**.

20 From the Tool Bar, select the 🖨 **Print** icon to print a copy of the worksheet.

21 You can now complete the input of the monthly figures, this time using a named cell, as follows. Select cell **B29**; from the Formula Bar, click on ▼| in the **Name** box and key in **OHEADS**; press ↵ (**Enter**).

22 The weekly figure in the named cells now needs to be converted into a monthly figure (calculating a month based on four weeks for simplicity), as follows:

Select cell **B13** and key in **=OHEADS*4**; click the ✔ **Enter** box in the Formula Bar; position the mouse pointer at the bottom right edge of cell **B13** until it changes to a ✛ (cross); click and drag to cell **G13** to replicate this formula across to the other cells.

Select cell **C29** and key in **=OHEADS*4**; click the ✔ **Enter** box in the Formula Bar.

23 Cross-check your work to see if the results are the same, as follows. Select cell **B8** and compare it with **C24**; select cell **B15** and compare it with **C31**; select cell **B17** and compare it with **C33**.

24 It would also be useful for the garden centre manager if the totals for the row headings were available, as follows:

Select cell **H3** and key in **TOTAL**; select cell **H5** and from the Tool Bar, click Σ **Autosum** and ensure that **=SUM(B5:G5)** is displayed in the Formula Bar; click the ✔ **Enter** box in the Formula Bar, position the mouse pointer at the bottom right edge of cell **H5** until it changes to a ✛ (cross); click and drag down to cell **H8** to replicate this formula down to the other cells.

Select cell **H11** and from the Tool Bar, click Σ **Autosum** and ensure that **=SUM(B11:G11)** is displayed in the Formula Bar; click the ✔ **Enter** box in the Formula Bar; position the mouse pointer at the bottom right edge of cell **H11** until it changes to a ✛ (cross); click and drag down to cell **H15** to replicate this formula down to the other cells.

25 To enable the garden centre manager to see the annual total, extend the worksheet as follows:

Select cell **I3** and key in **TOTAL PA**; select cell **I5** and key in **=H5*2** to calculate the total pa (which is **TOTAL*2**); click the ✔ **Enter** box in the Formula Bar; position the mouse pointer at the bottom right edge of cell **I5** until it changes to a ✛ (cross); click and drag down to cell **I8** to replicate this formula down to the other cells.

Select cell **I11** and key in **H11*2**; click the ✔ **Enter** box in the Formula Bar; position the mouse pointer at the bottom right edge of cell **I11** until it changes to a ✛ (cross); click and drag down to cell **I15** to replicate this formula down to the other cells.

26 Replicate the formula for the **PROFIT/LOSS** to include the two new columns as follows. Select cell **G17**; position the mouse pointer at the bottom right edge of cell **G17** until it changes to a ✛ (cross); click and drag across to cell **I17** to copy the formula across.

27 Format the cells containing the key total figures, for currency, as follows:

Select cell **I8** and from the Menu Bar, select **Format**, **Cells**; select the **Number** tab and from **Category** select **Currency**; from **Decimal Places** select **0**; from **Symbol** select **£ English (British)**; click **OK**.

Select cell **I15** and from the Menu Bar, select **Edit**, **Repeat Format Cells**.

Select cell **I17** and from the Menu Bar, select **Edit**, **Repeat Format Cells**.

28 Select cell **A36** and amend the filename **EPTASK5D**.

29 From the Menu Bar, select **File**, **Print Preview** to check the appearance of your worksheet. As it extends to two A4 pages, it is probably best to display it in landscape format as follows. From the current **Print Preview** screen select the **Set Up** button and in the **Page Setup** dialogue box click once on the **Landscape** button and click **OK**. Ensure that your worksheet corresponds with the key. Click once to zoom in and once again to zoom out. Click **Close** when finished.

30 From the Menu Bar, select **File**, **Save As** and save the worksheet as **EPTASK5D**.

31 From the Tool Bar, select the 🖨 **Print** icon to print a copy of the worksheet.

32 Show the formulae (cell contents) and ensure that the printout will display the entire width of each formula used as follows. From the Menu Bar, select **Tools**, **Options** and click the **View** tab; from the **Window Options** column click on the checkbox beside **Formulae** to display √ and click **OK**. Your worksheet will now be shown with all the formulae displayed and the columns will be automatically widened to accommodate this. Try to decrease the width of the worksheet as follows. Place the mouse pointer between column **A** and **B** heading buttons until it changes to a double-headed arrow; click and drag to the left so that the column is sufficiently wide to display the longest label, i.e. **WAGES – CONSTRUCTION**; continue to alter the other columns widths in the same way so that the worksheet, including the formulae is displayed to best effect.

33 You are now required to protect the contents of the column of cells containing the annual totals, as follows. Select cell **A1** and drag down and across to cell **H36** to highlight this range of cells which you want to remain unlocked; from the Menu Bar, select **Format**, **Cells**; from the **Format Cells** dialogue box, select the **Protection** tab; click once on the **Locked** checkbox to remove the √ so that the locking is switched off; click **OK**; from the Menu Bar, select **Tools**, **Protection**, **Protect Sheet ...**; ignore the **Password optional** text box which is offered and click **OK** to apply the protection of the sheet without a password.

34 Select cell **A36** and amend the filename to **EPTASK5E**. Click on cell **I8** and try keying in your name – you will find that an information box will present the message that 'Locked cells cannot be changed'.

35 From the Menu Bar, select **File**, **Save As** and save the worksheet as **EPTASK5E**.

36 From the Menu Bar, select **File**, **Print Preview** to check the appearance of your worksheet and to ensure that it corresponds with the key. Click once to zoom in and once again to zoom out. Click **Close** when finished.

37 Since only the first two columns of the main part of the income and expenditure account need to be printed, select the range as follows. Select cell **A1** and drag down to cell **B15** to highlight this range; from the Menu Bar, select **File**, **Print**; in the **Print What** text box, select **Selection**; click **OK**.

38 From the Menu Bar, select **File**, **Close** to close the file.

39 You will find that **EPTASK5A** is revealed as it was still open underneath. From the Menu Bar, select **File**, **Close** to close the file.

Don't forget to complete the Record of Progress sheet to indicate that you have finished this unit successfully.

— | **YOYO5A (You're On Your Own Task 5A)** | **▼ ▲**

1 Load Excel and open the file **YOYO4D**.

2 It has been noticed that Jayne Taylor's clock card indicated by mistake that she worked in the Ards Division. Her employment is actually with the Donard Division, so the worksheet needs to be extended to include this. Add a row between Jean Madden and Julie Broady and enter the following:

NAME	WEEKLY HOURS	OVERTIME
Jayne Taylor	**42**	**10**

Ensure that the formulae to generate the **TOTAL WEEKLY HOURS** includes this row.

Extend the formulae for **GROSS**, **TAX**, **NI** and **NET** to include the new row.

3 Another omission has been made – details for Brian Green should also have been recorded in the Donard Division, so the worksheet needs to be extended to include this. Add a row above Mary Bradley and enter the following:

NAME	WEEKLY HOURS	OVERTIME
Brian Green	**42**	**12.5**

Amend the formula to generate the **TOTAL WEEKLY HOURS** to include this new row; copy this formula across to **TOTAL OVERTIME** and **TOTAL NET**:

Extend the formulae for **GROSS**, **TAX**, **NI** and **NET** to include the new row.

4 It has been realised that the details for Helen Stevens were entered for the Donard Division by mistake, as she actually works for the Ards Division. The worksheet needs to be reduced to reflect this. Using the Menu Bar, delete this row containing Helen Stevens' details. Select cell **B41** to check that the worksheet has recalculated automatically to take account of this deletion.

5 Other errors have been discovered on the worksheet. Make the following amendments to the data:

- The **WEEKLY HOURS** for **Mary Bradley** should be **40**, not 42.
- The **OVERTIME** for **Anna Gee** should be **12**, not 10.
- **Margaret Smyth** has been spelt incorrectly and should be spelt **Margaret Smythe**.
- **Jean Madden** is not the complete name and should be **Billy-Jean Madden**.
- The **WEEKLY HOURS** for **Diane Henderson** should be **40**, not 42.
- **Rose Cullen** has been spelt incorrectly and should be spelt **Rosie Cullen**.

Check that the amendments you have made are correct as total accuracy is required.

6 Within the worksheet, projected figures have been used for the potential employment of a number of new staff. The manager would prefer to see the actual cost of wages for week 32 separated from the estimated cost were these new staff to be employed. This will require you to divide the worksheet into two sections and to insert new rows as follows:

Insert a row above row **6**; select cell **A6** and key in **CURRENT EMPLOYEES**; insert two rows above row **19**; select cell **A20** and key in **POTENTIAL EMPLOYEES**.

Change the column width of the first column from its current settings so that the new information can be displayed in full, leaving at least two character spaces at the end of the longest label.

Check that the formulae used to calculate the totals are correct by selecting cells **B44**, **C44** and **G44** and ensuring that rows **7** to **43** are included.

7 It has been decided that the summary information on the worksheets would be more useful to the manager if it related to **NET** figures rather than **HOURS**. Delete the cell contents in the range from cell **B46** to cell **G49**; select cell **A46** and amend the entry to **AVERAGE WEEKLY WAGE**; select cell **A47** and amend the entry to **HIGHEST WEEKLY WAGE**; select cell **A48** and amend the entry to **LOWEST WEEKLY WAGE**.

- Enter a formula using the **AVERAGE** function to calculate the average **NET** wages for a member of staff and enter this in the second column alongside the label **AVERAGE WEEKLY WAGE**.
- Enter a formula using the **MAXIMUM** function to calculate the maximum net wages for a member of staff and enter this in the second column alongside the label **HIGHEST WEEKLY WAGE**.
- Enter a formula using the **MINIMUM** function to calculate the minimum net wages for a member of staff and enter this in the second column alongside the label **LOWEST WEEKLY WAGE**.
- Enter a formula using the **COUNT** function to calculate the number of staff employed and enter this in the second column alongside the label **NO OF EMPLOYEES**.

8 The **AVERAGE WEEKLY WAGE** should be displayed in integer format (no decimal places) using the Menu Bar.

9 The **HIGHEST** and **LOWEST WEEKLY WAGE** should be displayed in currency format to two decimal places, using the Menu Bar.

10 Insert four new rows (after the summary information) above row **52**; select cell **A52** and key in **CURRENT EMPLOYEES**; select cell **A53** and key in **GROSS WEEKLY WAGES**; select cell **B53** and enter a formula to calculate the TOTAL GROSS for CURRENT EMPLOYEES; select cell **A54** and key in **GROSS MONTHLY WAGES**; select cell **B54** and enter a formula to calculate the gross monthly wages, based on the assumption that there are four weeks in a month (**GROSS WEEKLY WAGES*4**).

11 Amend the filename on the worksheet to **YOYO5A**.

12 Display **Print Preview** to check the appearance of your worksheet and to ensure it corresponds with the key.

13 Save the worksheet as **YOYO5A**.

14 Print a copy of the worksheet.

15 Show the formulae (cell contents) and ensure that the printout will display the entire width of each formula. Your worksheet should now be shown with all the formulae displayed and the columns widened automatically to accommodate this. Decrease the width of the columns so that the column headings all fit on to one page and the formulae are fully displayed.

16 Amend the filename on the worksheet to **YOYO5AF**.

17 Display **Print Preview** to check the appearance of your worksheet and to ensure it corresponds with the key.

18 Save the worksheet as **YOYO5AF**.

19 Select cell **A44** and drag to cell **G57** to highlight this range; print a copy of the summary formulae only.

20 Close the worksheet.

YOYO5B (You're On Your Own Task 5B)

To enable the manager to estimate what the cash flow might be over a six-month period, you are required to plan a simple worksheet to show the predicted receipts and payments from Jan to Jul. The first section should include the **INCOME** from

SALES – MAIL ORDER
SALES – RETAIL OUTLET
SALES – OTHER

The second section should include **EXPENSES** for

WAGES – MAIL ORDER
WAGES – RETAIL OUTLET
OVERHEADS
MATERIALS

You will need to extract the information from the test data financial statistics below and you will have to link this worksheet with the worksheet from **YOYO5A**:

TEST DATA: FINANCIAL STATISTICS

- Monthly income from **SALES – MAIL ORDER** is **£54,000**.
- Monthly income from **SALES – RETAIL OUTLET** is **£6000**.
- Monthly income from **SALES – OTHER** is **£12,000**.
- Monthly **WAGES – MAIL ORDER** to be taken from the worksheet on wages.
- Monthly **WAGES – RETAIL OUTLET** is **£4320**.
- Weekly overheads amount is **£1080**.
- Monthly materials are estimated at 25% of monthly sales.

1 Open **YOYO5A** as you will now be required to link data from this worksheet with a new worksheet. With YOYO5A open on screen, using the Tool Bar, open a new workbook on to your screen. (YOYO5A is still there underneath this new workbook as you will need to refer to it later in this task.)

2 Select cell **A1** and enter the title **THE DESIGNER COLLECTION CASH FORECAST**.

3 Select cell **B3** and enter the heading **JAN**; position the mouse pointer at the edge of cell **B3** until it changes to a ✛ (cross) and drag to cell **G3** to fill the cells with the months **FEB, MAR, APR, MAY, JUN**.

4 Select cell **A4** and key in **INCOME**; select cell **A5** and key in **SALES – MAIL ORDER**; select cell **A6** and key in **SALES – RETAIL OUTLET**; select cell **A7** and key in **SALES – OTHER**; select cell **A8** and key in **TOTAL INCOME**.

5 Select cell **A10** and key in **EXPENSES**; select cell **A11** and key in **WAGES – MAIL ORDER**; select cell **A12** and key in **WAGES – RETAIL OUTLET**; select cell **A13** and key in **OVERHEADS**; select cell **A14** and key in **MATERIALS**; select cell **A15** and key in **TOTAL EXPENSES**.

6 Select cell **A17** and key in **STATISTICAL ANALYSIS**; place the mouse pointer between column **A** and **B** heading buttons so that the column is sufficiently widened; select cell **B17** and key in **WEEKLY**; select cell **C17** and key in **MONTHLY**; select cell **A4** and drag down to cell **A15** to highlight this range; using the Tool Bar, copy this range and paste it in cell **A18** to place a copy of the row headings from row **18** to **29**.

7 Refer to the **FINANCIAL STATISTICS** and enter the test data that has been provided as follows. Select cell **C19** and enter the sales – mail order monthly income; select cell **C20** and enter the sales – retail outlet monthly income; select cell **C21** and enter the sales – other monthly income; select cell **C25**, which is to be linked to the worksheet on wages to generate the mail-order staff wages amount; link this cell with the **GROSS MONTHLY WAGES** figure in **YOYO5A** (cell **B54**).

8 Select cell **C26** and enter the monthly wages – retail outlet; select cell **B27** and enter the weekly overheads amount; select cell **C28** and enter a formula to calculate 25% of monthly sales (in the STATISTICAL ANALYSIS section i.e. TOTAL INCOME MONTHLY*25%) – this will appear as 0 at this stage.

9 Select cell **A31** and key in **YOUR NAME**; select cell **A32** and key in **YOYO5B**.

10 Display **Print Preview** to check the appearance of your worksheet and to ensure it corresponds with the key.

11 Save the worksheet as **YOYO5B**.

12 Print a copy of the worksheet.

13 You are now required to extract the data from the statistical analysis to produce the predictions for the cash forecast. We will use absolute cell references for the monthly figures as follows:

Select cell **B5** and key in an absolute cell reference for the SALES – MAIL ORDER in the STATISTICAL ANALYSIS section; position the mouse pointer at the edge of cell **B5** until it changes to a ✛ (cross) and drag to cell **G5** to replicate this formula across to the other cells.

Select cell **B6** and key in an absolute cell reference for the SALES – RETAIL OUTLET in the STATISTICAL ANALYSIS section; position the mouse pointer at the edge of cell **B6** until it changes to a ✛ (cross) and drag to cell **G6** to replicate this formula across to the other cells.

Select cell **B7** and key in an absolute cell reference for the SALES – OTHER in the STATISTICAL ANALYSIS section; position the mouse pointer at the edge of cell **B7** until it changes to a ✛ (cross) and drag to cell **G7** to replicate this formula across to the other cells.

Select cell **B11** and key in an absolute cell reference for the WAGES – MAIL ORDER in the STATISTICAL ANALYSIS section; position the mouse pointer at the edge of cell **B11** until it changes to a ✛ (cross) and drag to cell **G11** to replicate this formula across to the other cells.

Select cell **B12** and key in an absolute cell reference for the WAGES – RETAIL OUTLET in the STATISTICAL ANALYSIS section; position the mouse pointer at the edge of cell **B12** until it changes to a ✛ (cross) and drag to cell **G12** to replicate this formulae across to the other cells.

Select cell **B14** and key in an absolute cell reference for the MATERIALS in the STATISTICAL ANALYSIS section; position the mouse pointer at the edge of cell **B14** until it changes to a ✛ (cross) and drag to cell **G14** to replicate this formula across to the other cells.

14 To enable you to perform a cross-check on the test data later you can, at this stage, set up the formulae that will calculate the totals, as follows:

Select cell **B8**; from the Tool Bar, use **Autosum** to generate the TOTAL INCOME for JAN; position the mouse pointer at the edge of cell **B8** until it changes to a ✛ (cross) and drag to cell **G8** to replicate this formula across to the other cells.

Select cell **B15**; from the Tool Bar, use **Autosum** to generate the TOTAL EXPENSES for JAN; position the mouse pointer at the edge of cell **B15** until it changes to a ✛ (cross) and drag to cell **G15** to replicate this formula across to the other cells.

Select cell **C22**; from the Tool Bar, use **Autosum** to generate the MONTHLY TOTAL INCOME.

Select cell **C29**; from the Tool Bar, use **Autosum** to generate the MONTHLY TOTAL EXPENSES.

15 Since it would also be useful to display the potential profit or loss, insert two blank rows for this calculation as follows. Select row **17** heading button and drag to row **18** heading button to highlight these two rows; using the Menu Bar, insert two rows; select cell **A17** and key in **PROFIT/LOSS**; select cell **B17** and enter a formula to generate the profit or loss for JAN (TOTAL INCOME JAN – TOTAL EXPENSES JAN); position the mouse pointer at the edge of cell **B17** until it changes to a ✚ (cross) and drag to cell **G17** to replicate this formula across to the other cells. The figures will not be completely accurate at this stage since not all the data has been input yet.

16 Also to help you cross-check your data later you can input a formula for the monthly profit or loss in the statistical analysis. Select row **33** heading button and drag to row **34** heading button to highlight these two rows; using the Menu Bar, insert two rows; select cell **A33** and key in **PROFIT/LOSS**; select cell **C33** and enter a formula to generate the monthly profit or loss (TOTAL INCOME MONTHLY – TOTAL EXPENSES MONTHLY).

17 Amend the filename on the worksheet to **YOYO5C**.

18 Display **Print Preview** to check the appearance of your worksheet and to ensure it corresponds with the key.

19 Save the worksheet as **YOYO5C**.

20 Print a copy of the worksheet.

21 Next complete the input of the monthly figures, using a named cell: select cell **B29** and name this cell **OHEADS**.

22 The weekly figure in the named cell now needs to be converted into a monthly figure (based on four weeks representing a month for simplicity), as follows:

Select cell **B13** and enter a formula to give a monthly figure for overheads (**OHEADS*4**); position the mouse pointer at the edge of cell **B13** until it changes to a ✚ (cross) and drag to cell **G13** to replicate this formula across to the other cells.

Select cell **C29** and enter a formula to give a monthly figure for overheads (**OHEADS*4**).

23 Cross-check your work to see if the results are the same, as follows. Select cell **B8** and compare it with **C24**; select cell **B15** and compare it with **C31**; select cell **B17** and compare it with **C33**.

24 It would also be useful for the Garden Centre Manager if the totals for the row headings were available:

Select cell **H3** and key in **TOTAL**; select cell **H5** and, from the Tool Bar, use **Autosum** to generate the total; position the mouse pointer at the edge of cell **H5** until it changes to a ✚ (cross) and drag to cell **H8** to replicate this formula down to the other cells.

Select cell **H11** and, from the Tool Bar, use **Autosum** to generate the total; position the mouse pointer at the edge of cell **H11** until it changes to a ✚ (cross) and drag down to cell **H15** to replicate this formula down to the other cells.

25 To enable the Garden Centre Manager to see the annual total, extend the worksheet as follows:

Select cell **I3** and key in **TOTAL PA**; select cell **I5** and enter a formula to calculate the total per annum (**TOTAL*2**); position the mouse pointer at the edge of cell **I5** until it changes to a ✚ (cross) and drag to cell **I8** to replicate this formula across to the other cells.

Select cell **I 11** and enter a formula to calculate the total per annum (**TOTAL*2**); position the mouse pointer at the edge of cell **I 11** until it changes to a ✛ (cross) and drag down to cell **I 15** to replicate this formula down to the other cells.

26 Replicate the formula for the **PROFIT/LOSS** to include the two new columns; select the cell **G17**; position the mouse pointer at the edge of cell **G17** until it changes to a ✛ (cross) and drag to cell **I 17** to copy the formula across.

27 Format the cells containing the key total figures to zero decimal places and display the £ sign in cell **I 8**; select cell **I 15** and, using the Menu Bar, repeat the format of this cell; select cell **I 17** and, using the Menu Bar, repeat the format of this cell.

28 Amend the filename on the worksheet to **YOYO5D**.

29 Display **Print Preview** to check the appearance of your worksheet. Display it in landscape format. Ensure that your worksheet corresponds with the key.

30 Save the worksheet as **YOYO5D**.

31 Print a copy of the worksheet.

32 Show the formulae (cell contents) and ensure that the printout will display the entire width of each formula used.

33 You are now required to protect the contents of the column of cells containing the annual totals. (Remember first to select the range of cells which you want to remain unlocked; select the appropriate commands to remove the locking; select the appropriate commands to protect the worksheet.)

34 Amend the filename on the worksheet to **YOYO5E**. Click on cell **I 36** and try keying in your name – you will find that an information box will inform you that the cells are protected and cannot be changed.

35 Save the worksheet as **YOYO5E**.

36 Since only the first two columns of the main part of the income and expenditure account need to be printed, select this range and print this selection.

37 Close the file.

38 You will find that **YOYO5A** is revealed, as it was still open underneath. Close this file and exit from Excel.

Don't forget to complete the Record of Progress sheet to indicate that you have finished this unit successfully.

Congratulations! You have now completed all the work necessary for you to be able to do the RSA Integrated Business Technology (Spreadsheets) Stage II examination and the RSA Spreadsheets Stage II examination. Turn now to Section B Consolidation and work through the mock assignments to prepare you for these examinations. There are no helpful suggestions about which menu/Tool Bar options or keyboard strokes you might use but you are allowed to refer to the Memory Jogger to meet IBT II and Spreadshees II objectives and any notes that you might have made.

consolidation 1

RSA Integrated Business Technology (spreadsheets) Stage II

The Integrated Business Technology Stage II (IBT II) Scheme was developed to encourage those who can use computers and information technology at a basic level to build on their skills using integrated software packages.

The scheme is made up of five applications including spreadsheets. The mock assignments which follow will prepare you for the spreadsheet application in IBT II.

Assessment

Assessment of the Spreadsheet Module is through an assignment, which is made up of practical tasks using a spreadsheet application, such as MS Excel. There is one element of certification, i.e. create and use a spreadsheet to aid problem-solving.

To attain this element, you must achieve 10 assessment objectives. Assessment objectives are the operations you *must* be able to do to prove your ability and the performance criteria define the level of accuracy to which these objectives must be carried out.

A maximum of three data entry errors in text is permitted, but numeric information must be entered with 100% accuracy.

Exam tips

1 An assignment must be completed within a two-hour period, although printing may be done outside this time.

2 All instructions must be followed exactly.

3 Unique filenames for each assignment must be used. These should be concise and meaningful (e.g. SMQ5P1 is composed of S for spreadsheet, M for mock, Q5 for question 5 and P1 for printout 1).

4 Make sure you key in your name and filename on each spreadsheet before you save and print it.

5 When an assignment has been completed, the printouts should be assembled in the correct order and handed to the tutor with the copy of the assignment.

6 If you are not successful in the first assignment, a second completely fresh attempt is permitted.

7 There are two mock assignments to prepare you for the final assignment. The spreadsheet assignment for Mock 2 should not be commenced until Mock 1 has been checked for accuracy. Your printouts should match the keys exactly - otherwise you may fail an objective and therefore fail the entire assignment.

8 You should not speak to anyone when you are working on an assignment and must not ask your tutor any questions.

9 You are permitted to use your own notes, centre-prepared manuals or manufacturers' manuals.

IBT II Spreadsheet Mock Assignment 1

Scenario

You work as a receptionist at the Ballinascreen Optical Illusions Opticians with additional responsibility for the book-keeping and record keeping of all patients. Details have to be extracted from different sections of the patient record cards on a regular basis (see pages 134–5). Each patient is allocated a unique patient reference code, composed of the patient's date of birth and his or her status code, which is indicated by the final two letters. Regular patients, i.e. those who required two-yearly examinations, are identified by the letters RP; frequent patients, i.e. those who require more frequent examinations, are identified by FP; lapsed patients, i.e. those who have not attended their most recent retest examination appointments, are identified by LP; and new patients, i.e. those who have had an initial examination during the last year, are identified by NP.

You are going to create a spreadsheet to show the patients with a retest date for Week 1. It should group each patient under one of the three status code subheadings (RP, FP or NP). The LP, i.e. lapsed patients, should *not* be included.

2.3(a) **1** Using the information on the patient record cards (Section A) create a spreadsheet with the title **BALLINASCREEN OPTICAL ILLUSIONS**.

On a line below this, key in the subtitle **NON-PAYING ADULTS, JANUARY WEEK 1**.

The spreadsheet must include the following – the headings **SPEC** (spectacles), **CL** (contact lenses) and **ACC** (accessories) have been abbreviated although you may abbreviate others if you wish:

PATIENT NAME	SPEC CODE	CL CODE	PRESCRIPTION COST	SPEC ACC	CL ACC	TOTAL COST

RP – REGULAR PATIENTS

FP – FREQUENT PATIENTS

NP – NEW PATIENTS

TOTAL FOR WEEK 1

2.1(a)	2	Enter the text and numeric data for the RP, FP and NP patients with a retest date for **WEEK 1**. Ensure that
2.2(a), (b), (c), (d), (e)		• all text in the first column is left aligned; • the text and figures in the other columns are right aligned; • the figures for the SPEC ACC, CL ACC and TOTAL are right aligned and displayed to two decimal places; and • all other figures are right aligned and displayed in integer format.
2.3(a), (b)		When you have entered the data, check that it is correct.
2.4(a), (b)	3	Using appropriate formula generate a figure for the first patient in the **TOTAL COST** column (PRESCRIPTION COST plus SPEC ACC plus CL ACC). Replicate this formula for each of the other patients.
2.4(a)	4	Using the appropriate formula generate the totals for Week 1 on the **TOTAL FOR WEEK 1** row, for the columns **PRESCRIPTION COST**, **SPEC ACC**, **CL ACC** and **TOTAL** *only*.
2.7(a), (b), (c) 2.8 (a) 2.9(a), (b), (c)		Save the spreadsheet using a unique filename and record the details on the Record of Progress sheet. Print the title, column headings and data for the whole spreadsheet.
2.9(a), (b), (c)	5	Print the data for the **PATIENT NAME**, **SPEC CODE** and **CL CODE** columns for **REGULAR PATIENTS** *only*.
2.7(a), (b), (c), (d) 2.8(a)		Save the spreadsheet using a unique filename and record the details on the Record of Progress sheet indicating that this extract will be used later.
2.5(a), (b) 2.4(a), (b)	6	The NHS have decided to increase **PRESCRIPTION COSTS** by **6%**.
2.2(b), (c), (d), (e), (f)		Insert a column headed **PRESCRIPTION INCREASE** after the column headed PRESCRIPTION COSTS and before the column SPEC ACC. Use the appropriate formula to calculate the new prescription costs (106%) for the first patient. Replicate this formula for each of the other patients.
		Ensure that the column heading and figures are right aligned and the format set to display integer.
		Amend the formula for the TOTAL COST to use the **PRESCRIPTION INCREASE** amount (PRESCRIPTION INCREASE plus SPEC ACC plus CL ACC) for the first patient. Replicate this formula for each of the other patients. Ensure that the format for the TOTAL COST column is set to display currency to two decimal places. Ensure that this change is also reflected in the TOTAL FOR WEEK 1 row.
2.7(a), (b), (c) 2.8(a) 2.9(a), (b), (c)	7	Save the spreadsheet using a unique filename and record the details on the Record of Progress sheet. Print the title, columns headings and data for the whole spreadsheet.
2.6(a), (b)	8	The PRESCRIPTION INCREASE was insufficient and is now to be changed to **12%**. Amend the column heading from PRESCRIPTION INCREASE to **PRESCRIPTION INCREASE 12%** and adjust the values in the column to show the new rate (112%). Ensure that this change is reflected in the TOTAL COST column.
2.7(a), (b), (c) 2.8(a) 2.9(a), (b), (c)	9	Save the spreadsheet using a unique name and record the details on the Record of Progress sheet. Print the title, column headings and data for the whole spreadsheet.
2.10(a)	10	Print the formulae in the **PRESCRIPTION INCREASE 12%** column ensuring that the formulae are fully displayed.

PATIENT RECORD CARD (Section A)

NAME: E ALLEN
REF: 18/10/57/FP
SPEC CODE: S000461
CL CODE: N/A
PRESCRIPTION COST: 72
SP ACC: 2.50
CL ACC: 0
RETEST DATE: WEEK 1

PATIENT RECORD CARD (Section A)

NAME: J CRILLY
REF: 21/11/56/NP
SPEC CODE: S000501
CL CODE: C000450
PRESCRIPTION COST: 108
SP ACC: 4.99
CL ACC: 7.99
RETEST DATE: WEEK 1

PATIENT RECORD CARD (Section A)

NAME: J FARLEY
REF: 05/10/48/LP
SPEC CODE: S000209
CL CODE: N/A
PRESCRIPTION COST: 0
SP ACC: 0
CL ACC: 0
RETEST DATE: WEEK 1

PATIENT RECORD CARD (Section A)

NAME: M BOYLE
REF: 11/03/70/RP
SPEC CODE: S000432
CL CODE: C000382
PRESCRIPTION COST: 66
SP ACC: 2.50
CL ACC: 7.99
RETEST DATE: WEEK 1

PATIENT RECORD CARD (Section A)

NAME: O CHARLTON
REF: 12/10/49/RP
SPEC CODE: S000441
CL CODE: C00392
PRESCRIPTION COST: 78
SP ACC: 0
CL ACC: 22.50
RETEST DATE: WEEK 2

PATIENT RECORD CARD (Section A)

NAME: P TONER
REF: 04/07/71/LP
SPEC CODE: S000307
CL CODE: N/A
PRESCRIPTION COST: 0
SP ACC: 0
CL ACC: 0
RETEST DATE: WEEK 1

PATIENT RECORD CARD (Section A)

NAME: R CALDWELL
REF: 18/09/51/RP
SPEC CODE: S000210
CL CODE: N/A
PRESCRIPTION COST: 14
SP ACC: 3.99
CL ACC: 0
RETEST DATE: WEEK 1

PATIENT RECORD CARD (Section A)

NAME: G MCFLYNN
REF: 21/03/72/RP
SPEC CODE: S000306
CL CODE: N/A
PRESCRIPTION COST: 14
SP ACC: 0
CL ACC: 0
RETEST DATE: WEEK 1

PATIENT RECORD CARD (Section A)

NAME: T MARTIN
REF: 22/04/56/RP
SPEC CODE: S000196
CL CODE: N/A
PRESCRIPTION COST: 64
SP ACC: 2.50
CL ACC: 0
RETEST DATE: WEEK 2

PATIENT RECORD CARD (Section A)

NAME: K EWING
REF: 01/01/73/FP
SPEC CODE: S000224
CL CODE: C000174
PRESCRIPTION COST: 64
SP ACC: 3.99
CL ACC: 7.99
RETEST DATE: WEEK 1

PATIENT RECORD CARD (Section A)

NAME: T JENKINS
REF: 27/02/62/NP
SPEC CODE: S000502
CL CODE: N/A
PRESCRIPTION COST: 83
SP ACC: 1.99
CL ACC: 0
RETEST DATE: WEEK 1

PATIENT RECORD CARD (Section A)

NAME: S ROSS
REF: 11/06/70/FP
SPEC CODE: S000333
CL CODE: C000284
PRESCRIPTION COST: 89
SP ACC: 0
CL ACC: 11.99
RETEST DATE: WEEK 2

PATIENT RECORD CARD (Section A)

NAME: P NICHOLL
REF: 05/06/55/NP
SPEC CODE: S000503
CL CODE: N/A
PRESCRIPTION COST: 14
SP ACC: 2.10
CL ACC: 0
RETEST DATE: WEEK 1

PATIENT RECORD CARD (Section A)

NAME: B HAWKES
REF: 28/03/62/FP
SPEC CODE: S000316
CL CODE: N/A
PRESCRIPTION COST: 14
SP ACC: 0
CL ACC: 0
RETEST DATE: WEEK 1

PATIENT RECORD CARD (Section A)

NAME: F PATTERSON
REF: 20/01/56/FP
SPEC CODE: S000327
CL CODE: N/A
PRESCRIPTION COST: 14
SP ACC: 0
CL ACC: 0
RETEST DATE: WEEK 1

PATIENT RECORD CARD (Section A)

NAME: S RICHARDS
REF: 28/11/61/FP
SPEC CODE: S000162
CL CODE: C000113
PRESCRIPTION COST: 70
SP ACC: 0
CL ACC: 22.50
RETEST DATE: WEEK 2

PATIENT RECORD CARD (Section A)

NAME: G SIMPSON
REF: 16/03/63/FP
SPEC CODE: S000333
CL CODE: C000283
PRESCRIPTION COST: 39
SP ACC: 7.99
CL ACC: 14.50
RETEST DATE: WEEK 1

PATIENT RECORD CARD (Section A)

NAME: D SINCLAIR
REF: 17/05/56/RP
SPEC CODE: S000318
CL CODE: C000268
PRESCRIPTION COST: 14
SP ACC: 3.99
CL ACC: 7.99
RETEST DATE: WEEK 1

PATIENT RECORD CARD (Section A)

NAME: M YOUNG
REF: 15/04/57/LP
SPEC CODE: S000187
CL CODE: C000138
PRESCRIPTION COST: 0
SP ACC: 0
CL ACC: 0
RETEST DATE: WEEK 1

PATIENT RECORD CARD (Section A)

NAME: A WYLIE
REF: 18/06/55/FP
SPEC CODE: S000211
CL CODE: N/A
PRESCRIPTION COST: 70
SP ACC: 0
CL ACC: 0
RETEST DATE: WEEK 1

IBT II Spreadsheet Mock Assignment 2

Scenario

You work in the Accounts Department of Mourne Collegiate, which offers a range of courses, one category of which is Information Technology (IT). Details of each course are entered on a course file form and each is identified by a unique course reference (see pages 137–8). There are two methods of course delivery, either PART-TIME DAY (PTD) or PART-TIME EVENING (PTE) which is indicated by the final three letters of the course reference. Although many software applications are delivered, the most popular are Word Processing, Desk Top Publishing and Database.

You are going to create a spreadsheet to show the PART-TIME DAY (PTD) Information Technology (IT) courses at Mourne Collegiate. It should group together the appropriate courses under the software subheadings WORD PROCESSING, DESK TOP PUBLISHING and DATABASE.

2.3(a) **1** Using the information on the course file forms, create a spreadsheet with the title **MOURNE COLLEGIATE IT COURSES**.

The spreadsheet must include the following (headings can be abbreviated):

COURSE TITLE	NO OF CLASSES	STUDENT NO	STUDENT TOTAL	COURSE FEE	TOTAL FEE	COURSE REF	ROOMS	LENGTH

WORD PROCESSING

DESK TOP PUBLISHING

DATABASE

TOTALS

2.1(a) **2** Enter the text and numeric data for the **PART-TIME DAY (PTD)** courses at Mourne Collegiate. Ensure that

2.2(a)
(b), (c), (d),
(e), (f)
- all text in the first column is left aligned;
- the text and figures in the other columns are right aligned;
- monetary amounts are right aligned and displayed to two decimal places; and
- all other figures are right aligned and displayed in integer format.

2.3(a), (b) When you have entered the data, check that it is correct.

2.4(a), (b) **3** Using the appropriate formula, generate a figure for the first course in the **STUDENT TOTAL** column (NO OF CLASSES multiplied by STUDENT NO). Replicate this formula for each of the other courses.

2.4(a), (b) **4** Using the appropriate formula generate the **TOTAL FEE** (STUDENT TOTAL multiplied by COURSE FEE) for the first course. Replicate this formula for each of the other courses.

2.4(a) **5** Using the appropriate formula, generate the **TOTALS** for the columns **STUDENT TOTAL** and **TOTAL FEE** *only* on the **TOTALS** row.

2.7 (a), (b), (c)		Save the spreadsheet using a unique filename and record the details on the Record of Progress sheet. Print the title, column headings and data for the whole spreadsheet.
2.8 (a)		
2.9 (a), (b), (c)		
2.9 (a), (b), (c)	**6**	Print the column headings and data for the **COURSE TITLE**, **NO OF CLASSES**, **STUDENT NO**, **STUDENT TOTAL** and **COURSE FEE** columns in **WORD PROCESSING** applications *only*.
2.7(a), (b), (c), (d)		Save the spreadsheet using a unique filename and record the details on the Record of Progress sheet, indicating that this extract will be used later.
2.8(a)		
2.5(a), (b)	**7**	Due to an increase in the number of computers, the classes can now accommodate more students. The **STUDENT NO** for each of the courses is to be increased by **30%**.
2.4(a), (b)		
2.2(b), (c), (d)		Insert a column headed **STUDENT INCREASE** after the column headed STUDENT NO and before the column STUDENT TOTAL. Use the appropriate formula to calculate the increased number of students (130%) who can be accommodated by the first course. Replicate this formula for each of the other courses.
		Ensure that the column heading and figures are right aligned and the format set to display one decimal place.
		Amend the formula for the STUDENT TOTAL to use the **STUDENT INCREASE** amount (NO OF CLASSES multiplied by STUDENT INCREASE) for the first course. Replicate this formula for each of the other courses. Ensure that the format for the entire **STUDENT TOTAL** column is set to display integers. Ensure that this change is reflected in the **TOTAL FEE** column.
2.7(a), (b), (c)	**8**	Save the spreadsheet using a unique filename and record the details on the Record of Progress sheet. Print the title, column headings and data for the whole spreadsheet.
2.8(a)		
2.9(a), (b), (c)		
2.6(a), (b)	**9**	The STUDENT INCREASE was too optimistic and is now to be changed to **15%**. Amend the column heading from STUDENT INCREASE to **STUDENTS EXPECTED** and adjust the values in the column to show the new rate (115%). Ensure that this change is reflected in the **TOTAL FEE** column.
2.7(a), (b), (c)	**10**	Save the spreadsheet using a unique name and record the details on the Record of Progress sheet. Print the title, column headings and data for the whole spreadsheet.
2.8(a)		
2.9(a), (b), (c)		
2.10(a)	**11**	Print the formulae in the **STUDENTS EXPECTED** column ensuring that the formulae are fully displayed.

Note:
LENGTH: 2H × 10W = 2 HOURS PER WEEK FOR 10 WEEKS

COURSE FILE FORM **COURSE TITLE:** WORD **COURSE REF:** WP31PTE **FEE:** 35.50 **NO OF CLASSES:** 5 **ROOMS:** G1-G5 **LENGTH:** 2H × 10W **STUDENT NO:** 15 **SOFTWARE:** WORD PROCESSING	**COURSE FILE FORM** **COURSE TITLE:** PRESSWORKS **COURSE REF:** DT41PTD **FEE:** 65 **NO OF CLASSES:** 2 **ROOMS:** F6-F7 **LENGTH:** 2H × 10W **STUDENT NO:** 8 **SOFTWARE:** DESK TOP PUBLISHING
COURSE FILE FORM **COURSE TITLE:** WORD **COURSE REF:** WP30PTD **FEE:** 35.50 **NO OF CLASSES:** 5 **ROOMS:** G1-G5 **LENGTH:** 2H × 10W **STUDENT NO:** 15 **SOFTWARE:** WORD PROCESSING	**COURSE FILE FORM** **COURSE TITLE:** APPROACH **COURSE REF:** DB50PTD **FEE:** 39.99 **NO OF CLASSES:** 3 **ROOMS:** E1-E3 **LENGTH:** 2H × 10W **STUDENT NO:** 12 **SOFTWARE:** DATABASE
COURSE FILE FORM **COURSE TITLE:** WORDPERFECT **COURSE REF:** WP32PTE **FEE:** 35.50 **NO OF CLASSES:** 5 **ROOMS:** G11-G15 **LENGTH:** 2H × 10W **STUDENT NO:** 15 **SOFTWARE:** WORD PROCESSING	**COURSE FILE FORM** **COURSE TITLE:** ACCESS **COURSE REF:** DB51PTE **FEE:** 39.99 **NO OF CLASSES:** 3 **ROOMS:** E1-E3 **LENGTH:** 2H × 10W **STUDENT NO:** 12 **SOFTWARE:** DATABASE
COURSE FILE FORM **COURSE TITLE:** WORDPERFECT **COURSE REF:** WP33PTD **FEE:** 35.50 **NO OF CLASSES:** 4 **ROOMS:** G16-G19 **LENGTH:** 2H × 10W **STUDENT NO:** 12 **SOFTWARE:** WORD PROCESSING	**COURSE FILE FORM** **COURSE TITLE:** WORDSTAR **COURSE REF:** WP34PTE **FEE:** 35.50 **NO OF CLASSES:** 3 **ROOMS:** G16-G19 **LENGTH:** 2H × 10W **STUDENT NO:** 12 **SOFTWARE:** WORD PROCESSING
COURSE FILE FORM **COURSE TITLE:** PAGEMAKER **COURSE REF:** DT40PTD **FEE:** 65 **NO OF CLASSES:** 5 **ROOMS:** F1–F5 **LENGTH:** 2H × 10W **STUDENT NO:** 6 **SOFTWARE:** DESK TOP PUBLISHING	**COURSE FILE FORM** **COURSE TITLE:** WORDSTAR **COURSE REF:** WP35PTD **FEE:** 35.50 **NO OF CLASSES:** 3 **ROOMS:** G20–G23 **LENGTH:** 2H × 10W **STUDENT NO:** 12 **SOFTWARE:** WORD PROCESSING

COURSE FILE FORM

COURSE TITLE: SERIF PAGEPLUS
COURSE REF: DT42PTD
FEE: 65
NO OF CLASSES: 1
ROOMS: F8
LENGTH: 2H × 10W
STUDENT NO: 8
SOFTWARE: DESK TOP PUBLISHING

COURSE FILE FORM

COURSE TITLE: PARADOX
COURSE REF: DB53PTD
FEE: 39.99
NO OF CLASSES: 5
ROOMS: E10-E15
LENGTH: 2H × 10W
STUDENT NO: 12
SOFTWARE: DATABASE

COURSE FILE FORM

COURSE TITLE: QUARKXPRESS
COURSE REF: DT43PTD
FEE: 65
NO OF CLASSES: 2
ROOMS: F9-F10
LENGTH: 2H × 10W
STUDENT NO: 6
SOFTWARE: DESK TOP PUBLISHING

COURSE FILE FORM

COURSE TITLE: DATAEASE
COURSE REF: DB54PTE
FEE: 39.99
NO OF CLASSES: 5
ROOMS: E4-E9
LENGTH: 2H × 10W
STUDENT NO: 12
SOFTWARE: DATABASE

COURSE FILE FORM

COURSE TITLE: QUARKXPRESS
COURSE REF: DT44PTE
FEE: 65
NO OF CLASSES: 2
ROOMS: F9-F10
LENGTH: 2H × 10W
STUDENT NO: 6
SOFTWARE: DESK TOP PUBLISHING

COURSE FILE FORM

COURSE TITLE: VENTURA
COURSE REF: DT46PTD
FEE: 65
NO OF CLASSES: 5
ROOMS: F6-F11
LENGTH: 2H × 10W
STUDENT NO: 6
SOFTWARE: DESK TOP PUBLISHING

COURSE FILE FORM

COURSE TITLE: VENTURA
COURSE REF: DT45PTE
FEE: 65
NO OF CLASSES: 2
ROOMS: F6-F7
LENGTH: 2H × 10W
STUDENT NO: 6
SOFTWARE: DESK TOP PUBLISHING

COURSE FILE FORM

COURSE TITLE: DATAEASE
COURSE REF: DB55PTD
FEE: 39.99
NO OF CLASSES: 3
ROOMS: E4-E7
LENGTH: 2H × 10W
STUDENT NO: 12
SOFTWARE: DATABASE

COURSE FILE FORM

COURSE TITLE: ACCESS
COURSE REF: DB52PTD
FEE: 39.99
NO OF CLASSES: 5
ROOMS: E4-E9
LENGTH: 2H × 10W
STUDENT NO: 12
SOFTWARE: DATABASE

COURSE FILE FORM

COURSE TITLE: WORDPRO
COURSE REF: WP36PTD
FEE: 35.50
NO OF CLASSES: 3
ROOMS: G20-G23
LENGTH: 2H × 10W
STUDENT NO: 10
SOFTWARE: WORD PROCESSING

consolidation 2

RSA Spreadsheets Stage II

The Spreadsheets Stage II Scheme was developed to encourage those who can use computers and information technology at a basic level to build on their skills and to test their ability to create new spreadsheets as well as to use and maintain existing spreadsheets. Achievement of the qualification indicates that the candidate has a sound competence in the subject and can be recommended for employment.

Assessment

Assessment consists of an examination paper which is made up of practical tasks using a spreadsheet application, such as MS Excel. There are two elements of certification:

1 Amend, update and manipulate an existing spreadsheet.
2 Create, enter and test a spreadsheet.

For each of these elements, there are assessment objectives. Assessment objectives are the operations you *must* be able to do to prove your ability and the performance criteria define the level of accuracy to which these objectives must be carried out.

A maximum of three data entry errors in text input is permitted. Amendments have to be made to 5–7 specified cells in an existing spreadsheet with no errors.

Exam tips

1 The examination must be completed within a three-hour period, although printing may be done outside this time.

2 All instructions must be followed exactly.

3 The filenames used to save your files should be concise and meaningful (e.g. TIM1Q16 is composed of T1 for Task 1, M1 for mock 1, Q16 for question 16).

4 Make sure you key in your name, filename and centre number on each spreadsheet before you save and print it. (Alternatively you can write your name and centre number on each page of every document either at the top or bottom of the page.)

5 When the examination has been completed, the printouts should be assembled in the correct order and handed to the tutor with the copy of the examination paper.

6 There are two mock assignments to prepare you for the final examination. The

spreadsheet assignment for Mock 2 should not be commenced until Mock 1 has been checked for accuracy. Your printouts should match the keys exactly – otherwise you may fail an objective and therefore fail the entire assignment.

7   You should not speak to anyone when you are working on an assignment or in the examination and must not ask your tutor any questions.

8   You are permitted to use centre-prepared or manufacturers' manuals, as well as English and mother-tongue dictionaries, spellcheckers and calculators.

9   You are permitted to take an additional 15 minutes as a break in the course of the examination and the invigilator will tell you the arrangements for this.

◻ Spreadsheet Stage II Mock Assignment 1   ▼ ▲

Task 1

Element 1 – Amend, update and manipulate an existing spreadsheet.

Before you start Task 1 make sure you have on disk the file saved at Step 9 in IBT II Spreadsheet Mock Assignment 1 containing the spreadsheet to be loaded.

You are required to amend, update and display a spreadsheet for Ballinascreen Optical Illusions, showing the Section A details for non-paying adults, January, Week 1.

1.1(a)	**1**	Load a spreadsheet package.
1.1(b)	**2**	Load the file saved at Step 9 in the IBT II Spreadsheet Mock Assignment 1.
1.2(a)	**3**	Details for a patient **J FARLEY** should have been included. Add a row between RP (REGULAR PATIENTS) and M BOYLE and enter the following details:

> **PATIENT NAME:** J FARLEY
> **SPEC CODE:** S000209
> **CL CODE:** N/A
> **PRESCRIPTION COST:** 60
> **SPEC ACC:** 0
> **CL ACC:** 0

> Ensure that the formula to generate the figure for **TOTAL COST** is entered for this row.

1.8(a)	**4**	Check that the formulae used to calculate the totals in the **TOTAL FOR WEEK 1** row are correct and if not correct where necessary.
1.3(a) 1.8(a)	**5**	The information for **PRESCRIPTION INCREASE 12%** is no longer required. Delete the whole column including the column title. Check that the formulae used to calculate the TOTAL for each row are correct and if not correct where necessary.
1.4(a)	**6**	Make the following amendments to the data:

- The **SPEC ACC** amount for **G MCFLYNN** should be **2.50** not 0.
- The **CL ACC** amount for **K EWING** should be **17.99** not 7.99.
- **B HAWKES** has recently ordered contact lenses and his **CL CODE** should display **C000451** not N/A.
- M BOYLE has changed her name to **M BOYLE-BEN**.
- J CRILLY should read **JJ CRILLY**.
- The **SPEC CODE** for **P NICHOL** should read **S000530** not S000503.

		Check that the amendments you have made are correct as total accuracy is required.
1.2	7	Add the following information below the **TOTAL FOR WEEK 1** row at the bottom of the spreadsheet:

NEW PATIENTS SUMMARY
NO OF NEW PATIENTS
AVERAGE PRESCRIPTION COST
TOTAL COSTS

BOI/NP/

1.5(a)	8	Change the column width of the first column from its current setting so that all the information in the first column can be displayed in full. Leave at least two clear spaces at the end of the longest label in the first column.
1.9(a)	9	Amend the reference at the bottom of the spreadsheet from BOI/NP/ to also include your name at the end of it.
1.10(a)	10	**T JENKINS** is considering the purchase of contact lenses. Increase his **PRESCRIPTION COST** amount from 83 to **178.**
1.10(b)	11	As a decision has not yet been made on this, write down the new **TOTAL COST** value for **T JENKINS** as Step 11 on the Record of Progress sheet.
1.10(c)	12	Return the spreadsheet to the original values before that change was made.
	13	You must use functions for the following instructions. No other method of calculation will be accepted. In the **NEW PATIENTS SUMMARY** section:
1.7(b)		Use the **COUNT** function to calculate the number of new patients and enter this in the second column alongside the label **NO OF NEW PATIENTS**.
1.7(c)		Use the **AVERAGE** function to calculate the average cost of prescriptions for new patients and enter this in the second column alongside the label **AVERAGE PRESCRIPTION COST**.
1.7(a)		Use the **SUM** function to calculate the total cost for all the new patients and enter this in the second column alongside the label **TOTAL COSTS**.
1.6(a)	14	The **AVERAGE PRESCRIPTION COST** should be displayed in integer format (no decimal places).
1.6(b), (c)	15	The **TOTAL COSTS** should be displayed in currency format with two decimal places.
1.11(a)	16	Save the spreadsheet. Ask someone to verify this.
1.12(a)	17	Print a copy of the complete spreadsheet (or it may be printed later).
1.12(b)	18	Print a copy *only* of the **TOTAL FOR WEEK 1** row and the rows containing the **NEW PATIENTS SUMMARY** section of the spreadsheet (including your name). Show the formulae (cell contents) and ensure that the printout will display the entire width of each formula used in this extract. Your software package may require you to increase the column width.

The documents may be printed after the examination. This may be done by the invigilator or person appointed by the local secretary.

Task 2

Element 2 – Create, enter and test a spreadsheet.

Read the information given below before you start this task.

Ballinacreen Optical Illusions wish to make a projection on what the income in the coming year might be. This will be based on figures already available for JANUARY, WEEK 1. A spreadsheet needs to be planned in two sections, one to show the income for JANUARY, WEEK 1 and the other to show the PROJECTED ANNUAL INCOME.

The first section will include a breakdown of the income for JANUARY WEEK 1 under three headings: NON-PAYING ADULTS, NON-PAYING CHILDREN – i.e. those entitled to free NHS sight tests by reason of age, health condition, income support, etc., and OTHER – i.e. those who have to pay for sight tests, lenses, frames, etc.

The second section will include the projected annual income from JAN to DEC.

It will also be necessary for the spreadsheet to calculate for each month the GROUP TOTAL, GROUP AVERAGE and TOTAL INCOME.

You should be able to construct your spreadsheet with five columns and 32 rows.

You will link this spreadsheet with the spreadsheet saved at Step 16 in Task 1.

2.1(a) **1** Enter the title:

BALLINASCREEN OPTICAL ILLUSIONS
INCOME FOR JANUARY, WEEK 1

2.3(a) **2** Enter the column headings **ITEM, NON-PAYING ADULTS, NON-PAYING CHILDREN, OTHER, TOTAL INCOME**.

2.3(b) **3** Enter the row headings and test data as shown below. Check that the data is entered correctly as 100% accuracy is required:

ITEM	NON-PAYING ADULTS	NON-PAYING CHILDREN	OTHER	TOTAL INCOME
SIGHT TEST			**364**	
SPECTACLE FRAMES			**1144**	
SPECTACLE LENSES			**754**	
SP ACCESSORIES			**103.74**	
CONTACT LENSES			**660**	
CL ACCESSORIES			**135**	
INDUSTRIAL SPECS			**160**	
FRAME REPAIRS			**143**	
TOTAL			**3463.74**	
PROJECTED ANNUAL INCOME				
PERIOD				
JAN			**3463.74**	
FEB				
MAR				
APR				
MAY				
JUN				
JUL				
AUG				
SEP				
OCT				

NOV
DEC
GROUP TOTAL
GROUP AVERAGE

2.8(a)	4	In the **INCOME FOR JANUARY, WEEK 1** section select the cell where the **TOTAL** for **NON-PAYING ADULTS** is to be input and link to the **TOTAL COST** in the **TOTAL FOR WEEK 1** row from the spreadsheet saved at Step 16 in Task 1. Ask someone to verify this.
2.7(a)	5	In the **INCOME FOR JANUARY, WEEK 1** section select the **JAN** cell for **NON-PAYING ADULTS** and enter a formula that will multiply the cell containing **TOTAL** for **NON-PAYING ADULTS** by **4** to obtain a monthly figure. Name this cell **NPA**.
2.7(b)	6	As projected income for NON-PAYING ADULTS is expected to increase by 6% in FEB enter a formula in this cell using the named cell **NPA** multiplied by **106%** and replicate this for the other months. Formulae which use the cell reference instead of the name **NPA** will not be accepted.
2.4(a), (b)	7	Since non-paying children generate the equivalent of about 25% of the non-paying adults' income, in the **INCOME FOR JANUARY, WEEK 1** section select the **TOTAL** cell for **NON-PAYING CHILDREN** and enter a formula to multiply the **TOTAL** for **NON-PAYING ADULTS** by **25%**. Replicate this formula for **NON-PAYING CHILDREN** for each of the months from **JAN** to **DEC**.
2.5(b)	8	In the **INCOME FOR JANUARY, WEEK 1** section calculate the **TOTAL INCOME** in the **TOTAL** row. Replicate this for the months **JAN–DEC**.
2.4(a), (b)	9	Calculate the **GROUP TOTAL** for **NON-PAYING ADULTS** (sum the range from JAN to DEC). Replicate this for the **NON-PAYING CHILDREN**, **OTHER** and **TOTAL INCOME** columns.
2.2(b), (c)	10	Display the **GROUP TOTAL** row in currency format to two decimal places and widen the column if necessary.
2.4(a), (b)	11	Calculate the **GROUP AVERAGE** for **NON-PAYING ADULTS** (GROUP TOTAL divided by 12 or use the AVERAGE function – either is acceptable). Replicate this for the **NON-PAYING CHILDREN** and **OTHER** columns.
2.2(a)	12	Display the **GROUP AVERAGE** row in integer format (no decimal places).
2.9	13	On a row below the last row enter your name in the first column and save the spreadsheet. Ask someone to verify this.
2.11(a)	14	Print a copy of the complete spreadsheet.
2.11(b)	15	Print a copy of the complete spreadsheet showing the formulae (cell contents).
2.6	16	Protect the contents of the row of cells showing the **GROUP TOTAL**. Ask someone to verify this.
2.10	17	Display the spreadsheet values again and print *only* the second section of the spreadsheet, i.e. from the row containing the heading **PROJECTED ANNUAL INCOME** down to and including the row containing **YOUR NAME**.

The documents may be printed after the examination. The printouts for this task must be generated by the candidate.

Spreadsheet Stage II Mock Assignment 2

Task 1

Element 1 – Amend, update and manipulate an existing spreadsheet.

Before you start Task 1 make sure you have on disk the file saved at Step 10 in IBT II Spreadsheet Mock Assignment 2 containing the spreadsheet to be loaded.

You are required to amend, update and display a spreadsheet for Mourne Collegiate, showing the revenue earned by some of its IT courses.

1.1(a)	**1**	Load a spreadsheet package.
1.1(b)	**2**	Load the file saved at Step 10 in IBT II Spreadsheet Mock Assignment 2.
1.2(a)	**3**	Details for a Word Processing course CLARIS have not been included. Add a row between **WORD PROCESSING** and **WORD** and enter the following details:

COURSE TITLE: CLARIS
NO OF CLASSES: 2
STUDENT NO: 12
COURSE FEE: 35.50
COURSE REF: WP37PTD
ROOMS: G24-G25
LENGTH: 2H × 10W

Ensure that the formula to generate the figures for **STUDENTS EXPECTED**, **STUDENT TOTAL** and **TOTAL FEE** is entered for this row.

1.8(a)	**4**	Check that the formulae used to calculate the totals in the **TOTALS** row are correct and, if not, correct where necessary.
1.3(a)	**5**	It has been found that the information for the **WORDPRO** course has been entered by mistake as this course is only available in the evenings. Delete the whole row including the course title. If your software package does not recalculate automatically you may need to recalculate the totals row.
1.4(a)	**6**	Make the following amendments to the data:

- The **NO OF CLASSES** for **WORDPERFECT** should be **5** not 4.
- The **LENGTH** for **CLARIS** should be **3H × 10W** not 2H × 10W.
- The **STUDENT NO** for **QUARKXPRESS** should be **8** not 6.
- **COURSE TITLE** should read **COURSE TITLES**.
- The description **LENGTH** should read **DURATION**.
- The **ROOMS** for **PRESSWORKS** should be **F9–F10** not F6–F7.

Check that the amendments you have made are correct as total accuracy is required.

1.2	**7**	Add the following information below the **TOTALS** row at the bottom of the spreadsheet:

IT STATISTICS
OVERALL TOTAL FEES
NO OF COURSES
AVERAGE STUDENT NO

MC/IT

1.5(a)	**8**	Change the column width of the first column from its current setting so that all the information in the first column can be

displayed in full. Leave at least two clear spaces at the end of the longest label in the first column (including the IT statistics).

1.9(a)   **9**   Amend the reference at the bottom of the spreadsheet from MC/IT to also show **YOUR NAME** and **TODAY'S DATE**.

1.10(a)   **10**   Due to demand it may be possible to offer extra **WORD** classes on Saturdays as well as during the week. Increase the **NO OF CLASSES** for **WORD** from 5 to **8**.

1.10 (b)   **11**   As this increase is only a projection if the college was to open on Saturdays write down the new **TOTAL FEE** value for **WORD** as Step 11 on the Record of Progress sheet.

1.10(c)   **12**   Return the spreadsheet to the original values before the change was made.

13   You must use **FUNCTIONS** for the following instructions. No other method of calculation will be accepted.

In the **IT STATISTICS** section:

1.7(a)   Use the **SUM** function to calculate the overall total fees of all courses and enter this in the second column alongside the label OVERALL TOTAL FEES.

1.7(b)   Use the **COUNT** function to calculate the number of course references and enter this in the second column alongside the label NO OF COURSES.

1.7(c)   Use the **AVERAGE** function to calculate the average number of students and enter this in the second column alongside the label AVERAGE STUDENT NO.

1.6(b)   **14**   The numberic data for **OVERAL TOTAL FEES** should be in currency format with two decimal places.

1.6(c)   **15**   The numeric data for **NO OF COURSES** should be displayed to two decimal places.

1.6(a)   **16**   The **AVERAGE STUDENT NO** should be displayed in integer format (no decimal places).

1.11(a)   **17**   Save the spreadsheet. Ask someone to verify this.

1.12(a)   **18**   Print a copy of the complete spreadsheet (or it may be printed later).

1.12(b)   **19**   Print a copy *only* of the **TOTALS** row and the rows containing the **IT STATISTICS** section of the spreadsheet (including your name). Show the formulae (cell contents) and ensure that the printout will display the entire width of each formula used in this extract. Your software package may require you to increase the column width.

The documents may be printed after the examination. This may be done by the invigilator or person appointed by the local secretary.

— ▓   **Spreadsheet Stage II Mock Assignment 2**   ▼ ▲

Task 2

Element 2 – Create, enter and test a spreadsheet.

Background information

Please read the information given below you start this task.

Mourne Collegiate intend to develop further courses in Desk Top Publishing. These will be delivered on a much more flexible basis than traditional standard college courses and will be offered six days a week throughout the entire year. Prior to the introduction of this initiative a spreadsheet needs to be planned to show the costing of such courses. The spreadsheet will be in two sections. The first section will include the **INCOME** from

COURSE FEES
COURSE FUNDING

The second section will include **EXPENDITURE** for

SALARIES
CRECHE
OTHER OVERHEADS

It will also be necessary for the spreadsheet to calculate for each quarter the

TOTAL INCOME
TOTAL EXPENDITURE
NET PROFIT/LOSS

You should be able to construct the spreadsheet with six columns and 29 rows.

You will link this spreadsheet with the spreadsheet saved at Step 17 in Task 1.

2.1(a)	**1**	Enter the title:
		COSTING FOR DTP COURSES
2.3(a)	**2**	Enter the column headings **ITEM, JUN–AUG, SEP–NOV, DEC–FEB, MAR–MAY, TOTAL PA**.
2.3(b) 2.5(a)	**3**	Enter the row headings and test data as shown below. Check that the data is entered correctly as 100% accuracy is required:

ITEM	JUN–AUG	SEP–NOV	DEC–FEB	MAR–MAY	TOTAL PA
INCOME					
COURSE FEES					
COURSE FUNDING	3701.25	3701.25	3701.25	3701.25	
TOTAL INCOME					
EXPENDITURE					
SALARIES					
CRECHE	210	210	210	210	
OTHER OVERHEADS	2775	3165	3240	3189	
TOTAL EXPENDITURE					
NET PROFIT/LOSS					
RATE PER HR (£)	33				

2.8(a) 2.5(b)	**4**	In the cell where the JUN–AUG COURSE FEES are to be input, link this to the **TOTAL FEE** for the **SERIF PAGEPLUS** course from the spreadsheet saved at Step 17 in Task 1. Ask someone to verify this. Replicate for the other three quarters.

2.7(a)	5	Each course lasts 20 hours and this figure should be used in the appropriate cell to calculate the **SALARIES** for **JUN–AUG**, i.e. by multiplying the RATE PER HR by the number of hours, i.e. 20 (RATE PER HR*20). Name this cell **SALARY**.
2.7(b)	6	Staff salaries are to include an annual increment of 3% payable from September onwards. In the **SEP–NOV** column against **SALARIES** enter a formula using the named cell **SALARY** multiplied by **103%**. Replicate this for the other quarters. Formulae which use the cell reference instead of the name **SALARY** will not be accepted.
2.5(b)	7	Calculate the **TOTAL INCOME** and **TOTAL EXPENDITURE** for **MAR–MAY** and replicate this for the other quarters. Calculate the **TOTAL PA** for each item of income and expenditure including the totals.
2.4(a), (b)	8	Calculate the **NET PROFIT/LOSS** for **JUN–AUG** (TOTAL INCOME minus TOTAL EXPENDITURE) and replicate this for the other months.
2.2(a)	9	Display the **TOTAL INCOME** and **TOTAL EXPENDITURE** rows in integer format (no decimal places).
2.2b)	10	Display the **NET PROFIT/LOSS** and **RATE PER HR** rows in currency format to two decimal places.
2.2(c)	11	Display the remainder of the spreadsheet to two decimal places.
2.9	12	On a row below the last row enter you name in the first column. Enter the filename beneath this. Save your spreadsheet. Ask someone to verify this.
2.11(a)	13	Print a copy of the complete spreadsheet.
2.11(b)	14	Print a copy of the complete spreadsheet showing the formulae (cell contents).
2.6	15	Protect the contents of the column of cells showing the **TOTAL PA**. Ask someone to verify this.
2.10	16	Display the spreadsheet values again and print *only* the first two columns down to and including the row containing your name.

The documents may be printed after the examination. The printouts for this task must be generated by the candidate.

key to tasks

Task 1C   Sheet 1

CAR SALES

TYPE	JAN	FEB	MAR	APR	MAY	JUN	TOTAL
SALOON	3	8	10	7	12	11	
COUPE	1	1	2	1	2	3	
TOURER	10	12	12	15	16	15	
ESTATE	8	8	11	12	14	17	
VAN	8	12	10	9	7	8	
PICK UP	6	7	9	10	9	12	
TOTAL							

YOUR NAME
TASK 1C

Task 1F   Sheet 1

CAR SALES

TYPE	JAN	FEB	MAR	APR	MAY	JUN	TOTAL	TOTAL PA
SALOON	3	8	10	7	12	11	51	102
COUPE	1	1	2	1	2	3	10	20
TOURER	10	12	12	15	16	15	80	160
ESTATE	8	8	11	12	14	17	70	140
VAN	8	12	10	9	7	8	54	108
PICK UP	6	7	9	10	9	12	53	106
TOTAL	36	48	54	54	60	66		
AVERAGE	6	8	9	9	10	11		

YOUR NAME
TASK 1F

Extra Practice Task 1   Sheet 1

CONFECTIONERY SALES

ITEM	JUL	AUG	SEP	OCT	NOV	DEC	TOTAL	TOTAL PA
TOFFEES	19	18	11	17	22	23	110	220
FUDGE	10	10	11	14	17	18	80	160
GUMS	8	7	8	12	11	24	70	140
BONBON	14	12	11	12	13	11	73	146
MINTS	18	19	20	17	16	15	105	210
ROCK	21	24	17	12	11	11	96	192
TOTAL	90	90	78	84	90	102		
AVERAGE	15	15	13	14	15	17		

YOUR NAME
EPTASK 1

YOYO Task 1

WINE SALES

BOTTLE	JUL	AUG	SEP	OCT	NOV	DEC	TOTAL	TOTAL PA
CHABLIS	16	17	15	15	15	18	96	192
CLARET	20	14	11	14	17	22	98	196
MERLOT	28	17	18	22	21	24	130	260
HOCK	24	26	27	26	24	28	155	310
RIOJA	21	20	22	21	28	31	143	286
CHIANTI	23	26	27	22	21	21	140	280
TOTAL	132	120	120	120	126	144		
AVERAGE	22	20	20	20	21	24		

YOUR NAME
YOYO1

Task 2B

Sheet 1

VEHICLE SALES

TYPE	JAN	FEB	MAR	APR	MAY	JUN	TOTAL	TOTAL PA
SALOON 4DR	3	8	10	7	12	11	51	102
COUPE	7	1	2	1	2	3	16	32
CAMPER	10	12	12	15	16	15	80	160
ESTATE	8	8	11	12	14	17	70	140
HATCHBACK 5DR	8	12	10	15	7	8	60	120
TRUCK	6	7	9	10	9	12	53	106
TOTAL	42	48	54	60	60	66		
AVERAGE	7	8	9	10	10	11		

YOUR NAME
TASK2B

Page 1

Task 2C

Sheet 1

VEHICLE SALES

TYPE	JAN	FEB	MAR	APR	MAY	JUN	JUL	TOTAL	TOTAL PA
SALOON 4DR	3	8	10	7	12	2	11	53	106
COUPE	7	1	2	1	2	0	3	16	32
CAMPER	10	12	12	15	16	1	15	81	162
ESTATE	8	8	11	12	14	8	17	78	156
HATCHBACK 5DR	8	12	10	15	7	5	8	65	130
TRUCK	6	7	9	10	9	6	12	59	118
CABRIOLET	0	0	6	6	6	6	6	30	
TOTAL	42	48	60	66	66	28	72		
AVERAGE									

YOUR NAME
TASK 2C

Page 1

Task 2D

Sheet 1

VEHICLE SALES

TYPE	JAN	FEB	MAR	APR	MAY	JUN	TOTAL	TOTAL PA
SALOON 4DR	3	8	10	7	12	11	51	102
COUPE	7	1	2	1	2	3	16	32
CAMPER	10	12	12	15	16	15	80	160
ESTATE	8	8	11	12	14	17	70	140
HATCHBACK 5DR	8	12	10	15	7	8	60	120
TRUCK	6	7	9	10	9	12	53	106
TOTAL	42	48	54	60	60	66		
AVERAGE								

YOUR NAME
TASK2D

Page 1

Extra Practice Task 2   Sheet 1

SALES OF CONFECTIONERY

ITEM	JUL	AUG	SEP	OCT	NOV	DEC	TOTAL	TOTAL PA
BUTTER TOFFEES	19	18	11	17	22	23	110	220
FUDGE	16	10	11	14	17	18	86	172
GUMS	8	7	8	12	11	24	70	140
JELLIES	14	12	11	12	13	11	73	146
MINTOS	18	19	20	17	16	15	105	210
LIQUORICE	21	24	17	12	11	5	90	180
TOTAL	96	90	78	84	90	96		
AVERAGE	16	15	13	14	15	16		

YOUR NAME
EPTASK2

YOYO Task 2

SALES OF POPULAR WINES

BOTTLE	JUL	AUG	SEP	OCT	NOV	DEC	TOTAL	TOTAL PA
CHABLIS	16	17	15	15	15	18	96	192
CLARET	14	14	11	14	17	22	92	184
MERLOT	28	17	18	22	21	24	130	260
SHIRAZ CABERNET	24	26	27	26	24	28	155	310
RIOJA	21	20	22	21	28	31	143	286
SEMILLON	23	26	27	22	21	27	146	292
TOTAL	126	120	120	120	126	150		
AVERAGE	21	20	20	20	21	25		

YOUR NAME
YOYO2

Task 3C   Sheet 1
VEHICLE SALES

TYPE	JAN	FEB	MAR	APR	MAY	JUN	TOTAL	COST
SALOON 4DR	3	8	10	7	12	11	**51**	10499
COUPE	3	6	6	7	10	9	**41**	17000
CAMPER	10	12	12	15	16	15	**80**	20500
ESTATE	8	8	11	12	14	17	**70**	12499
HATCHBACK 5DR	8	12	10	15	7	8	**60**	10500
OFF ROADER	6	7	9	10	9	12	**53**	25500
TOTAL	**38**	**53**	**58**	**66**	**68**	**72**	**355**	
AVERAGE							**59.17**	

YOUR NAME
TASK3C

Task 3D

VEHICLE SALES

TYPE	JAN	FEB	MAR	APR	MAY	JUN	TOTAL	COST
SALOON 4DR	3	8	10	7	12	11	**51**	£10,499
COUPE	3	6	6	7	10	9	**41**	£17,000
CAMPER	10	12	12	15	16	15	**80**	£20,500
ESTATE	8	8	11	12	14	17	**70**	£12,499
HATCHBACK 5DR	8	12	10	15	7	8	**60**	£10,500
OFF ROADER	6	7	9	10	9	12	**53**	£25,500
TOTAL	**38**	**53**	**58**	**66**	**68**	**72**	**355**	
AVERAGE							**59**	

YOUR NAME
TASK3D

Task 3E

VEHICLE SALES

TYPE	JAN	FEB	MAR	APR	MAY	JUN	JUL	AUG	SEP	TOTAL	COST
SALOON 4DR	3	8	10	7	12	11				51	£10,499
CABRIOLET											
HATCHBACK 3DR											
COUPE	3	6	6	7	10	9				41	£17,000
CAMPER	10	12	12	15	16	15				80	£20,500
ESTATE	8	8	11	12	14	17				70	£12,499
HATCHBACK 5DR	8	12	10	15	7	8				60	£10,500
OFF ROADER	6	7	9	10	9	12				53	£25,500
TOTAL	38	53	58	66	68	72				355	
AVERAGE										59	

YOUR NAME
TASK3E

Page 1

Task 3F   Sheet 1

VEHICLE SALES

TYPE	JAN	FEB	MAR	APR	MAY	JUN	JUL	AUG	SEP	TOTAL	COST
SALOON 4DR	3	8	10	7	12	11	3	3	3	60	£10,499
CABRIOLET	2	2	2	2	2	2	3	3	3	21	£19,999
HATCHBACK 3DR	5	5	5	5	5	5	6	6	6	48	£10,000
COUPE	3	6	6	7	10	9	6	6	6	59	£17,000
CAMPER	10	12	12	15	16	15	6	6	6	98	£20,500
ESTATE	8	8	11	12	14	17	6	6	6	88	£12,499
HATCHBACK 5DR	8	12	10	15	7	8	6	6	6	78	£10,500
OFF ROADER	6	7	9	10	9	12	6	6	6	71	£25,500
TOTAL	45	60	65	73	75	79	42	42	42	523	
AVERAGE	6	8	8	9	9	10	5	5	5	65	

YOUR NAME
TASK3F

Page 1

Task 3H   Sheet 1

VEHICLE SALES

TYPE	TOTAL JAN-JUL	TOTAL JUL-DEC	ANNUAL TOTAL	COST PRICE	STOCK VALUE	SELLING PRICE	PROFIT PER CAR
SALOON 4DR	51	63	114	£10,499	£1,196,886	£11,999	£1,500
CABRIOLET	12	14	26	£19,999	£519,974	£22,999	£3,000
HATCHBACK 3DR	30	49	79	£10,000	£790,000	£11,499	£1,499
COUPE	35	38	73	£17,000	£1,241,000	£19,499	£2,499
CAMPER	80	67	147	£20,500	£3,013,500	£21,999	£1,499
ESTATE	70	63	133	£12,499	£1,662,367	£14,499	£2,000
HATCHBACK 5DR	60	59	119	£10,500	£1,249,500	£11,999	£1,499
OFF ROADER	53	46	99	£25,500	£2,524,500	£28,499	£2,999
TOTAL	391	399	790	£126,497	£12,197,727	£142,992	£16,495
AVERAGE	49	50	99				

YOUR NAME
TASK3H

Page 1

Task 3I   Sheet 1

VEHICLE SALES

TYPE	TOTAL JAN-JUN	TOTAL JUL-DEC
SALOON 4DR	51	63
CABRIOLET	12	14
HATCHBACK 3DR	30	49
COUPE	35	38
CAMPER	80	67
ΓSTATE	70	63
HATCHBACK 5DR	60	59
OFF ROADER	53	46
TOTAL	=SUM(B5:B12)	=SUM(C5:C12)
AVERAGE	=B13/8	=C13/8

YOUR NAME
TASK31

Page 1

Task 3I (continued)   Sheet 1

ANNUAL TOTAL	COST PRICE	STOCK VALUE	SELLING PRICE
=B5+C5	10499	=D5*E5	11999
=B6+C6	19999	=D6*E6	22999
=B7+C7	10000	=D7*E7	11499
=B8+C8	17000	=D8*E8	19499
=B9+C9	20500	=D9*E9	21999
=B10+C10	12499	=D10*E10	14499
=B11+C11	10500	=D11*E11	11999
=B12+C12	25500	=D12*E12	28499
=SUM(D5:D12)	=SUM(E5:E12)	=SUM(F5:F12)	=SUM(G5:G12)
=D13/8			

Page 2

Task 3I (continued)   Sheet 1

PROFIT PER CAR

=G5-E5
=G6-E6
=G7-E7
=G8-E8
=G9-E9
=G10-E10
=G11-E11
=G12-E12
=SUM(H5:H12)

Page 3

Extra Practice Task 3A   Sheet 1

SALES OF CONFECTIONERY

ITEM	JUL	AUG	SEP	OCT	NOV	DEC	JAN	FEB	MAR	TOTAL	COST
BUTTER TOFFEES	19	18	11	17	22	23	13	13	13	**149**	£0.75
NUTTY TOFFEES	20	20	20	20	20	20	13	13	13	**159**	£0.80
NUTTY FUDGE	15	15	15	15	15	15	16	16	16	**138**	£0.70
FUDGE	11	12	17	17	20	22	16	16	16	**147**	£0.65
GUMS	8	7	8	12	11	24	16	16	16	**118**	£0.55
JELLIES	14	12	11	12	13	11	16	16	16	**121**	£0.65
MINTOS	18	19	20	17	16	15	16	16	16	**153**	£0.65
ROCK	21	24	17	12	11	5	16	16	16	**138**	£0.45
TOTAL	126	127	119	122	128	135	122	122	122	1123	
AVERAGE	16	16	15	15	16	17	15	15	15	140	

YOUR NAME
EPTASK3A

Page 1

Extra Practice Task 3B   Sheet 1

SALES OF CONFECTIONERY

ITEM	TOTAL JAN-JUN	TOTAL JUL-DEC	ANNUAL TOTAL	COST PRICE	STOCK VALUE	SELLING PRICE	PROFIT PER PACK
BUTTER TOFFEES	88	110	198	£0.75	£148.50	£0.85	£0.10
NUTTY TOFFEES	96	120	216	£0.80	£172.80	£0.90	£0.10
NUTTY FUDGE	92	90	182	£0.70	£127.40	£0.80	£0.10
FUDGE	106	99	205	£0.65	£133.25	£0.75	£0.10
GUMS	80	70	150	£0.55	£82.50	£0.60	£0.05
JELLIES	85	73	158	£0.65	£102.70	£0.75	£0.10
MINTOS	110	105	215	£0.65	£139.75	£0.75	£0.10
ROCK	98	90	188	£0.45	£84.60	£0.50	£0.05
TOTAL	755	757	1512	£5.20	£991.50	£5.90	£0.70
AVERAGE	94	95	189				

YOUR NAME
EPTASK3B

Extra Practice Task 3C

SALES OF CONFECTIONERY

ITEM	TOTAL JAN-JUN	TOTAL JUL-DEC
BUTTER TOFFEES	88	110
NUTTY TOFFEES	96	120
NUTTY FUDGE	92	90
FUDGE	106	99
GUMS	80	70
JELLIES	85	73
MINTOS	110	105
ROCK	98	90
TOTAL	=SUM(B5:B12)	=SUM(C5:C12)
AVERAGE	=B13/8	=C13/8

YOUR NAME
EPTASK3C

Extra Practice Task 3C (continued)

ANNUAL TOTAL	COST PRICE	STOCK VALUE	SELLING PRICE
=B5+C5	0.75	=D5*E5	0.85
=B6+C6	0.8	=D6*E6	0.9
=B7+C7	0.7	=D7*E7	0.8
=B8+C8	0.65	=D8*E8	0.75
=B9+C9	0.55	=D9*E9	0.6
=B10+C10	0.65	=D10*E10	0.75
=B11+C11	0.65	=D11*E11	0.75
=B12+C12	0.45	=D12*E12	0.5
=SUM(D5:D12)	=SUM(E5:E12)	=SUM(F5:F12)	=SUM(G5:G12)
=D13/8			

Extra Practice Task 3C (continued)

PROFIT PER PACK
=G5-E5
=G6-E6
=G7-E7
=G8-E8
=G9-E9
=G10-E10
=G11-E11
=G12-E12
=SUM(H5:H12)

YOYO Task 3A

SALES OF POPULAR WINES

BOTTLE	JUL	AUG	SEP	OCT	NOV	DEC	JAN	FEB	MAR	TOTAL	COST
CHABLIS	16	17	15	15	15	18	23	23	23	**165**	£5.30
BEAUJOLAIS	20	20	20	20	20	20	23	23	23	**189**	£2.60
BURGUNDY	25	25	25	25	25	25	26	26	26	**228**	£3.30
CLARET	21	16	17	18	20	24	26	26	26	**194**	£3.30
MERLOT	28	17	18	22	21	24	26	26	26	**208**	£1.90
SHIRAZ CABERNET	24	26	27	26	24	28	26	26	26	**233**	£2.60
RIOJA	21	20	22	21	28	31	26	26	26	**221**	£4.60
SAUVIGNON	23	26	27	22	21	27	26	26	26	**224**	£2.60
TOTAL	**178**	**167**	**171**	**169**	**174**	**197**	**202**	**202**	**202**	1662	
AVERAGE	**22**	**21**	**21**	**21**	**22**	**25**	**25**	**25**	**25**	208	

YOUR NAME
YOYO3A

YOYO Task 3B

SALES OF POPULAR WINES

BOTTLE	TOTAL JAN-JUN	TOTAL JUL-DEC	ANNUAL TOTAL	COST PRICE	STOCK VALUE	SELLING PRICE	PROFIT PER BOTTLE
CHABLIS	96	138	234	£5.30	£1,240.20	£13.25	£7.95
BEAUJOLAIS	120	138	258	£2.60	£670.80	£6.50	£3.90
BURGUNDY	150	156	306	£3.30	£1,009.80	£8.25	£4.95
CLARET	116	156	272	£3.30	£897.60	£8.25	£4.95
MERLOT	130	156	286	£1.90	£543.40	£4.75	£2.85
SHIRAZ CABERNET	155	156	311	£2.60	£808.60	£6.50	£3.90
RIOJA	143	156	299	£4.60	£1,375.40	£11.50	£6.90
SAUVIGNON	146	156	302	£2.60	£785.20	£6.50	£3.90
TOTAL	1056	1212	2268	£26.20	£7,331.00	£65.50	£39.30
AVERAGE	132	152	284				

YOUR NAME
YOYO3B

YOYO Task 3C

SALES OF POPULAR WINES

BOTTLE	TOTAL JAN-JUN	TOTAL JUL-DEC	ANNUAL TOTAL	COST PRICE	STOCK VALUE	SELLING PRICE	PROFIT PER BOTTLE
CHABLIS	96	138	=B5+C5	5.3	=D5*E5	13.25	=G5-E5
BEAUJOLAIS	120	138	=B6+C6	2.6	=D6*E6	6.5	=G6-E6
BURGUNDY	150	156	=B7+C7	3.3	=D7*E7	8.25	=G7-E7
CLARET	116	156	=B8+C8	3.3	=D8*E8	8.25	=G8-E8
MERLOT	130	156	=B9+C9	1.9	=D9*E9	4.75	=G9-E9
SHIRAZ CABERNET	155	156	=B10+C10	2.6	=D10*E10	6.5	=G10-E10
RIOJA	143	156	=B11+C11	4.6	=D11*E11	11.5	=G11-E11
SAUVIGNON	146	156	=B12+C12	2.6	=D12*E12	6.5	=G12-E12
TOTAL	=SUM(B5:B12)	=SUM(C5:C12)	=SUM(D5:D12)	=SUM(E5-E12)	=SUM(F5-F12)	=(SUM(G5:G12)	=(SUM(H5:H12)
AVERAGE	=B13/8	=C13/8	=D13/8				

YOUR NAME
YOYO3C

CLAIT Spreadsheet Mock Assignment 1

SLAVE TO FASHION
INVOICE – AGENCY NO 1-G8500-513

DESCRIPTION	LOCATION	SIZE	QUANTITY	PRICE	ITEM NO
ORANGE PARKA JACKET	844-15D	16	1	14.99	2063UY
GREEN SKIRT	832-12E	14	1	29.99	0580UX
TEAL JOG PANTS	451-11G	12	2	10.99	0836CA
GREEN JERSEY CARDIGAN	832-13E	14	1	23.99	0597UM
CREAM STRETCH BLOUSE	616-09B	14	2	32.99	7223WX
CREAM VELOUR TOP	616-24B	16	3	16.99	9818WA
BROWN STITCH BOOT	825-12H	7	1	39.99	2389NM
TOTAL			11	169.93	

YOUR NAME
SMOCK1P1

CLAIT Spreadsheet Mock Assignment 1 (continued)

SLAVE TO FASHION
INVOICE – AGENCY NO 1-G8500-513

DESCRIPTION	SIZE	QUANTITY	PRICE	COST	ITEM NO
ORANGE PARKA JACKET	16	1	14.99	14.99	2063UY
GREEN STRETCH SKIRT	14	1	29.99	29.99	0580UX
TEAL JOG PANTS	14	2	10.99	21.98	0836CA
GREEN JERSEY CARDIGAN	14	1	23.99	23.99	0597UM
CREAM STRETCH BLOUSE	14	2	32.99	65.98	7223WX
CREAM VELOUR TOP	16	3	16.99	50.97	9818WA
WHITE JOG PANTS	14	1	10.99	10.99	0801BL
BROWN STITCH BOOT	7	1	39.99	39.99	2389NM
TOTAL		12	180.92	258.88	

YOUR NAME
SMOCK1P2

CLAIT Spreadsheet Mock Assignment 1 (continued)

SLAVE TO FASHION
INVOICE – AGENCY NO 1-G8

DESCRIPTION	SIZE	QUANTITY	PRICE	COST	ITEM NO
ORANGE PARKA JACKET	16	1	14.99	=C5*D5	2063UY
GREEN STRETCH SKIRT	14	1	29.99	=C6*D6	0580UX
TEAL JOG PANTS	14	2	10.99	=C7*D7	0836CA
GREEN JERSEY CARDIGAN	14	1	23.99	=C8*D8	0597UM
CREAM STRETCH BLOUSE	14	2	32.99	=C9*D9	7223WX
CREAM VELOUR TOP	16	3	16.99	=C10*D10	9818WA
WHITE JOG PANTS	14	1	10.99	=C11*D11	0801BL
BROWN STITCH BOOT	6.5	1	39.99	=C12*D12	2389NM
TOTAL		=SUM(C5:C12)	=SUM(D5:D12)	=SUM(E5:E12)	

YOUR NAME
SMOCK1P3

CLAIT Spreadsheet Mock Assignment 2

QUARTERLY SALES FIGURES – FABRICS

FABRIC DESCRIPTION	JAN	FEB	MAR	QT	CP(M)	SP(M)
FIONULA	17	18	16	51.00	5.70	9.50
ORLA STRIPE	8	13	12	33.00	5.75	9.50
AISLIN	10	15	16	41.00	5.75	8.95
TARA LATTICE	7	5	4	16.00	5.25	7.50
FIONA	6	9	9	24.00	5.95	7.95
ELLEN BRIAR	16	15	12	43.00	6.00	8.50
DEIRDRE PLAID	20	18	16	54.00	5.50	9.00

YOUR NAME
SMOCK2P1

CLAIT Spreadsheet Mock Assignment 2 (continued)

QUARTERLY SALES FIGURES – FABRICS

FABRIC DESCRIPTION	JAN	FEB	MAR	QT	PROFIT	CP(M)	SP(M)
FIONULA	17	18	16	51	3.80	5.70	9.50
ORLA STRIPE	12	13	12	37	3.75	5.75	9.50
AISLIN TARTAN	10	15	16	41	3.20	5.75	8.95
FIONA	6	9	9	24	2.00	5.95	7.95
ELLEN BRIAR	16	15	12	43	2.50	6.00	8.50
DIERDRE PLAID	20	18	16	54	3.50	5.50	9.00

YOUR NAME
SMOCK2P2

CLAIT Spreadsheet Mock Assignment 2 (continued)

QUARTERLY SALES FIGURES – FABRICS

FABRIC DESCRIPTION	JAN	FEB	MAR	QT	PROFIT	CP(M)	SP(M)
FIONULA	17	18	16	=SUM(B5:D5)	=H5-G5	5.7	9.5
ORLA STRIPE	12	13	12	=SUM(B6:D6)	=H6-G6	5.75	9.5
AISLIN TARTAN	10	15	16	=SUM(B7:D7)	=H7-G7	5.75	8.95
FIONA	6	9	9	=SUM(B8:D8)	=H8-G8	5.95	7.95
ELLEN BRIAR	16	15	12	=SUM(B9:D9)	=H9-G9	6	8.5
DEIRDRE PLAID	20	18	16	=SUM(B10:D10)	=H10-G10	5.5	9

YOUR NAME
SMOCK2P3

Task 4B   Sheet 1

SPERRIN VIEW COMMUNITY CLUB – WAGES FOR WEEK 32

NAME	WEEKLY HOURS	OVER-TIME	GROSS	TAX	NI	NET
Vera Brown	40.0	5.5	478.75	119.69	33.51	325.55
Paul Gibson	40.0	7.0	497.50	124.38	34.83	338.30
Adrian Lang	35.0	0.0	358.75	89.69	25.11	243.95
Jake Johnston	40.0	7.5	503.75	125.94	35.26	342.55
Kevin Barrat	40.0	2.5	441.25	110.31	30.89	300.05
Mike Green	40.0	7.5	503.75	125.94	35.26	342.55
Gary Boyle	40.0	0.0	410.00	102.50	28.70	278.80
Brian Bradley	40.0	9.5	528.75	132.19	37.01	359.55
Bob Dunn	40.0	5.5	478.75	119.69	33.51	325.55
Martin Grey	40.0	7.5	503.75	125.94	35.26	342.55
TOTAL	395.0	52.5				3199.4

YOUR NAME
TASK4B

Task 4E   Sheet 1

SPERRIN VIEW COMMUNITY CLUB – WAGES FOR WEEK 32

NAME	WEEKLY HOURS	OVER-TIME	GROSS	TAX	NI	NET
Keith Daley	40.0	7.5	503.75	125.94	35.26	342.55
Vera Brown	40.0	5.5	478.75	119.69	33.51	325.55
Paul Gibson	40.0	7.0	497.50	124.38	34.83	338.30
Adrian Lang	35.0	0.0	358.75	89.69	25.11	243.95
Jake Johnston	40.0	7.5	503.75	125.94	35.26	342.55
Kevin Barrat	40.0	2.5	441.25	110.31	30.89	300.05
Mike Green	40.0	7.5	503.75	125.94	35.26	342.55
Gary Boyle	40.0	0.0	410.00	102.50	28.70	278.80
Brian Bradley	40.0	9.5	528.75	132.19	37.01	359.55
Bob Dunn	40.0	5.5	478.75	119.69	33.51	325.55
Martin Grey	40.0	7.5	503.75	125.94	35.26	342.55
TOTAL	435.0	60.0				3542.0
AVERAGE	40	5	474	118	33	322
HIGHEST	40.0					
LOWEST	35.0					
NO OF EMPLOYEES	11.0					
PROJECTION	3576.8					

YOUR NAME
TASK4E

Task 4G

NEW STREET MOTORS   YOUR NAME

VEHICLE SALES

TYPE	TOTAL JAN-JUN	TOTAL JUL-DEC	ANNUAL TOTAL	COST PRICE	STOCK VALUE	SELLING PRICE	PROFIT PER CAR
SALOON 4DR	51	63	=B5+C5	10499	=D5*E5	11999	=G5-E5
CABRIOLET	12	14	=B6+C6	16999	=D6*E6	19999	=G6-E6
HATCHBACK 3DR	30	49	=B7+C7	10000	=D7*E7	11499	=G7-E7
COUPE	35	38	=B8+C8	14000	=D8*E8	16499	=G8-E8
CAMPER	80	67	=B9+C9	20500	=D9*E9	21999	=G9-E9
ESTATE	70	63	=B10+C10	12499	=D10*E10	14499	=G10-E10
HATCHBACK 5DR	60	59	=B11+C11	10500	=D11*E11	11999	=G11-E11
OFF ROADER	53	46	=B12+C12	25500	=D12*E12	26499	=G12-E12
TOTAL	=SUM(B5:B12)	=SUM(C5:C12)	=SUM(D5:D12)	=SUM(E5:E12)	=SUM(F5:F12)	=SUM(G5:G12)	=SUM(H5:H12)
AVERAGE	=B13/8	=C13/8	=D13/8				

YOUR NAME
TASK4G

Date: 3/25/97   Page 1

Task 4H

SPERRIN VIEW COMMUNITY CLUB – WAGES FOR WEEK 32

NAME	WEEKLY HOURS	OVER-TIME	GROSS	TAX	NI	NET
Keith Daley	40.0	7.5	503.75	125.94	35.26	342.55
Vera Brown	40.0	5.5	478.75	119.69	33.51	325.55
Paul Gibson	40.0	7.0	497.50	124.38	34.83	338.30
Adrian Lang	35.0	0.0	358.75	89.69	25.11	243.95
Jake Johnston	40.0	7.5	503.75	125.94	35.26	342.55
Kevin Barrat	40.0	2.5	441.25	110.31	30.89	300.05
Mike Green	40.0	7.5	503.75	125.94	35.26	342.55
Gary Boyle	40.0	0.0	410.00	102.50	28.70	278.80
Brian Bradley	40.0	9.5	528.75	132.19	37.01	359.55
Bob Dunn	40.0	5.5	478.75	119.69	33.51	325.55
Martin Grey	40.0	7.5	503.75	125.94	35.26	342.55
TOTAL	435.0	60.0				3542.0
AVERAGE	40	5	474	118	33	322
HIGHEST	40.0					
LOWEST	35.0					
NO OF EMPLOYEES	11					
PROJECTION	3576.8					

YOUR NAME
TASK4H

Task 4J

SPERRIN VIEW COMMUNITY CLUB – WAGES FOR WEEK 32

NAME	WEEKLY HOURS	OVER-TIME	GROSS	TAX	NI	NET
Keith Daley	40.0	7.5	503.75	125.94	35.26	342.55
Vera Brown	40.0	5.5	478.75	119.69	33.51	325.55
Paul Gibson	40.0	7.0	497.50	124.38	34.83	338.30
Adrian Lang	35.0	0.0	358.75	89.69	25.11	243.95
Jake Johnston	40.0	7.5	503.75	125.94	35.26	342.55
Kevin Barrat	40.0	2.5	441.25	110.31	30.89	300.05
Mike Green	40.0	7.5	503.75	125.94	35.26	342.55
Gary Boyle	40.0	0.0	410.00	102.50	28.70	278.80
Brian Bradley	40.0	9.5	528.75	132.19	37.01	359.55
Bob Dunn	40.0	5.5	478.75	119.69	33.51	325.55
Martin Grey	40.0	7.5	503.75	125.94	35.26	342.55
Martin Grey	40.0	7.5	503.75	125.94	35.26	342.55
Martin Grey	40.0	7.5	503.75	125.94	35.26	342.55
Martin Grey	40.0	7.5	503.75	125.94	35.26	342.55
Martin Grey	40.0	7.5	503.75	125.94	35.26	342.55
Martin Grey	40.0	7.5	503.75	125.94	35.26	342.55
Martin Grey	40.0	7.5	503.75	125.94	35.26	342.55
Martin Grey	40.0	7.5	503.75	125.94	35.26	342.55
Martin Grey	40.0	7.5	503.75	125.94	35.26	342.55
Martin Grey	40.0	7.5	503.75	125.94	35.26	342.55
Martin Grey	40.0	7.5	503.75	125.94	35.26	342.56
Martin Grey	40.0	7.5	503.75	125.94	35.26	342.55
Martin Grey	40.0	7.5	503.75	125.94	35.26	342.55
Martin Grey	40.0	7.5	503.75	125.94	35.26	342.55
Martin Grey	40.0	7.5	503.75	125.94	35.26	342.55
Martin Grey	40.0	7.5	503.75	125.94	35.26	342.55
Martin Grey	40.0	7.5	503.75	125.94	35.26	342.55
Martin Grey	40.0	7.5	503.75	125.94	35.26	342.55

Task 4J (continued)

NAME	WEEKLY HOURS	OVER-TIME	GROSS	TAX	NI	NET
Martin Grey	40.0	7.5	503.75	125.94	35.26	342.55
Martin Grey	40.0	7.5	503.75	125.94	35.26	342.55
Martin Grey	40.0	7.5	503.75	125.94	35.26	342.55
TOTAL	1335.0	232.5				11420.6
AVERAGE	40	7	494	123	35	336
HIGHEST	40.0					
LOWEST	35.0					

NO OF EMPLOYEES   34

YOUR NAME
TASK4J

Extra Practice Task 4A   Sheet 1

SPERRIN SKYWAY GARDEN CENTRE
Construction Employees, Dart Division

NAME	WEEKLY HOURS	OVER-TIME	GROSS	TAX	NI	NET
Anne Moore	42.0	7.0	518.00	129.50	36.26	352.24
Louise Atkinson	42.0	7.5	524.25	131.06	36.70	356.49
Sylvia Cheshire	42.0	2.5	461.75	115.44	32.32	313.99
Mike Brown	42.0	7.5	524.25	131.06	36.70	356.49
Michelle Blackman	42.0	7.0	518.00	129.50	36.26	352.24
Denise Birch	42.0	7.5	524.25	131.06	36.70	356.49
Margery Bartram	42.0	9.5	549.25	137.31	38.45	373.49
Jolanta Hughes	42.0	9.0	543.00	135.75	38.01	369.24
Christine Gilman	42.0	7.5	524.25	131.06	36.70	356.49
Bob Nangle	42.0	7.0	518.00	129.50	36.26	352.24
TOTAL	420.00	72.0				3539.40

YOUR NAME
EPTASK4A

Extra Practice Task 4B   Sheet 1

SPERRIN SKYWAY GARDEN CENTRE
Construction Employees, Dart Division

NAME	WEEKLY HOURS	OVER-TIME	GROSS	TAX	NI	NET
Joanne Fisher	42.0	10.0	555.50	138.88	38.89	377.74
Anne Moore	42.0	7.0	518.00	129.50	36.26	352.24
Louise Atkinson	42.0	7.5	524.25	131.06	36.70	356.49
Sylvia Cheshire	42.0	2.5	461.75	115.44	32.32	313.99
Mike Brown	42.0	7.5	524.25	131.06	36.70	356.49
Michelle Blackman	42.0	7.0	518.00	129.50	36.26	352.24
Denise Birch	42.0	7.5	524.25	131.06	36.70	356.49
Margery Bartram	42.0	9.5	549.25	137.31	38.45	373.49
Jolanta Hughes	42.0	9.0	543.00	135.75	38.01	369.24
Christine Gilman	42.0	7.5	524.25	131.06	36.70	356.49
Bob Nangle	42.0	7.0	518.00	129.50	36.26	352.24
TOTAL	462.0	82.0				3917.14
AVERAGE	42	7	524	131	37	356
HIGHEST		10.0				
LOWEST		2.5				
NO OF EMPLOYEES	11.0					

PROJECTION   3955.4

YOUR NAME
EPTASK4B

Extra Practice Task 4C

SPERRIN SKYWAY

SPERRIN SKYWAY GARDEN CENTRE
Construction Employees, Dart Division

NAME	WEEKLY HOURS	OVER-TIME	GROSS	TAX	NI	NET
Joanne Fisher	42.0	10.0	555.50	138.88	38.89	377.74
Anne Moore	42.0	7.0	518.00	129.50	36.26	352.24
Louise Atkinson	42.0	7.5	524.25	131.06	36.70	356.49
Sylvia Cheshire	42.0	2.5	461.75	115.44	32.32	313.99
Mike Brown	42.0	7.5	524.25	131.06	36.70	356.49
Michelle Blackman	42.0	7.0	518.00	129.50	36.26	352.24
Denise Birch	42.0	7.5	524.25	131.06	36.70	356.49
Margery Bartram	42.0	9.5	549.25	137.31	38.45	373.49
Jolanta Hughes	42.0	9.0	543.00	135.75	38.01	369.24
Christine Gilman	42.0	7.5	524.25	131.06	36.70	356.49
Bob Nangle	42.0	7.0	518.00	129.50	36.26	352.24
TOTAL	462.0	82.0				3917.14
AVERAGE	42	7	524	131	37	356
HIGHEST		10.0				
LOWEST		2.5				
NO OF EMPLOYEES	11.0					
PROJECTION	3955.4					

YOUR NAME
EPTASK4B

Extra Practice Task 4D

SPERRIN SKYWAY

SPERRIN SKYWAY GARDEN CENTRE
Construction Employees, Dart Division

NAME	WEEKLY HOURS	OVER-TIME	GROSS	TAX	NI	NET
Joanne Fisher	42.0	10.0	555.50	138.88	38.89	377.74
Anne Moore	42.0	7.0	518.00	129.50	36.26	352.24
Louise Atkinson	42.0	7.5	524.25	131.06	36.70	356.49
Sylvia Cheshire	42.0	2.5	461.75	115.44	32.32	313.99
Mike Brown	42.0	7.5	524.25	131.06	36.70	356.49
Michelle Blackman	42.0	7.0	518.00	129.50	36.26	352.24
Denise Birch	42.0	7.5	524.25	131.06	36.70	356.49
Margery Bartram	42.0	9.5	549.25	137.31	38.45	373.49
Jolanta Hughes	42.0	9.0	543.00	135.75	38.01	369.24
Christine Gilman	42.0	7.5	524.25	131.06	36.70	356.49
Bob Nangle	42.0	7.0	518.00	129.50	36.26	352.24
Bob Nangle	42.0	7.0	518.00	129.50	36.26	352.24
Bob Nangle	42.0	7.0	518.00	129.50	36.26	352.24
Bob Nangle	42.0	7.0	518.00	129.50	36.26	352.24
Bob Nangle	42.0	7.0	518.00	129.50	36.26	352.24
Bob Nangle	42.0	7.0	518.00	129.50	36.26	352.24
Bob Nangle	42.0	7.0	518.00	129.50	36.26	352.24
Bob Nangle	42.0	7.0	518.00	129.50	36.26	352.24
Bob Nangle	42.0	7.0	518.00	129.50	36.26	352.24
Bob Nangle	42.0	7.0	518.00	129.50	36.26	352.24
Bob Nangle	42.0	7.0	518.00	129.50	36.26	352.24
Bob Nangle	42.0	7.0	518.00	129.50	36.26	352.24
Bob Nangle	42.0	7.0	518.00	129.50	36.26	352.24
Bob Nangle	42.0	7.0	518.00	129.50	36.26	352.24
Bob Nangle	42.0	7.0	518.00	129.50	36.26	352.24
Bob Nangle	42.0	7.0	518.00	129.50	36.26	352.24
Bob Nangle	42.0	7.0	518.00	129.50	36.26	352.24
Bob Nangle	42.0	7.0	518.00	129.50	36.26	352.24

Extra Practice Task 4D (continued)

SPERRIN SKYWAY

GARDEN CENTRE ACCOUNTS

NAME	WEEKLY HOURS	OVER-TIME	GROSS	TAX	NI	NET
Bob Nangle	42.0	7.0	518.00	129.50	36.26	352.24
Bob Nangle	42.0	7.0	518.00	129.50	36.26	352.24
Bob Nangle	42.0	7.0	518.00	129.50	36.26	352.24
TOTAL	1428.0	243.0				12018.66
AVERAGE	42	7	520	130	36	353
HIGHEST		10.0				
LOWEST		2.5				
NO OF EMPLOYEES	34.0					

YOUR NAME
EPTASK4D

Prepared by YOUR NAME, Date: 3/24/97   Page 2

YOYO Task 4A

THE DESIGNER COLLECTION
Mail Order Employees, Donard Division

NAME	WEEKLY HOURS	OVER-TIME	GROSS	TAX	NI	NET
Margaret Smythe	42.0	8.0	324.98	81.25	22.75	220.99
Rose Cullen	42.0	8.5	328.89	82.22	23.02	223.64
Kathy Crowe	42.0	4.5	297.65	74.41	20.84	202.40
John Masters	42.0	12.0	356.22	89.06	24.94	242.23
Jean Madden	42.0	8.0	324.98	81.25	22.75	220.99
Julie Broady	42.0	8.5	328.89	82.22	23.02	223.64
Diane Henderson	42.0	8.0	324.98	81.25	22.75	220.99
Anna Gee	42.0	10.0	340.60	85.15	23.84	231.61
Helen Stevens	42.0	8.5	328.89	82.22	23.02	223.64
Jim Mather	42.0	8.0	324.98	81.25	22.75	220.99
TOTAL	420.0	84.0				2231.11

YOUR NAME
YOYO4A

YOYO Task 4B

THE DESIGNER COLLECTION
Mail Order Employees, Donard Division

NAME	WEEKLY HOURS	OVER-TIME	GROSS	TAX	NI	NET
Mary Bradley	42.0	10.0	340.60	85.15	23.84	231.61
Margaret Smyth	42.0	8.0	324.98	81.25	22.75	220.99
Rose Cullen	42.0	8.5	328.89	82.22	23.02	223.64
Kathy Crowe	42.0	4.5	297.65	74.41	20.84	202.40
John Masters	42.0	12.0	356.22	89.06	24.94	242.23
Jean Madden	42.0	8.0	324.98	81.25	22.75	220.99
Julie Broady	42.0	8.5	328.89	82.22	23.02	223.64
Diane Henderson	42.0	8.0	324.98	81.25	22.75	220.99
Anna Gee	42.0	10.0	340.60	85.15	23.84	231.61
Helen Stevens	42.0	8.5	328.89	82.22	23.02	223.64
Jim Mather	42.0	8.0	324.98	81.25	22.75	220.99
TOTAL	462.0	94.0				2462.72
AVERAGE	42	9	329	82	23	224
HIGHEST		12.0				
LOWEST		4.5				
NO OF EMPLOYEES	11.0					
PROJECTION	2481.3					

YOUR NAME
YOYO4B

YOYO Task 4C

THE DESIGNER COLLECTION
THE DESIGNER COLLECTION
Mail Order Employees, Donard Division

ACCOUNTS

NAME	WEEKLY HOURS	OVER- TIME	GROSS	TAX	NI	NET
Mary Bradley	42.0	10.0	340.60	85.15	23.84	231.61
Margaret Smyth	42.0	8.0	324.98	81.25	22.75	220.99
Rose Cullen	42.0	8.5	328.89	82.22	23.02	223.64
Kathy Crowe	42.0	4.5	297.65	74.41	20.84	202.40
John Masters	42.0	12.0	356.22	89.06	24.94	242.23
Jean Madden	42.0	8.0	324.98	81.25	22.75	220.99
Julie Broady	42.0	8.5	328.89	82.22	23.02	223.64
Diane Henderson	42.0	8.0	324.98	81.25	22.75	220.99
Anna Gee	42.0	10.0	340.60	85.15	23.84	231.61
Helen Stevens	42.0	8.5	328.89	82.22	23.02	223.64
Jim Mather	42.0	8.0	324.98	81.25	22.75	220.99
TOTAL	462.0	94.0				2462.72
AVERAGE	42	9	329	82	23	224
HIGHEST		12.0				
LOWEST		4.5				
NO OF EMPLOYEES	11.0					
PROJECTION	2481.3					

YOUR NAME
YOYO4C

YOYO Task 4D

THE DESIGNER COLLECTION
THE DESIGNER COLLECTION
Mail Order Employees, Donard Division

ACCOUNTS

NAME	WEEKLY HOURS	OVER- TIME	GROSS	TAX	NI	NET
Mary Bradley	42.0	10.0	340.60	85.15	23.84	231.61
Margaret Smythe	42.0	8.0	324.98	81.25	22.75	220.99
Rose Cullen	42.0	8.5	328.89	82.22	23.02	223.64
Kathy Crowe	42.0	4.5	297.65	74.41	20.84	202.40
John Masters	42.0	12.0	356.22	89.06	24.94	242.23
Jean Madden	42.0	8.0	324.98	81.25	22.75	220.99
Julie Broady	42.0	8.5	328.89	82.22	23.02	223.64
Diane Henderson	42.0	8.0	324.98	81.25	22.75	220.99
Anna Gee	42.0	10.0	340.60	85.15	23.84	231.61
Helen Stevens	42.0	8.5	328.89	82.22	23.02	223.64
Jim Mather	42.0	8.0	324.98	81.25	22.75	220.99
Jim Mather	42.0	8.0	324.98	81.25	22.75	220.99
Jim Mather	42.0	8.0	324.98	81.25	22.75	220.99
Jim Mather	42.0	8.0	324.98	81.25	22.75	220.99
Jim Mather	42.0	8.0	324.98	81.25	22.75	220.99
Jim Mather	42.0	8.0	324.98	81.25	22.75	220.99
Jim Mather	42.0	8.0	324.98	81.25	22.75	220.99
Jim Mather	42.0	8.0	324.98	81.25	22.75	220.99
Jim Mather	42.0	8.0	324.98	81.25	22.75	220.99
Jim Mather	42.0	8.0	324.98	81.25	22.75	220.99
Jim Mather	42.0	8.0	324.98	81.25	22.75	220.99
Jim Mather	42.0	8.0	324.98	81.25	22.75	220.99
Jim Mather	42.0	8.0	324.98	81.25	22.75	220.99
Jim Mather	42.0	8.0	324.98	81.25	22.75	220.99
Jim Mather	42.0	8.0	324.98	81.25	22.75	220.99
Jim Mather	42.0	8.0	324.98	81.25	22.75	220.99
Jim Mather	42.0	8.0	324.98	81.25	22.75	220.99
Jim Mather	42.0	8.0	324.98	81.25	22.75	220.99

YOYO Task 4D (continued)

THE DESIGNER COLLECTION

NAME	WEEKLY HOURS	OVER-TIME	GROSS	TAX	NI	NET
Jim Mather	42.0	8.0	324.98	81.25	22.75	220.99
Jim Mather	42.0	8.0	324.98	81.25	22.75	220.99
Jim Mather	42.0	8.0	324.98	81.25	22.75	220.99
TOTAL	1428.0	278.0				7545.40
AVERAGE	42	8	326	82	23	222
HIGHEST		12.0				
LOWEST		4.5				
NO OF EMPLOYEES	34.0					

YOUR NAME
YOYO4D

Prepared by YOUR NAME, Date: 6/23/97

Task 5A

SPERRIN VIEW COMMUNITY CLUB – WAGES FOR WEEK 32

NAME	WEEKLY HOURS	OVER-TIME	GROSS	TAX	NI	NET
CURRENT EMPLOYEES						
Julie White	42.0	12.5	586.75	146.69	41.07	398.99
Keith Daley	42.0	7.5	524.25	131.06	36.70	356.49
Vera Brown	42.0	5.5	499.25	124.81	34.95	339.49
Paul Gibson-Greene	40.0	7.0	497.50	124.38	34.83	338.30
Adrian Long	35.0	0.0	358.75	89.69	25.11	243.95
Jake Johnston	40.0	12.5	566.25	141.56	39.64	385.05
Kevin Barratt	40.0	2.5	441.25	110.31	30.89	300.05
Angela Black	40.0	0.0	410.00	102.50	28.70	278.80
Mike Green	40.0	7.5	503.75	125.94	35.26	342.55
Gary Boyle	40.0	0.0	410.00	102.50	28.70	278.80
Brian Bradley	40.0	9.5	528.75	132.19	37.01	359.55
Martin Grey	40.0	7.5	503.75	125.94	35.26	342.55
POTENTIAL EMPLOYEES						
Martin Grey	40.0	7.5	503.75	125.94	35.26	342.55
Martin Grey	40.0	7.5	503.75	125.94	35.26	342.55
Martin Grey	40.0	7.5	503.75	125.94	35.26	342.55
Martin Grey	40.0	7.5	503.75	125.94	35.26	342.55
Martin Grey	40.0	7.5	503.75	125.94	35.26	342.55
Martin Grey	40.0	7.5	503.75	125.94	35.26	342.55
Martin Grey	40.0	7.5	503.75	125.94	35.26	342.55
Martin Grey	40.0	7.5	503.75	125.94	35.26	342.55
Martin Grey	40.0	7.5	503.75	125.94	35.26	342.55
Martin Grey	40.0	7.5	503.75	125.94	35.26	342.55
Martin Grey	40.0	7.5	503.75	125.94	35.26	342.55
Martin Grey	40.0	7.5	503.75	125.94	35.26	342.55
Martin Grey	40.0	7.5	503.75	125.94	35.26	342.55
Martin Grey	40.0	7.5	503.75	125.94	35.26	342.55
Martin Grey	40.0	7.5	503.75	125.94	35.26	342.55
Martin Grey	40.0	7.5	503.75	125.94	35.26	342.55

Task 5A (continued)

NAME	WEEKLY HOURS	OVER TIME	GROSS	TAX	NI	NET
Martin Grey	40.0	7.5	503.75	125.94	35.26	342.55
Martin Grey	40.0	7.5	503.75	125.94	35.26	342.55
Martin Grey	40.0	7.5	503.75	125.94	35.26	342.55
Martin Grey	40.0	7.5	503.75	125.94	35.26	342.55
Martin Grey	40.0	7.5	503.75	125.94	35.26	342.55
Martin Grey	40.0	7.5	503.75	125.94	35.26	342.55
Martin Grey	40.0	7.5	503.75	125.94	35.26	342.55
TOTAL	1401.0	244.5				11843.2

AVERAGE WEEKLY WAGE	338
HIGHEST WEEKLY WAGE	£398.99
LOWEST WEEKLY WAGE	£243.95
NO OF EMPLOYEES	35

CURRENT EMPLOYEES
GROSS WEEKLY WAGES	5830.3
GROSS MONTHLY WAGES	23321.0

YOUR NAME
TASK5A

Task 5AF

SPERRIN VIEW COMMUNITY CLUB

NAME	WEEKLY HOURS	OVER-TIME	GROSS	TAX	NI	NET
CURRENT EMPLOYEES						
Julie White	42	12.5	=(B7*10.25)+(C7*12.5)	=D7*25%	=D7*7%	=D7-E7-F7
Keith Daley	42	7.5	=(B8*10.25)+(C8*12.5)	=D8*25%	=D8*7%	=D8-E8-F8
Vera Brown	42	7.5	=(B9*10.25)+(C9*12.5)	=D9*25%	=D9*7%	=D9-E9-F9
Paul Gibson-Greene	40	7	=(B10*10.25)+(C10*12.5)	=D10*25%	=D10*7%	=D10-E10-F10
Adrian Long	35	0	=(B11*10.25)+(C11*12.5)	=D11*25%	=D11*7%	=D11-E11-F11
Jake Johnston	40	12.5	=(B12*10.25)+(C12*12.5)	=D12*25%	=D12*7%	=D12-E12-F12
Kevin Barratt	40	2.5	=(B13*10.25)+(C13*12.5)	=D13*25%	=D13*7%	=D13-E13-F13
Angela Black	40	0	=(B14*10.25)+(C14*12.5)	=D14*25%	=D14*7%	=D14-E14-F14
Mike Green	40	7.5	=(B15*10.25)+(C15*12.5)	=D15*25%	=D15*7%	=D15-E15-F15
Gary Boyle	40	0	=(B16*10.25)+(C16*12.5)	=D16*25%	=D16*7%	=D16-E16-F16
Brian Bradley	40	9.5	=(B17*10.25)+(C17*12.5)	=D17*25%	=D17*7%	=D17-E17-F17
Martin Grey	40	7.5	=(B18*10.25)+(C18*12.5)	=D18*25%	=D18*7%	=D18-E18-F18
POTENTIAL EMPLOYEES						
Martin Grey	40	7.5	=(B21*10.25)+(C21*12.5)	=D21*25%	=D21*7%	=D21-E21-F21
Martin Grey	40	7.5	=(B22*10.25)+(C22*12.5)	=D22*25%	=D22*7%	=D22-E22-F22
Martin Grey	40	7.5	=(B23*10.25)+(C23*12.5)	=D23*25%	=D23*7%	=D23-E23-F23
Martin Grey	40	7.5	=(B24*10.25)+(C24*12.5)	=D24*25%	=D24*7%	=D24-E24-F24
Martin Grey	40	7.5	=(B25*10.25)+(C25*12.5)	=D25*25%	=D25*7%	=D25-E25-F25
Martin Grey	40	7.5	=(B26*10.25)+(C26*12.5)	=D26*25%	=D26*7%	=D26-E26-F26
Martin Grey	40	7.5	=(B27*10.25)+(C27*12.5)	=D27*25%	=D27*7%	=D27-E27-F27
Martin Grey	40	7.5	=(B28*10.25)+(C28*12.5)	=D28*25%	=D28*7%	=D28-E28-F28
Martin Grey	40	7.5	=(B29*10.25)+(C29*12.5)	=D29*25%	=D29*7%	=D29-E29-F29
Martin Grey	40	7.5	=(B30*10.25)+(C30*12.5)	=D30*25%	=D30*7%	=D30-E30-F30
Martin Grey	40	7.5	=(B31*10.25)+(C31*12.5)	=D31*25%	=D31*7%	=D31-E31-F31
Martin Grey	40	7.5	=(B32*10.25)+(C32*12.5)	=D32*25%	=D32*7%	=D32-E32-F32
Martin Grey	40	7.5	=(B33*10.25)+(C33*12.5)	=D33*25%	=D33*7%	=D33-E33-F33
Martin Grey	40	7.5	=(B34*10.25)+(C34*12.5)	=D34*25%	=D34*7%	=D34-E34-F34
Martin Grey	40	7.5	=(B35*10.25)+(C35*12.5)	=D35*25%	=D35*7%	=D35-E35-F35
Martin Grey	40	7.5	=(B36*10.25)+(C36*12.5)	=D36*25%	=D36*7%	=D36-E36-F36

Task 5AF (continued)

NAME	WEEKLY HOURS	OVER-TIME	GROSS	TAX	NI	NET
Martin Grey	40	7.5	=(B37*10.25)+(C37*12.5)	=D37*25%	=D37*7%	=D37-E37-F37
Martin Grey	40	7.5	=(B38*10.25)+(C38*12.5)	=D38*25%	=D38*7%	=D38-E38-F38
Martin Grey	40	7.5	=(B39*10.25)+(C39*12.5)	=D39*25%	=D39*7%	=D39-E39-F39
Martin Grey	40	7.5	=(B40*10.25)+(C40*12.5)	=D40*25%	=D40*7%	=D40-E40-F40
Martin Grey	40	7.5	=(B41*10.25)+(C41*12.5)	=D41*25%	=D41*7%	=D41-E41-F41
Martin Grey	40	7.5	=(B42*10.25)+(C42*12.5)	=D42*25%	=D42*7%	=D42-E42-F42
Martin Grey	40	7.5	=(B43*10.25)+(C43*12.5)	=D43*25%	=D43*7%	=D43-E43-F43
TOTAL	=SUM(B7:B43)	=SUM(C7:C43)				=SUM(G7:G43)

AVERAGE WEEKLY WAGE	=AVERAGE(G7:G43)
HIGHEST WEEKLY WAGE	=MAX(G7:G43)
LOWEST WEEKLY WAGE	=MIN(G7:G43)
NO EMPLOYEES	=COUNT(G7:G43)
CURRENT EMPLOYEES	
GROSS WEEKLY WAGES	=SUM(D7:D18)
GROSS MONTHLY WAGES	=B53*4

YOUR NAME
TASK5AF

Task 5B

Sheet 1

SPERRIN VIEW COMMUNITY CLUB INCOME AND EXPENDITURE ACCOUNT

	JAN	FEB	MAR	APR	MAY	JUN
INCOME						
SUBSCRIPTIONS						
FEES						
BAR SALES						
TOTAL INCOME						
EXPENDITURE						
WAGES – INSTRUCTORS						
WAGES – OTHER						
OVERHEADS						
BAR SUPPLIES						
TOTAL EXPENDITURE						

STATISTICAL ANALYSIS	WEEKLY	MONTHLY
INCOME		
SUBSCRIPTIONS		15080
FEES		6940
BAR SALES	5950	
TOTAL INCOME		
EXPENDITURE		
WAGES – INSTRUCTORS		23321
WAGES – OTHER		4200
OVERHEADS	1200	
BAR SUPPLIES	2957	
TOTAL EXPENDITURE		

YOUR NAME
TASK5B

Task 5C

SPERRIN VIEW COMMUNITY CLUB INCOME AND EXPENDITURE ACCOUNT

	JAN	FEB	MAR	APR	MAY	JUN
INCOME						
SUBSCRIPTIONS	15080	15080	15080	15080	15080	15080
FEES	6940	6940	6940	6940	6940	6940
BAR SALES						
TOTAL INCOME	22020	22020	22020	22020	22020	22020
EXPENDITURE						
WAGES – INSTRUCTORS	23321	23321	23321	23321	23321	23321
WAGES – OTHER	4200	4200	4200	4200	4200	4200
OVERHEADS						
BAR SUPPLIES						
TOTAL EXPENDITURE	27521	27521	27521	27521	27521	27521
PROFIT/LOSS	–5501	–5501	–5501	–5501	–5501	–5501

STATISTICAL ANALYSIS	WEEKLY	MONTHLY
INCOME		
SUBSCRIPTIONS		15080
FEES		6940
BAR SALES	5950	
TOTAL INCOME		22020
EXPENDITURE		
WAGES – INSTRUCTORS		23321
WAGES – OTHER		4200
OVERHEADS	1200	
BAR SUPPLIES	2957	
TOTAL EXPENDITURE		27521
PROFIT/LOSS		–5501

YOUR NAME
TASK5C

Task 5D

SPERRIN VIEW COMMUNITY CLUB INCOME AND EXPENDITURE ACCOUNT

	JAN	FEB	MAR	APR	MAY	JUN	TOTAL	TOTAL PA
INCOME								
SUBSCRIPTIONS	15080	15080	15080	15080	15080	15080	90480	180960
FEES	6940	6940	6940	6940	6940	6940	41640	83280
BAR SALES	23800	23800	23800	23800	23800	23800	142800	285600
TOTAL INCOME	45820	45820	45820	45820	45820	45820	274920	£549,840
EXPENDITURE								
WAGES – INSTRUCTORS	23321	23321	23321	23321	23321	23321	139926	279852
WAGES – OTHER	4200	4200	4200	4200	4200	4200	25200	50400
OVERHEADS	4800	4800	4800	4800	4800	4800	28800	57600
BAR SUPPLIES	11828	11828	11828	11828	11828	11828	70968	141936
TOTAL EXPENDITURE	44149	44149	44149	44149	44149	44149	264894	£529,788
PROFIT/LOSS	1671	1671	1671	1671	1671	1671	10026	£20,052

STATISTICAL ANALYSIS	WEEKLY	MONTHLY
INCOME		
SUBSCRIPTIONS		15080
FEES		6940
BAR SALES	5950	23800
TOTAL INCOME		45820
EXPENDITURE		
WAGES – INSTRUCTORS		23321
WAGES – OTHER		4200
OVERHEADS	1200	4800
BAR SUPPLIES	2957	11828
TOTAL EXPENDITURE		44149
PROFIT/LOSS		1671

YOUR NAME
TASK5D

Task 5E   Sheet 1

SPERRIN VIEW COMMUNITY CLUB

	JAN	FEB
INCOME		
SUBSCRIPTIONS	=$C$21	=$C$21
FEES	=$C$22	=$C$22
BAR SALES	=BSALES*4	=BSALES*4
TOTAL INCOME	=SUM(B5:B7)	=SUM(C5:C7)
EXPENDITURE		
WAGES – INSTRUCTORS	=$C$27	=$C$27
WAGES – OTHER	=$C$28	=$C$28
OVERHEADS	=OHEADS*4	=OHEADS*4
BAR SUPPLIES	=BSUPPS*4	=BSUPPS*4
TOTAL EXPENDITURE	=SUM(B11:B14)	=SUM(C11:C14)
PROFIT/LOSS	=B8-B15	=C8-C15

STATISTICAL ANALYSIS	WEEKLY	MONTHLY
INCOME		
SUBSCRIPTIONS		15080
FEES		6940
BAR SALES	5950	=BSALES*4
TOTAL INCOME		=SUM(C21:C23)
EXPENDITURE		
WAGES – INSTRUCTORS		='C:\GAL\KEYS\[TASK5A.xls]Sheet1'!$B$54
WAGES – OTHER		4200
OVERHEADS	1200	=OHEADS*4
BAR SUPPLIES	2957	=BSUPPS*4
TOTAL EXPENDITURE		=SUM(C27:C30)
PROFIT/LOSS		=C24-C31

YOUR NAME
TASK5E

Page 1

Extra Practice Task 5A

SPERRIN SKYWAY   GARDEN CENTRE ACCOUNTS

SPERRIN SKYWAY GARDEN CENTRE
Construction Employees, Dart Division

NAME	WEEKLY HOURS	OVER-TIME	GROSS	TAX	NI	NET
CURRENT EMPLOYEES						
Gregory Smith	42.0	12.5	586.75	146.69	41.07	398.99
Joanne Fisher	40.0	10.0	535.00	133.75	37.45	363.80
Anne-Marie Moore	42.0	7.0	518.00	129.50	36.26	352.24
Louise Atkinson	42.0	7.5	524.25	131.06	36.70	356.49
Sylvia Cheshire	42.0	2.5	461.75	115.44	32.32	313.99
Mike Browne	42.0	7.5	524.25	131.06	36.70	356.49
Michelle Blackham	42.0	7.0	518.00	129.50	36.26	352.24
Kathy Bowker	42.0	9.0	543.00	135.75	38.01	369.24
Denise Birch	42.0	7.5	524.25	131.06	36.70	356.49
Margery Bartram	40.0	9.5	528.75	132.19	37.01	359.55
Jolanta Hughes	42.0	10.0	555.50	138.88	38.89	377.74
Bob Nangle	42.0	7.0	518.00	129.50	36.26	352.24
POTENTIAL EMPLOYEES						
Bob Nangle	42.0	7.0	518.00	129.50	36.26	352.24
Bob Nangle	42.0	7.0	518.00	129.50	36.26	352.24
Bob Nangle	42.0	7.0	518.00	129.50	36.26	352.24
Bob Nangle	42.0	7.0	518.00	129.50	36.26	352.24
Bob Nangle	42.0	7.0	518.00	129.50	36.26	352.24
Bob Nangle	42.0	7.0	518.00	129.50	36.26	352.24
Bob Nangle	42.0	7.0	518.00	129.50	36.26	352.24
Bob Nangle	42.0	7.0	518.00	129.50	36.26	352.24
Bob Nangle	42.0	7.0	518.00	129.50	36.26	352.24
Bob Nangle	42.0	7.0	518.00	129.50	36.26	352.24
Bob Nangle	42.0	7.0	518.00	129.50	36.26	352.24
Bob Nangle	42.0	7.0	518.00	129.50	36.26	352.24
Bob Nangle	42.0	7.0	518.00	129.50	36.26	352.24
Bob Nangle	42.0	7.0	518.00	129.50	36.26	352.24
Bob Nangle	42.0	7.0	518.00	129.50	36.26	352.24
Bob Nangle	42.0	7.0	518.00	129.50	36.26	352.24

Prepared by YOUR NAME, Date: 3/25/97.   Page 1

Extra Practice Task 5A (continued)

SPERRIN SKYWAY

NAME	WEEKLY HOURS	OVER-TIME	GROSS	TAX	NI	NET
Bob Nangle	42.0	7.0	518.00	129.50	36.26	352.24
Bob Nangle	42.0	7.0	518.00	129.50	36.26	352.24
Bob Nangle	42.0	7.0	518.00	129.50	36.26	352.24
Bob Nangle	42.0	7.0	518.00	129.50	36.26	352.24
Bob Nangle	42.0	7.0	518.00	129.50	36.26	352.24
Bob Nangle	42.0	7.0	518.00	129.50	36.26	352.24
Bob Nangle	42.0	7.0	518.00	129.50	36.26	352.24
TOTAL	1466.0	258.0				12411.0

AVERAGE WEEKLY WAGE	355
HIGHEST WEEKLY WAGE	£398.99
LOWEST WEEKLY WAGE	£313.99
NO EMPLOYEES	35

CURRENT EMPLOYEES
GROSS WEEKLY WAGES	6337.5
GROSS MONTHLY WAGES	25350.0

YOUR NAME
EPTASK5A

Prepared by YOUR NAME, Date: 3/25/97

Extra Practice Task 5A (continued)

SPERRIN SKYWAY
SPERRIN SKYWAY GARDEN CENTRE
Construction Employees, Dart Division

NAME	WEEKLY HOURS	OVER-TIME	GROSS	TAX	NI	NET
CURRENT EMPLOYEES						
Gregory Smith	42	12.5	=(B7*10.25)+(C7*12.5)	=D7*25%	=D7*7%	=D7-E7-F7
Joanne Fisher	40	10	=(B8*10.25)+(C8*12.5)	=D8*25%	=D8*7%	=D8-E8-F8
Anne-Marie Moore	42	7	=(B9*10.25)+(C9*12.5)	=D9*25%	=D9*7%	=D9-E9-F9
Louisa Atkinson	42	7.5	=(B10*10.25)+(C10*12.5)	=D10*25%	=D10*7%	=D10-E10-F10
Sylvia Cheshire	42	2.5	=(B11*10.25)+(C11*12.5)	=D11*25%	=D11*7%	=D11-E11-F11
Mike Browne	42	7.5	=(B12*10.25) ı (C12*12.5)	=D12*25%	=D12*7%	=D12-E12-F12
Michelle Blackham	42	7	=(B13*10.25)+(C13*12.5)	=D13*25%	=D13*7%	=D13-E13-F13
Kathy Bowker	42	9	=(B14*10.25)+(C14*12.5)	=D14*25%	=D14*7%	=D14-E14-F14
Denise Birch	42	7.5	=(B15*10.25)+(C15*12.5)	=D15*25%	=D15*7%	=D15-E15-F15
Margery Bartram	40	9.5	=(B16*10.25)+(C16*12.5)	=D16*25%	=D16*7%	=D16-E16-F16
Jolanta Hughes	42	10	=(B17*10.25)+(C17*12.5)	=D17*25%	=D17*7%	=D17-E17-F17
Bob Nangle	42	7	=(B18*10.25)+(C18*12.5)	=D18*25%	=D18*7%	=D18-E18-F18
POTENTIAL EMPLOYEES						
Bob Nangle	42	7	=(B21*10.25)+(C21*12.5)	=D21*25%	=D21*7%	=D21-E21-F21
Bob Nangle	42	7	=(B22*10.25)+(C22*12.5)	=D22*25%	=D22*7%	=D22-E22-F22
Bob Nangle	42	7	=(B23*10.25)+(C23*12.5)	=D23*25%	=D23*7%	=D23-E23-F23
Bob Nangle	42	7	=(B24*10.25)+(C24*12.5)	=D24*25%	=D24*7%	=D24-E24-F24
Bob Nangle	42	7	=(B25*10.25)+(C25*12.5)	=D25*25%	=D25*7%	=D25-E25-F25
Bob Nangle	42	7	=(B26*10.25)+(C26*12.5)	=D26*25%	=D26*7%	=D26-E26-F26
Bob Nangle	42	7	=(B27*10.25)+(C27*12.5)	=D27*25%	=D27*7%	=D27-E27-F27
Bob Nangle	42	7	=(B28*10.25)+(C28*12.5)	=D28*25%	=D28*7%	=D28-E28-F28
Bob Nangle	42	7	=(B29*10.25)+(C29*12.5)	=D29*25%	=D29*7%	=D29-E29-F29
Bob Nangle	42	7	=(B30*10.25)+(C30*12.5)	=D30*25%	=D30*7%	=D30-E30-F30
Bob Nangle	42	7	=(B31*10.25)+(C31*12.5)	=D31*25%	=D31*7%	=D31-E31-F31
Bob Nangle	42	7	=(B32*10.25)+(C32*12.5)	=D32*25%	=D32*7%	=D32-E32-F31
Bob Nangle	42	7	=(B33*10.25)+(C33*12.5)	=D33*25%	=D33*7%	=D33-E33-F33
Bob Nangle	42	7	=(B34*10.25)+(C34*12.5)	=D34*25%	=D34*7%	=D34-E34-F34
Bob Nangle	42	7	=(B35*10.25)+(C35*12.5)	=D35*25%	=D35*7%	=D35-E35-F35
Bob Nangle	42	7	=(B36*10.25)+(C36*12.5)	=D36*25%	=D36*7%	=D36-E36-F36

Prepared by YOUR NAME, Date: 3/25/97.

Extra Practice Task 5A (continued)

SPERRIN SKYWAY

GARDEN CENTRE ACCOUNTS

NAME	WEEKLY HOURS	OVER-TIME	GROSS	TAX	NI	NET
Bob Nangle	42	7	=(B37*10.25)+(C37*12.5)	=D37*25%	=D37*7%	=D37-E37-F37
Bob Nangle	42	7	=(B38*10.25)+(C38*12.5)	=D38*25%	=D38*7%	=D38-E38-F38
Bob Nangle	42	7	=(B39*10.25)+(C39*12.5)	=D39*25%	=D39*7%	=D39-E39-F39
Bob Nangle	42	7	=(B40*10.25)+(C40*12.5)	=D40*25%	=D40*7%	=D40-E40-F40
Bob Nangle	42	7	=(B41*10.25)+(C41*12.5)	=D41*25%	=D41*7%	=D41-E41-F41
Bob Nangle	42	7	=(B42*10.25)+(C42*12.5)	=D42*25%	=D42*7%	=D42-E42-F42
Bob Nangle	42	7	=(B43*10.25)+(C43*12.5)	=D43*25%	=D43*7%	=D43-E43-F43
TOTAL	=SUM(B7:B43)	=SUM(C7:C43)				=SUM(G7:G43)

AVERAGE WEEKLY WAGE	=AVERAGE(G7:G43)
HIGHEST WEEKLY WAGE	=MAX(G7:G43)
LOWEST WEEKLY WAGE	=MIN(G7:G43)
NO EMPLOYEES	=COUNT(G7:G43)

CURRENT EMPLOYEES	
GROSS WEEKLY WAGES	=SUM(D7:D18)
GROSS MONTHLY WAGES	=B53*4

YOUR NAME
EPTASK5AF

Prepared by YOUR NAME, Date: 3/25/97

Page 2

Extra Practice Task 5B

SPERRIN SKYWAY GARDEN CENTRE CASH FORECAST

	JAN	FEB	MAR	APR	MAY	JUN
INCOME						
SALES – MAIL ORDER						
CASH SALES – OTHER						
CREDIT SALES – OTHER						
TOTAL INCOME						
EXPENSES						
WAGES – CONSTRUCTION						
WAGES – CULTIVATION						
OVERHEADS						
MATERIALS						
TOTAL EXPENSES						

STATISTICAL ANALYSIS	WEEKLY	MONTHLY
INCOME		
SALES – MAIL ORDER		45000
CASH SALES – OTHER		5000
CREDIT SALES – OTHER		10000
TOTAL INCOME		
EXPENSES		
WAGES – CONSTRUCTION		25350
WAGES – CULTIVATION		3600
OVERHEADS	900	
MATERIALS		0
TOTAL EXPENSES		

YOUR NAME
EPTASK5B

Extra Practice Task 5C

SPERRIN SKYWAY GARDEN CENTRE CASH FORECAST

	JAN	FEB	MAR	APR	MAY	JUN
INCOME						
SALES – MAIL ORDER	45000	45000	45000	45000	45000	45000
CASH SALES – OTHER	5000	5000	5000	5000	5000	5000
CREDIT SALES – OTHER	10000	10000	10000	10000	10000	10000
TOTAL INCOME	60000	60000	60000	60000	60000	60000
EXPENSES						
WAGES – CONSTRUCTION	25350	25350	25350	25350	25350	25350
WAGES – CULTIVATION	3600	3600	3600	3600	3600	3600
OVERHEADS						
MATERIALS	15000	15000	15000	15000	15000	15000
TOTAL EXPENSES	28950	28950	28950	28950	28950	28950
PROFIT/LOSS	16050	16050	16050	16050	16050	16050

STATISTICAL ANALYSIS	WEEKLY	MONTHLY
INCOME		
SALES – MAIL ORDER		45000
CASH SALES – OTHER		5000
CREDIT SALES – OTHER		10000
TOTAL INCOME		60000
EXPENSES		
WAGES – CONSTRUCTION		25350
WAGES – CULTIVATION		3600
OVERHEADS	900	
MATERIALS		15000
TOTAL EXPENSES		43950
PROFIT/LOSS		16050

YOUR NAME
EPTASK5C

Extra Practice Task 5D

SPERRIN SKYWAY GARDEN CENTRE CASH FORECAST

	JAN	FEB	MAR	APR	MAY	JUN	TOTAL	TOTAL PA
INCOME								
SALES – MAIL ORDER	45000	45000	45000	45000	45000	45000	270000	540000
CASH SALES – OTHER	5000	5000	5000	5000	5000	5000	30000	60000
CREDIT SALES – OTHER	10000	10000	10000	10000	10000	10000	60000	120000
TOTAL INCOME	60000	60000	60000	60000	60000	60000	360000	£720,000
EXPENSES								
WAGES – CONSTRUCTION	25350	25350	25350	25350	25350	25350	152100	304200
WAGES – CULTIVATION	3600	3600	3600	3600	3600	3600	21600	43200
OVERHEADS	3600	3600	3600	3600	3600	3600	21600	43200
MATERIALS	15000	15000	15000	15000	15000	15000	90000	180000
TOTAL EXPENSES	47550	47550	47550	47550	47550	47550	285300	£570,600
PROFIT/LOSS	12450	12450	12450	12450	12450	12450	74700	£149,400

STATISTICAL ANALYSIS	WEEKLY	MONTHLY
INCOME		
SALES – MAIL ORDER		45000
CASH SALES – OTHER		5000
CREDIT SALES – OTHER		10000
TOTAL INCOME		60000
EXPENSES		
WAGES – CONSTRUCTION		25350
WAGES – CULTIVATION		3600
OVERHEADS	900	3600
MATERIALS		15000
TOTAL EXPENSES		47550
PROFIT/LOSS		12450

YOUR NAME
EPTASK5D

Extra Practice Task 5E

SPERRIN SKYWAY GARDEN CENTRE CASH FORECAST

	JAN	FEB	MAR	APR	MAY	JUN
INCOME						
SALES – MAIL ORDER	=$C$21	=$C$21	=$C$21	=$C$21	=$C$21	=$C$21
CASH SALES – OTHER	=$C$22	=$C$22	=$C$22	=$C$22	=$C$22	=$C$22
CREDIT SALES – OTHER	=$C$23	=$C$23	=$C$23	=$C$23	=$C$23	=$C$23
TOTAL INCOME	=SUM(B5:B7)	=SUM(C5:C7)	=SUM(D5:D7)	=SUM(E5:E7)	=SUM(F5:F7)	=SUM(G5:G7)
EXPENSES						
WAGES – CONSTRUCTION	=$C$27	=$C$27	=$C$27	=$C$27	=$C$27	=$C$27
WAGES – CULTIVATION	=$C$28	=$C$28	=$C$28	=$C$28	=$C$28	=$C$28
OVERHEADS	=OHEADS*4	=OHEADS*4	=OHEADS*4	=OHEADS*4	=OHEADS*4	=OHEADS*4
MATERIALS	=$C$30	=$C$30	=$C$30	=$C$30	=$C$30	=$C$30
TOTAL EXPENSES	=SUM(B11:B14)	=SUM(C11:C14)	=SUM(D11:D14)	=SUM(E11:E14)	=SUM(F11:F14)	=SUM(G11:G14)
PROFIT/LOSS	=B8-B15	=C8-C15	=D8-D15	=E8-E15	=F8-F15	=G8-G15

	WEEKLY	MONTHLY
STATISTICAL ANALYSIS		
INCOME		
SALES – MAIL ORDER		45000
CASH SALES – OTHER		5000
CREDIT SALES – OTHER		10000
TOTAL INCOME		=SUM(C21:C23)
EXPENSES		
WAGES – CONSTRUCTION		='C:\Book3altkeys\[EPTASK5A.XLS]
WAGES CULTIVATION		3600
OVERHEADS	900	=OHEADS*4
MATERIALS		=C24*25%
TOTAL EXPENSES		=SUM(C27:C30)
PROFIT/LOSS		=C24-C31

YOUR NAME
EPTASK5E

EXTRA PRACTICE TASK 5E (continued)

TOTAL	TOTAL PA
=SUM(B5:G5)	=H5*2
=SUM(B6:G6)	=H6*2
=SUM(B7:G7)	=H7*2
=SUM(B8:G8)	=H8*2
=SUM(B11:G11)	=H11*2
=SUM(B12:G12)	=H12*2
=SUM(B13:G13)	=H13*2
=SUM(B14:G14)	=H14*2
=SUM(B15:G15)	=H15*2
=H8-H15	=I8-I15

YOYO Task 5A

THE DESIGNER COLLECTION

THE DESIGNER COLLECTION
Mail Order Employees, Donard Division

NAME	WEEKLY HOURS	OVER-TIME	GROSS	TAX	NI	NET
CURRENT EMPLOYEES						
Brian Green	42.0	12.5	360.13	90.03	25.21	244.89
Mary Bradley	40.0	10.0	328.10	82.03	22.97	223.11
Margaret Smythe	42.0	8.0	324.98	81.25	22.75	220.99
Rosie Cullen	42.0	8.5	328.89	82.22	23.02	223.64
Kathy Crowe	42.0	4.5	297.65	74.41	20.84	202.40
John Masters	42.0	12.0	356.22	89.06	24.94	242.23
Billy-Jean Madden	42.0	8.0	324.98	81.25	22.75	220.99
Jayne Taylor	42.0	10.0	340.60	85.15	23.84	231.64
Julie Broady	42.0	8.5	328.89	82.22	23.02	223.64
Diane Henderson	40.0	8.0	312.48	78.12	21.87	212.49
Anna Gee	42.0	12.0	356.22	89.06	24.94	242.23
Jim Mather	42.0	8.0	324.98	81.25	22.75	220.99
POTENTIAL EMPLOYEES						
Jim Mather	42.0	8.0	324.98	81.25	22.75	220.99
Jim Mather	42.0	8.0	324.98	81.25	22.75	220.99
Jim Mather	42.0	8.0	324.98	81.25	22.75	220.99
Jim Mather	42.0	8.0	324.98	81.25	22.75	220.99
Jim Mather	42.0	8.0	324.98	81.25	22.75	220.99
Jim Mather	42.0	8.0	324.98	81.25	22.75	220.99
Jim Mather	42.0	8.0	324.98	81.25	22.75	220.99
Jim Mather	42.0	8.0	324.98	81.25	22.75	220.99
Jim Mather	42.0	8.0	324.98	81.25	22.75	220.99
Jim Mather	42.0	8.0	324.98	81.25	22.75	220.99
Jim Mather	42.0	8.0	324.98	81.25	22.75	220.99
Jim Mather	42.0	8.0	324.98	81.25	22.75	220.99
Jim Mather	42.0	8.0	324.98	81.25	22.75	220.99
Jim Mather	42.0	8.0	324.98	81.25	22.75	220.99
Jim Mather	42.0	8.0	324.98	81.25	22.75	220.99
Jim Mather	42.0	8.0	324.98	81.25	22.75	220.99

Prepared by YOUR NAME, Date: 6/23/97

YOYO Task 5A (continued)

THE DESIGNER COLLECTION

NAME	WEEKLY HOURS	OVER-TIME	GROSS	TAX	NI	NET
Jim Mather	42.0	8.0	324.98	81.25	22.75	220.99
Jim Mather	42.0	8.0	324.98	81.25	22.75	220.99
Jim Mather	42.0	8.0	324.98	81.25	22.75	220.99
Jim Mather	42.0	8.0	324.98	81.25	22.75	220.99
Jim Mather	42.0	8.0	324.98	81.25	22.75	220.99
Jim Mather	42.0	8.0	324.98	81.25	22.75	220.99
Jim Mather	42.0	8.0	324.98	81.25	22.75	220.99
TOTAL	1466.0	294.0				7791.88

AVERAGE WEEKLY WAGE	223
HIGHEST WEEKLY WAGE	£244.89
LOWEST WEEKLY WAGE	£202.40
NO OF EMPLOYEES	35.0

CURRENT EMPLOYEES

GROSS WEEKLY WAGES	3984.1
GROSS MONTHLY WAGES	15936.4

YOUR NAME
YOYO5A

Prepared by YOUR NAME, Date: 6/23/97

YOYO Task 5AF

THE DESIGNER COLLECTION

ACCOUNTS

THE DESIGNER COLLECTION
Mail Order Employees, Donard Division

NAME	WEEKLY HOURS	OVER-TIME	GROSS	TAX	NI	NET	
CURRENT EMPLOYEES							
Brian Green	42	12.5	=(B7*6.25)+(C7*7.81)	=D7*25%	=D7*7%	=D7-E7-F7	
Mary Bradley	40	10	=(B8*6.25)+(C8*7.81)	=D8*25%	=D8*7%	=D8-E8-F8	
Margaret Smythe	42	8	=(B9*6.25)+(C9*7.81)	=D9*25%	=D9*7%	=D9-E9-F9	
Rosie Cullen	42	8.5	=(B10*6.25)+(C10*7.81)	=D10*25%	=D10*7%	=D10-E10-F10	
Kathy Crowe	42	4.5	=(B11*6.25)+(C11*7.81)	=D11*25%	=D11*7%	=D11-E11-F11	
John Masters	42	12	=(B12*6.25)+(C12*7.81)	=D12*25%	=D12*7%	=D12-E12-F12	
Billy-Jean Madden	42	8	=(B13*6.25)+(C13*7.81)	=D13*25%	=D13*7%	=D13-E13-F13	
Jayne Taylor	42	10	=(B14*6.25)+(C14*7.81)	=D14*25%	=D14*7%	=D14-E14-F14	
Julie Broady	42	8.5	=(B15*6.25)+(C15*7.81)	=D15*25%	=D15*7%	=D15-E15-F15	
Diane Henderson	40	8	=(B16*6.25)+(C16*7.81)	=D16*25%	=D16*7%	=D16-E16-F16	
Anna Gee	42	12	=(B17*6.25)+(C17*7.81)	=D17*25%	=D17*7%	=D17-E17-F17	
Jim Mather	42	8	=(B18*6.25)+(C18*7.81)	=D18*25%	=D18*7%	=D18-E18-F18	
POTENTIAL EMPLOYEES							
Jim Mather	42	8	=(B21*6.25)+(C21*7.81)	=D21*25%	=D21*7%	=D21-E21-F21	
Jim Mather	42	8	=(B22*6.25)+(C22*7.81)	=D22*25%	=D22*7%	=D22-E22-F22	
Jim Mather	42	8	=(B23*6.25)+(C23*7.81)	=D23*25%	=D23*7%	=D23-E23-F23	
Jim Mather	42	8	=(B24*6.25)+(C24*7.81)	=D24*25%	=D24*7%	=D24-E24-F24	
Jim Mather	42	8	=(B25*6.25)+(C25*7.81)	=D25*25%	=D25*7%	=D25-E25-F25	
Jim Mather	42	8	=(B26*6.25)+(C26*7.81)	=D26*25%	=D26*7%	=D26-E26-F26	
Jim Mather	42	8	=(B27*6.25)+(C27*7.81)	=D27*25%	=D27*7%	=D27-E27-F27	
Jim Mather	42	8	=(B28*6.25)+(C28*7.81)	=D28*25%	=D28*7%	=D28-E28-F28	
Jim Mather	42	8	=(B29*6.25)+(C29*7.81)	=D29*25%	=D29*7%	=D29-E29-F29	
Jim Mather	42	8	=(B30*6.25)+(C30*7.81)	=D30*25%	=D30*7%	=D30-E30-F30	
Jim Mather	42	8	=(B31*6.25)+(C31*7.81)	=D31*25%	=D31*7%	=D31-E31-F31	
Jim Mather	42	8	=(B32*6.25)+(C32*7.81)	=D32*25%	=D32*7%	=D32-E32-F32	
Jim Mather	42	8	=(B33*6.25)+(C33*7.81)	=D33*25%	=D33*7%	=D33-E33-F33	
Jim Mather	42	8	=(B34*6.25)+(C34*7.81)	=D34*25%	=D34*7%	=D34-E34-F34	
Jim Mather	42	8	=(B35*6.25)+(C35*7.81)	=D35*25%	=D35*7%	=D35-E35-F35	
Jim Mather	42	8	=(B36*6.25)+(C36*7.81)	=D36*25%	=D36*7%	=D36-E36-F36	

YOYO Task 5AF (continued)

THE DESIGNER COLLECTION

ACCOUNTS

NAME	WEEKLY HOURS	OVER-TIME	GROSS	TAX	NI	NET
Jim Mather	42	8	=(B37*6.25)+(C37*7.81)	=D37*25%	=D37*7%	=D37-E37-F37
Jim Mather	42	8	=(B38*6.25)+(C38*7.81)	=D38*25%	=D38*7%	=D38-E38-F38
Jim Mather	42	8	=(B39*6.25)+(C39*7.81)	=D39*25%	=D39*7%	=D39-E39-F39
Jim Mather	42	8	=(B40*6.25)+(C40*7.81)	=D40*25%	=D40*7%	=D40-E40-F40
Jim Mather	42	8	=(B41*6.25)+(C41*7.81)	=D41*25%	=D41*7%	=D41-E41-F41
Jim Mather	42	8	=(B42*6.25)+(C42*7.81)	=D42*25%	=D42*7%	=D42-E42-F42
Jim Mather	42	8	=(B43*6.25)+(C43*7.81)	=D43*25%	=D43*7%	=D43-E43-F43
TOTAL	=SUM(B7:B43)	=SUM(C7:C43)				=SUM(G7:G43)

AVERAGE WEEKLY WAGE	=AVERAGE(G7:G43)
HIGHEST WEEKLY WAGE	=MAX(G7:G43)
LOWEST WEEKLY WAGE	=MIN(G7:G43)
NO EMPLOYEES	=COUNT(G7:G43)
CURRENT EMPLOYEES	
GROSS WEEKLY WAGES	=SUM(D7:D18)
GROSS MONTHLY WAGES	=B53*4

YOUR NAME
YOYO5AF

YOYO Task 5B

THE DESIGNER COLLECTION CASH FORECAST

	JAN	FEB	MAR	APR	MAY	JUN
INCOME						
SALES – MAIL ORDER						
SALES – RETAIL OUTLET						
SALES – OTHER						
TOTAL INCOME						
EXPENSES						
WAGES – MAIL ORDER						
WAGES – RETAIL OUTLET						
OVERHEADS						
MATERIALS						
TOTAL EXPENSES						

STATISTICAL ANALYSIS	WEEKLY	MONTHLY
INCOME		
SALES – MAIL ORDER		54000
SALES – RETAIL OUTLET		6000
SALES – OTHER		12000
TOTAL INCOME		
EXPENSES		
WAGES – MAIL ORDER		15936.4
WAGES – RETAIL OUTLET		4320
OVERHEADS	1080	
MATERIALS		0
TOTAL EXPENSES		

YOUR NAME
YOYO5B

YOYO Task 5C

THE DESIGNER COLLECTION CASH FORECAST

	JAN	FEB	MAR	APR	MAY	JUN
INCOME						
SALES – MAIL ORDER	54000	54000	54000	54000	54000	54000
SALES – RETAIL OUTLET	6000	6000	6000	6000	6000	6000
SALES – OTHER	12000	12000	12000	12000	12000	12000
TOTAL INCOME	72000	72000	72000	72000	72000	72000
EXPENSES						
WAGES – MAIL ORDER	15936.4	15936.4	15936.4	15936.4	15936.4	15936.4
WAGES – RETAIL OUTLET	4320	4320	4320	4320	4320	4320
OVERHEADS						
MATERIALS	18000	18000	18000	18000	18000	18000
TOTAL EXPENSES	38256.4	38526.4	38526.4	38526.4	38526.4	38526.4
PROFIT/LOSS	33743.6	33743.6	33743.6	33743.6	33743.6	33743.6

STATISTICAL ANALYSIS	WEEKLY	MONTHLY
INCOME		
SALES – MAIL ORDER		54000
SALES – RETAIL OUTLET		6000
SQLES – OTHER		12000
TOTAL INCOME		72000
EXPENSES		
WAGES – MAIL ORDER		15936.4
WAGES – RETAIL OUTLET		4320
OVERHEADS	1080	
MATERIALS		18000
TOTAL EXPENSES		38256.4
PROFIT/LOSS		33743.6

YOUR NAME
YOYO5C

YOYO Task 5D

THE DESIGNER COLLECTION CASH FORECAST

	JAN	FEB	MAR	APR	MAY	JUN	TOTAL	TOTAL PA
INCOME								
SALES – MAIL ORDER	54000	54000	54000	54000	54000	54000	324000	648000
SALES – RETAIL OUTLET	6000	6000	6000	6000	6000	6000	36000	72000
SALES – OTHER	12000	12000	12000	12000	12000	12000	72000	144000
TOTAL INCOME	72000	72000	72000	72000	72000	72000	432000	£846,000
EXPENSES								
WAGES – MAIL ORDER	15936.4	15936.4	15936.4	15936.4	15936.4	15936.4	95618.4	191236.8
WAGES – RETAIL OUTLET	4320	4320	4320	4320	4320	4320	25920	51840
OVERHEADS	4320	4320	4320	4320	4320	4320	25920	51840
MATERIALS	18000	18000	18000	18000	18000	18000	108000	216000
TOTAL EXPENSES	42576.4	42576.4	42576.4	42576.4	42576.4	42576.4	255458.4	£510,917
PROFIT/LOSS	29423.6	29423.6	29423.6	29423.6	29423.6	29423.6	176541.6	£353,038

STATISTICAL ANALYSIS	WEEKLY	MONTHLY
INCOME		
SALES – MAIL ORDER		54000
SALES – RETAIL OUTLET		6000
SALES – OTHER		12000
TOTAL INCOME		72000
EXPENSES		
WAGES – MAIL ORDER		15936.4
WAGES – RETAIL OUTLET		4320
OVERHEADS	1080	4320
MATERIALS		18000
TOTAL EXPENSES		42576.4
PROFIT/LOSS		29423.6

YOUR NAME
YOYO5D

IBT II Spreadsheet Mock Assignment 1   Sheet 1

BALLINASCREEN OPTICAL ILLUSIONS
NON-PAYING ADULTS, JANUARY WEEK 1

PATIENT NAME	SPEC CODE	CL CODE	PRESCRIPTION COST	SPEC ACC	CL ACC	TOTAL COST
RP – REGULAR PATIENTS						
M BOYLE	S000432	C000382	66	2.50	7.99	76.49
R CALDWELL	S000210	N/A	14	3.99	0.00	17.99
G MCFLYNN	S000306	N/A	14	0.00	0.00	14.00
D SINCLAIR	S000318	C000268	14	3.99	7.99	25.98
FP – FREQUENT PATIENTS						
E ALLEN	S000461	N/A	72	2.50	0.00	74.50
K EWING	S000224	C000174	64	3.99	7.99	75.98
B HAWKES	S000316	N/A	14	0.00	0.00	14.00
F PATTERSON	S000327	N/A	14	0.00	0.00	14.00
G SIMPSON	S000333	C000283	39	7.99	14.50	61.49
A WYLIE	S000211	N/A	70	0.00	0.00	70.00
NP – NEW PATIENTS						
J CRILLY	S000501	C000450	108	4.99	7.99	120.98
T JENKINS	S000502	N/A	83	1.99	0.00	84.99
P NICHOLL	S000503	N/A	14	2.10	0.00	16.10
TOTAL FOR WEEK 1			586	34.04	46.46	666.5

SM1Q4P1

IBT II Spreadsheet Mock Assignment 1 (continued)   Sheet 1

BALLINASCREEN OPTICAL ILLUSIONS
NON-PAYING ADULTS, JANUARY WEEK 1

PATIENT NAME	SPEC CODE	CL CODE
RP – REGULAR PATIENTS		
M BOYLE	S000432	C000382
R CALDWELL	S000210	N/A
G MCFLYNN	S000306	N/A
D SINCLAIR	S000318	C000268

SM1Q5P2

IBT II Spreadsheet Mock Assignment 1 (continued)   Sheet 1

BALLINASCREEN OPTICAL ILLUSIONS
NON-PAYING ADULTS, JANUARY WEEK 1

PATIENT NAME	SPEC CODE	CL CODE	PRESCRIPTION COST	PRESCRIPTION INCREASE	SPEC ACC	CL ACC	TOTAL COST
RP – REGULAR PATIENTS							
M BOYLE	S000432	C000382	66	70	2.50	7.99	£80.45
R CALDWELL	S000210	N/A	14	15	3.99	0.00	£18.83
G MCFLYNN	S000306	N/A	14	15	0.00	0.00	£14.84
D SINCLAIR	S000318	C000268	14	15	3.99	7.99	£26.82
FP – FREQUENT PATIENTS							
E ALLEN	S000461	N/A	72	76	2.50	0.00	£78.82
K EWING	S000224	C000174	64	68	3.99	7.99	£79.82
B HAWKES	S000316	N/A	14	15	0.00	0.00	£14.84
F PATTERSON	S000327	N/A	14	15	0.00	0.00	£14.84
G SIMPSON	S000333	C000283	39	41	7.99	14.50	£63.83
A WYLIE	S000211	N/A	70	74	0.00	0.00	£74.20
NP – NEW PATIENTS							
J CRILLY	S000501	C000450	108	114	4.99	7.99	£127.46
T JENKINS	S000502	N/A	83	88	1.99	0.00	£89.97
P NICHOLL	S000503	N/A	14	15	2.10	0.00	£16.94
TOTAL FOR WEEK 1			586		34.04	46.46	£701.66

SM1Q7P3

IBT II Spreadsheet Mock Assignment 1 (continued)   Sheet 1

BALLINASCREEN OPTICAL ILLUSIONS
NON-PAYING ADULTS, JANUARY WEEK 1

PATIENT NAME	SPEC CODE	CL CODE	PRESCRIPTION COST	PRESCRIPTION INCREASE 12%	SPEC ACC	CL ACC	TOTAL COST
RP – REGULAR PARIENTS							
M BOYLE	S000432	C000382	66	74	2.50	7.99	£84.41
R CALDWELL	S000210	N/A	14	16	3.99	0.00	£19.67
G MCFLYNN	S000306	N/A	14	16	0.00	0.00	£15.68
D SINCLAIR	S000318	C000268	14	16	3.99	7.99	£27.66
FP – FREQUENT PATIENTS							
E ALLEN	S000416	N/A	72	81	2.50	0.00	£83.14
K EWING	S000224	C000174	64	72	3.99	7.99	£83.66
B HAWKES	S000316	N/A	14	16	0.00	0.00	£15.68
F PATTERSON	S000327	N/A	14	16	0.00	0.00	£15.68
G SIMPSON	S000333	C000283	39	44	7.99	14.50	£66.17
A WYLIE	S000211	N/A	70	78	0.00	0.00	£78.40
NP – NEW PATIENTS							
J CRILLY	S000501	C000450	108	121	4.99	7.99	£133.94
T JENKINS	S000502	N/A	83	93	1.99	0.00	£94.95
P NICHOLL	S000503	N/A	14	16	2.10	0.00	£17.78
TOTAL FOR WEEK 1			586	656.32	34.04	46.46	£736.82

SM1Q9P4

IBT II Spreadsheet Mock Assignment 1 (continued)   Sheet 1

PRESCRIPTION
INCREASE 12%

=D8*112%
=D9*112%
=D10*112%
=D11*112%

=D14*112%
=D15*112%
=D16*112%
=D17*112%
=D18*112%
=D19*112%

=D22*112%
=D23*112%
=D24*112%

=SUM(E8:E25)

SM1Q10P5

Page 1

IBT II Spreadsheet Mock Assignment 2   Sheet 1

MOURNE COLLEGIATE IT COURSES

COURSE TITLE	NO OF CLASSES	STUDENT NO	STUDENT TOTAL	COURSE FEE	TOTAL FEE	COURSE REF	ROOMS	LENGTH
WORD PROCESSING								
WORD	5	15	75	35.50	2662.50	WP30PTD	G1-G5	2H X 10W
WORDPERFECT	4	12	48	35.50	1704.00	WP33PTD	G16-G19	2H X 10W
WORDSTAR	3	12	36	35.50	1278.00	WP35PTD	G20-G23	2H X 10W
WORDPRO	3	10	30	35.50	1065.00	WP36PTD	G20-G23	2H X 10W
DESK TOP PUBLISHING								
PAGEMAKER	5	6	30	65.00	1950.00	DT40PTD	F1-F5	2H X 10W
PRESSWORKS	2	8	16	65.00	1040.00	DT41PTD	F6-F7	2H X 10W
SERIF PAGEPLUS	1	8	8	65.00	520.00	DT42PTD	F8	2H X 10W
QUARKXPRESS	2	6	12	65.00	780.00	DT43PTD	F9-F10	2H X 10W
VENTURA	5	6	30	65.00	1950.00	DT46PTD	F6-F11	2H X 10W
DATABASE								
APPROACH	3	12	36	39.99	1439.64	DB50PTD	E1-E3	2H X 10W
ACCESS	5	12	60	39.99	2399.40	DB52PTD	E4-E9	2H X 10W
PARADOX	5	12	60	39.99	2399.40	DB53PTD	E10-E15	2H X 10W
DATAEASE	3	12	36	39.99	1439.64	DB55PTD	E4-E7	2H X 10W
TOTALS			477		20627.58			

SM2Q5P1

Page 1

IBT II Spreadsheet Mock Assignment 2 (continued)   Sheet 1

MOURNE COLLEGIATE IT COURSES

COURSE TITLE	NO OF CLASSES	STUDENT NO	STUDENT TOTAL	COURSE FEE
WORD PROCESSING				
WORD	5	15	75	35.50
WORDPERFECT	4	12	48	35.50
WORDSTAR	3	12	36	35.50
WORDPRO	3	10	30	35.50

SM2Q6P2

Page 1

IBT II Spreadsheet Mock Assignment 2 (continued)   Sheet 1

MOURNE COLLEGIATE IT COURSES

COURSE TITLE	NO OF CLASSES	STUDENT NO	STUDENT INCREASE	STUDENT TOTAL	COURSE FEE	TOTAL FEE	COURSE REF	ROOMS	LENGTH
WORD PROCESSING									
WORD	5	15	19.5	98	35.50	3461.25	WP30PTD	G1-G5	2H X 10W
WORDPERFECT	4	12	15.6	62	35.50	2215.20	WP33PTD	G16-G19	2H X 10W
WORDSTAR	3	12	15.6	47	35.50	1661.40	WP35PTD	G20-G23	2H X 10W
WORDPRO	3	10	13.0	39	35.50	1384.50	WP36PTD	G20-G23	2H X 10W
DESK TOP PUBLISHING									
PAGEMAKER	5	6	7.8	39	65.00	2535.00	DT40PTD	F1-F5	2H X 10W
PRESSWORKS	2	8	10.4	21	65.00	1352.00	DT41PTD	F6-F7	2H X 10W
SERIF PAGEPLUS	1	8	10.4	10	65.00	676.00	DT42PTD	F8	2H X 10W
QUARKXPRESS	2	6	7.8	16	65.00	1014.00	DT43PTD	F9-F10	2H X 10W
VENTURA	5	6	7.8	39	65.00	2535.00	DT46PTD	F6-F11	2H X 10W
DATABASE									
APPROACH	3	12	15.6	47	39.99	1871.53	DB50PTD	E1-E3	2H X 10W
ACCESS	5	12	15.6	78	39.99	3119.22	DB52PTD	E4-E9	2H X 10W
PARADOX	5	12	15.6	78	39.99	3119.22	DB53PTD	E10-E15	2H X 10W
DATAEASE	3	12	15.6	47	39.99	1871.53	DB55PTD	E4-E7	2H X 10W
TOTALS				620		26815.85			

SM2Q8P3

Page 1

IBT II Spreadsheet Mock Assignment 2 (continued)   Sheet 1

MOURNE COLLEGAITE IT COURSES

COURSE TITLE	NO OF CLASSES	STUDENT NO	STUDENTS EXPECTED	STUDENT TOTAL	COURSE FEE	TOTAL FEE	COURSE REF	ROOMS	LENGTH
WORD PROCESSING									
WORD	5	15	17.3	86	35.50	3061.88	WP30PTD	G1-G5	2H X 10W
WORDPERFECT	4	12	13.8	55	35.50	1959.60	WP33PTD	G16-G19	2H X 10W
WORDSTAR	3	12	13.8	41	35.50	1469.70	WP35PTD	G20-G23	2H X 10W
WORDPRO	3	10	11.5	35	35.50	1224.75	WP36PTD	G20-G23	2H X 10W
DESK TOP PUBLISHING									
PAGEMAKER	5	6	6.9	35	65.00	2242.50	DT40PTD	F1-F5	2H X 10W
PRESSWORKS	2	8	9.2	18	65.00	1196.00	DT41PTD	F6-F7	2H X 10W
SERIF PAGEPLUS	1	8	9.2	9	65.00	589.00	DT42PTD	F8	2H X 10W
QUARKWPRESS	2	6	6.9	14	65.00	897.00	DT43PTD	F9-F10	2H X 10W
VENTURA	5	6	6.9	35	65.00	2242.50	DT46PTD	F6-F11	2H X 10W
DATABASE									
APPROACH	3	12	13.8	41	39.99	1655.59	DB50PTD	E1-E3	2H X 10W
ACCESS	5	12	13.8	69	39.99	2759.31	DB52PTD	E4-E9	2H X 10W
PARADOX	5	12	13.8	69	39.99	2759.31	DB53PTD	E10-E15	2H X 10W
DATAEASE	3	12	13.8	41	39.99	1655.59	DB55PTD	E4-E7	2H X 10W
TOTALS				549		23721.72			

SM2Q10P4

Page 1

IBT II Spreadsheet Mock Assignment 2 (continued)   Sheet 1

MOURNE COLLEGE IT COURSES

COURSE TITLE	NO OF CLASSES	STUDENT NO	STUDENTS EXPECTED	STUDENT TOTAL	COURSE FEE	TOTAL FEE	COURSE REF	ROOMS	LENGTH
WORD PROCESSING									
WORD	5	15	=C7*115%	=B7*D7	35.5	=E7*F7	WP30PTD	G1-G5	2H X 10W
WORDPERFECT	4	12	=C8*115%	=B8*D8	35.5	=E8*F8	WP33PTD	G16-G19	2H X 10W
WORDSTAR	3	12	=C9*115%	=B9*D9	35.5	=E9*F9	WP35PTD	G20-G23	2H X 10W
WORDPRO	3	10	=C10*115%	=B10*D10	35.5	=E10*F10	WP36PTD	G20-G23	2H X 10W
DESK TOP PUBLISHING									
PAGEMAKER	5	6	=C13*115%	=B13*D13	65	=E13*F13	DT40PTD	F1-F5	2H X 10W
PRESSWORKS	2	8	=C14*115%	=B14*D14	65	=E14*F14	DT41PTD	F6-F7	2H X 10W
SERIF PAGEPLUS	1	8	=C15*115%	=B15*D15	65	=E15*F15	DT42PTD	F8	2H X 10W
QUARKXPRESS	2	6	=C16*115%	=B16*D16	65	=E16*F16	DT43PTD	F9-F10	2H X 10W
VENTURA	5	6	=C17*115%	=B17*D17	65	=E17*F17	DT46PTD	F6-F11	2H X 10W
DATABASE									
APPROACH	3	12	=C20*115%	=B20*D20	39.99	=E20*F20	DB50PTD	E1-E3	2H X 10W
ACCESS	5	12	=C21*115%	=B21*D21	39.99	=E21*F21	DB52PTD	E4-E9	2H X 10W
PARADOX	5	12	=C22*115%	=B22*D22	39.99	=E22*F22	DB53PTD	E10-E15	2H X 10W
DATAEASE	3	12	=C23*115%	=B23*D23	39.99	=E23*F23	DB55PTD	E4-E7	2H X 10W
TOTALS				=SUM(E7:E23)		=SUM(G7:G23)			

SM2Q11P5

Page 1

RSA SP II Mock Assignment 1 Task 1   Sheet 1

BALLINASCREEN OPTICAL ILLUSIONS
NON-PAYING ADULTS, JANUARY WEEK 1

PATIENT NAME	SPEC CODE	CL CODE	PRESCRIPTION COST	SPEC ACC	CL ACC	TOTAL COST
RP – REGULAR PATIENTS						
J FARLEY	S000209	N/A	60	0	0	£60.00
M BOYLE-BEN	S000432	C000382	66	2.50	7.99	£76.49
R CALDWELL	S000210	N/A	14	3.99	0.00	£17.99
G MCFLYNN	S000306	N/A	14	2.50	0.00	16.50
D SINCLAIR	S000318	C000268	14	3.99	7.99	£25.98
FP – FREQUENT PATIENTS						
E ALLEN	S000461	N/A	72	2.50	0.00	£74.50
K EWING	S000224	C000174	64	3.99	17.99	£85.98
B HAWKES	S000316	C000451	14	0.00	0.00	£14.00
F PATTERSON	S000327	N/A	14	0.00	0.00	£14.00
G SIMPSON	S000333	C000283	39	7.99	14.50	£61.49
A WYLIE	S000211	N/A	70	0.00	0.00	£70.00
NP – NEW PATIENTS						
JJ CRILLY	S000501	C000450	108	4.99	7.99	£120.98
T JENKINS	S000502	N/A	83	1.99	0.00	£84.99
P NICHOLL	S000530	N/A	14	2.10	0.00	£16.10
TOTAL FOR WEEK 1			646	36.54	56.46	739

NEW PATIENTS SUMMARY
NO OF NEW PATIENTS	3
AVERAGE PRESCRIPTION COST	68
TOTAL COSTS	£222.07

BOI/NP/YOUR NAME
T1M1Q16

Page 1

RSA SP II Mock Assignment 1 Task 1 (continued)   Sheet 1

TOTAL FOR WEEK 1   =SUM(D8:D26)   =SUM(E8:E26)   =SUM(F8:F26)   =SUM(G8:G26)

NEW PATIENTS SUMMARY
NO OF NEW PATIENTS   =COUNTA(A23:A25)
AVERAGE PRESCRIPTION COST   =AVERAGE(D23:D25)
TOTAL COSTS   =SUM(G23:G25)

BOI/NP/YOUR NAME
T1M1Q18

Page 1

RSA SP II Mock Assignment 1 Task 2   Sheet 1

BALLINASCREEN OPTICAL ILLUSIONS
INCOME FOR JANUARY, WEEK 1

ITEM	NON-PAYING ADULTS	NON-PAYING CHILDREN	OTHER	TOTAL INCOME
SIGHT TEST			364	
SPECTACLE FRAMES			1144	
SPECTACLE LENSES			754	
SP ACCESSORIES			103.74	
CONTACT LENSES			660	
CL ACCESSORIES			135	
INDUSTRIAL SPECS			160	
FRAME REPAIRS			143	
TOTAL	739	184.75	3463.74	4387.49

PROJECTED ANNUAL INCOME

PERIOD				
JAN	2956	739	13854.96	17549.96
FEB	3133.36	783.34	13854.96	17771.66
MAR	3133.36	783.34	13854.96	17771.66
APR	3133.36	783.34	13854.96	17771.66
MAY	3133.36	783.34	13854.96	17771.66
JUN	3133.36	783.34	13854.96	17771.66
JUL	3133.36	783.34	13854.96	17771.66
AUG	3133.36	783.34	13854.96	17771.66
SEP	3133.36	783.34	13854.96	17771.66
OCT	3133.36	783.34	13854.96	17771.66
NOV	3133.36	783.34	13854.96	17771.66
DEC	3133.36	783.34	13854.96	17771.66
GROUP TOTAL	£37,422.96	£9,355.74	£166,259.52	£213,038.22
GROUP AVERAGE	3119	780	13855	

YOUR NAME
T2M1Q13

Page 1

RSA SP II Mock Assignment 1 Task 2 (continued)   Sheet 1

BALLINASCREEN OPTICAL ILLUSIONS
INCOME FOR JANUARY, WEEK 1

ITEM	NON-PAYING ADULTS	NON-PAYING CHILDREN	OTHER	TOTAL INCFOME
SIGHT TEST			364	
SPECTACLE FRAMES			1144	
SPECTACLE LENSES			754	
SP ACCESSORIES			103.74	
CONTACT LENSES			660	
CL ACCESSORIES			135	
INDUSTRIAL SPECS			160	
FRAME REPAIRS			143	
TOTAL	=[T1M1Q16.xls]Sheet1!$G$27	=B15*25%	=SUM(D7:D14)	=SUM(B15:D15)

PROJECTED ANNUAL

PERIOD				
JAN	=B15*4	=B20*25%	13854.96	=SUM(B20:D20)
FEB	=NPA*106%	=B21*25%	13854.96	=SUM(B21:D21)
MAR	=NPA*106%	=B22*25%	13854.96	=SUM(B22:D22)
APR	=NPA*106%	=B23*25%	13854.96	=SUM(B23:D23)
MAY	=NPA*106%	=B24*25%	13854.96	=SUM(B24:D24)
JUN	=NPA*106%	=B25*25%	13854.96	=SUM(B25:D25)
JUL	=NPA*106%	=B26*25%	13854.96	=SUM(B26:D26)
AUG	=NPA*106%	=B27*25%	13854.96	=SUM(B27:D27)
SEP	=NPA*106%	=B28*25%	13854.96	=SUM(B28:D28)
OCT	=NPA*106%	=B29*25%	13854.96	=SUM(B29:D29)
NOV	=NPA*106%	=B30*25%	13854.96	=SUM(B30:D30)
DEC	=NPA*106%	=B31*25%	13854.96	=SUM(B31:D31)
GROUP TOTAL	=SUM(B20:B31)	=SUM(C20:C31)	=SUM(D20:D31)	=SUM(E20:E31)
GROUP AVERAGE	=B32/12	=C32/12	=D32/12	

YOUR NAME
T2M1Q15

Page 1

RSA SP II Mock Assignment 1 Task 2 (continued)   Sheet 1

PROJECTED ANNUAL INCOME

PERIOD				
JAN	2956	739	13854.96	17549.96
FEB	3133.36	783.34	13854.96	17771.66
MAR	3133.36	783.34	13854.96	17771.66
APR	3133.36	783.34	13854.96	17771.66
MAY	3133.36	783.34	13854.96	17771.66
JUN	3133.36	783.34	13854.96	17771.66
JUL	3133.36	783.34	13854.96	17771.66
AUG	3133.36	783.34	13854.96	17771.66
SEP	3133.36	783.34	13854.96	17771.66
OCT	3133.36	783.34	13854.96	17771.66
NOV	3133.36	783.34	13854.96	17771.66
DEC	3133.36	783.34	13854.96	17771.66
GROUP TOTAL	£37,422.96	£9,355.74	£166,259.52	£213,038.22
GROUP AVERAGE	3119	780	13855	

YOUR NAME
T2M1Q17

Page 1

RSA SP II Mock Assignment 2 Task 1   Sheet 1

MOURNE COLLEGIATE IT COURSES

COURSE TITLES	NO OF CLASSES	STUDENT NO	STUDENTS EXPECTED	STUDENT TOTAL	COURSE FEE	TOTAL FEE	COURSE REF	ROOMS	LENGTH
WORD PROCESSING									
CLARIS	2	12	13.8	28	35.50	979.80	WP37PTD	G24-G25	3H X 10W
WORD	5	15	17.3	86	35.50	3061.88	WP30PTD	G1-G5	2H X 10W
WORDPERFECT	5	12	13.8	69	35.50	2449.50	WP33PTD	G16-G19	2H X 10W
WORDSTAR	3	12	13.8	41	35.50	1469.70	WP35PTD	G20-G23	2H X 10W
DESK TOP PUBLISHING									
PAGEMAKER	5	6	6.9	35	65.00	2242.50	DT40PTD	F1-F5	2H X 10W
PRESSWORKS	2	8	9.2	18	65.00	1196.00	DT41PTD	F9-F10	2H X 10W
SERIF PAGEPLUS	1	8	9.2	9	65.00	598.00	DT42PTD	F8	2H X 10W
QUARKXPRESS	2	8	9.2	18	65.00	1196.00	DT43PTD	F9-F10	2H X 10W
VENTURA	5	6	6.9	35	65.00	2242.50	DT46PTD	F6-F11	2H X 10W
DATABASE									
APPROACH	3	12	13.8	41	39.99	1655.59	DB50PTD	E1-E3	2H X 10W
ACCESS	5	12	13.8	69	39.99	2759.31	DB52PTD	E4-E9	2H X 10W
PARADOX	5	12	13.8	69	39.99	2759.31	DB53PTD	E10-E15	2H X 10W
DATAEASE	3	12	13.8	41	39.99	1655.59	DB55PTD	E4-E7	2H X 10W
TOTALS				560		24265.67			

IT STATISTICS
OVERALL TOTAL FEES   £24,265.67
NO OF COURSES   13.00
AVERAGE STUDENT NO   10

MC/IT/YOUR NAME/TODAY'S DATE
T1M2Q17

RSA SP II Mock Assignment 2 Task 1 (continued)   Sheet 1

TOTALS	=SUM(E7:E23)	=SUM(G7:G23)

IT STATISTICS
OVERALL TOTAL FEES   =SUM(G7:G23)
NO OF COURSES   =COUNTA(H:H23)
AVERAGE STUDENT NO   =AVERAGE(C7:C23)

MC/IT/YOUR NAME/TOD
T1M2Q19

RSA SP II Mock Assignment 2 Task 2   Sheet 1

COSTING FOR DTP COURSES

ITEM	JUN-AUG	SEP-NOV	DEC-FEB	MAR-MAY	TOTAL PA
INCOME					
COURSE FEES	598.00	598.00	598.00	598.00	2392.00
COURSE FUNDING	3701.25	3701.25	3701.25	3701.25	14805.00
TOTAL INCOME	4299	4299	4299	4299	17197
EXPENDITURE					
SALARIES	660.00	679.80	679.80	679.80	2699.40
CRECHE	210.00	210.00	210.00	210.00	840.00
OTHER OVERHEADS	2775.00	3165.00	3240.00	3189.00	12369.00
TOTAL EXPENDITURE	3645	4055	4130	4079	15908
NET PROFIT/LOSS	£654.25	£244.45	£169.45	£220.45	
RATE PER HR (£)	£33.00				

YOUR NAME
T2M2Q12

RSA SP II Mock Assignment 2 Task 2 (continued)   Sheet 1

COSTING FOR DTP COURSES

ITEM	JUN-AUG	SEP-NOV	DEC-FEB	MAR-MAY	TOTAL PA
INCOME					
COURSE FEES	=[T1M2Q17.XLS]Sheet1!$G$15	=[T1M2Q17.XLS]Sheet1!$G$15	=[T1M2Q17.XLS]Sheet1!$G$15	=[T1M2Q17.XLS]Sheet1!$G$15	=SUM(B7:E7)
COURSE FUNDING	3701.25	3701.25	3701.25	3701.25	=SUM(B8:E8)
TOTAL INCOME	=SUM(B7:B8)	=SUM(C7:C8)	=SUM(D7:D8)	=SUM(E7:E8)	=SUM(B9:E9)
EXPENDITURE					
SALARIES	=B19*20	=SALARY*103%	=SALARY*103%	=SALARY*103%	=SUM(B13:E13)
CRECHE	210	210	210	210	=SUM(B14:E14)
OTHER OVERHEADS	2775	3165	3240	3189	=SUM(B15:E15)
TOTAL EXPENDITURE	=SUM(B13:B15)	=SUM(C13:C15)	=SUM(D13:D15)	=SUM(E13:E15)	=SUM(B16:E16)
NET PROFIT/LOSS	=B9-B16	=C9-C16	=D9-D16	=E9-E16	
RATE PER HR (£)	33				

YOUR NAME
T2M2Q14

Page 1

RSA SP II Mock Assignment 2 Task 2 (continued)   Sheet 1

COSTING FOR DTP COURSES

ITEM	JUN-AUG
INCOME	
COURSE FEES	598.00
COURSE FUNDING	3701.25
TOTAL INCOME	4299
EXPENDITURE	
SALARIES	660.00
CRECHE	210.00
OTHER OVERHEADS	2775.00
TOTAL EXPENDITURE	3645
NET PROFIT/LOSS	£654.25
RATE PER HR (£)	£33.00

YOUR NAME
T2M2Q16

Page 1

record of progress

Date	Task no.	Step no.	Page no.	Filename

DATABANK

memory jogger

CLAIT, IBT II, SP II

Objective	Menu Bar *select ...*	Tool Bar *click ...*	Keyboard Shortcut *press ...*

align text as specified	• Select cells to be aligned.
	 • **Format**
	 • **Cells**
	 • **Alignment**
	 • Select the alignment required
	 • **OK**
	 • Deselect range.
		• Select cells to be aligned
		 • Click one of the following:
		   ■ **Align Left**
		   ■ **Align Centre**
		   ■ **Align Right**
		   ■ **Centre Across Columns**
			• Select cells to be aligned.
			 • **Ctrl + 1**
			 • **Alignment**
			 • Select the alignment required
			 • **OK**
			 • Deselect range.

apply percentages	The formula D6*25% would calculate 25% of the cell contents in D6. The formula D6*125% would increase the cell contents of D6 by 25% i.e. D6 contents (100%) plus 25%.		
assign a name to a cell	• Select the cell or cell range that you wish to name. • From the Formula Bar, click on ■ in the **Name** box. • Key in the name on the drop-down list. • Press ↵ **(Enter)**.		
change column width	• **Format** • **Column** • **Width** • **Key in width** • **OK**	• Place mouse pointer to the right edge of the chosen column heading button until it changes to a double-headed arrow. • Click and drag to the required width *or* double-click for the cell width to automatically widen.	
change values temporarily	When requested to change values temporarily, always check the formulae for accuracy after you have returned the spreadsheet to its former value.		
close a file	• **File** • **Close**	■ **Close window**	**Ctrl + F4**
close Print Preview	**Close**		**Alt + C**
correct erroneous formulae	Warning! Many candidates fail this objective. Tip: • After inserting or deleting rows or columns it is vital that you check *all* formulae on the spreadsheet to ensure that they accurately reflect the cells for calculation. • You are also required to locate an erroneous formula inserted by someone else, so it is always useful to have an estimate of what the overall calculation might be.		
create a new file	• **File** • **New**	▢ **New workbook**	**Ctrl + N**
delete a name from a named cell	• Select the named cell from which you wish to remove the name. • **Insert** • **Name** • **Define** • Select the name from the list. • Click the **Delete** button. • **OK**		
delete row or column	• Select the row/column heading button of the row/column that you want to delete to highlight entire row/column. • **Edit** • **Delete**		

Objective	Menu Bar *select ...*	Tool Bar *click ...*	Keyboard Shortcut *press ...*
display amount in sterling	• Select cells to be formatted. • **Format** • **Cells** • **Number** • From **Category**, select **Currency**; *to two decimal places:* From **Decimal Places**; *to the nearest pound:* From **Decimal Places**, select **0**; From **Symbol**, select **£ English (British)**. • **OK**	• Select cells to be formatted. ▦ **Currency Style**	
display data instead of formulae	Follow the instructions for 'Display formulae' but at the **Window Options** click on the checkbox beside **Formulae** to remove the √.		
display formulae	• **Tools** • **Options** • **View** • From the **Window Options** column click on the checkbox beside **Formulae** to display √. • **OK**		
edit data	• Select the cell (place mouse pointer in appropriate cell and click once). • In the Formula Bar, move the mouse pointer to where you wish to edit and click once so that it changes to an I beam. • Type the new data and/or delete what is not required using the **Delete** button on the keyboard. • Click once on the ▣ **Enter** box in the Formula Bar, or press ↵ **(Enter)**.		

enter formulae	• Select the cell where you want the result of your formula to appear (place the mouse pointer in appropriate cell and click once).
	• Type the **=** sign.
	• Type the formula, e.g. SUM(B5:B10).
	
	This will sum or add up the numbers in the range of cells (e.g. from B5 to B10). The range can be shown by keying in (within brackets) the beginning of the range and the end of the range, separated by a : sign. Other formulae are shown below:
	
	Formula *Sign* *Example*
	
	Addition + =B5+B6+B7 *or*
	         SUM =SUM(B5:B7)
	Subtraction – =B5-C5
	Multiplication * =B5*C5 *or*
	          =B5*8
	Division / =B5/C5 *or*
	          =B5/8
	• Click once on the ▣ **Enter** box in the Formula Bar or press ↵ **(Enter)**.		

enter text and numeric data	• Place the mouse pointer in the desired cell and click to select the cell. • Key in the data for that cell. • Click once on the ▣ **Enter** box in the Formula Bar or press ↵ **(Enter)** to confirm the entry.		
exit from Excel	• **File** • **Exit**	✕ **Close window**	**Alt + F4**
generate a formula using a named cell	• Select the cell where the formula is to appear. • Key in the **=** sign. • Key in the name of the named cell. • Complete the formula. • Click the ▣ **Enter** box.		
insert row or column	• Select the row/column heading button of the row/column where you wish to insert (to highlight entire row/column). • **Insert** • **Rows** or **Columns**		

Objective	Menu Bar *select …*	Tool Bar *click …*	Keyboard Shortcut *press …*
left or right justify text	• Select cells to be aligned. • **Format** • **Cells** • **Alignment** • Select the alignment required. • **OK** • Deselect range.	• Select cells to be aligned: ■**Align Left** *or* ■**Align Right** • Deselect range. • **OK** • Deselect range.	• Select cells to be aligned: • **Ctrl + 1** • **Alignment** • Select the alignment required.
load Excel	• ▣ Start • ▣ Programs ▶ • ▣ Microsoft Excel		
obtain data from another spreadsheet by linking	• Ensure that all the required worksheet files are opened. One will be placed on top of the other, the names of which will be displayed in a drop-down list if you click on **Window** in the Menu Bar. • On the worksheet where you wish to establish the link, select the cell that is to be linked. • Key in the = sign. • From the Menu Bar, select **Windows** and from the drop-down list, click once on the required worksheet filename. • On this worksheet, select the cell containing the data or formulae that you wish to be linked. • Click the ✓ **Enter** box in the Formula Bar or press ↵ **(Enter)**. The cell reference of the linked cell, preceded by the name of the workbook and the worksheet, will be displayed in the Formula Bar, e.g. [TASK5A]Sheet1!$B$54.		
open a file	• **File** • **Open**	▣ **Open**	**Ctrl + O**
print data or formulae	• **File** • **Print** • **OK**	▣ **Print**	• **CTRL + P** • press ↵ **(Enter)**
Print Preview	• **File** • **Print Preview**	▣ **Print Preview**	
print specified cells or information	• Select the range you wish to print. • **File** • **Print** • **Selection** • **OK** or press ↵ **(Enter)** to accept the other settings.	• Select the range you wish to print. ▣ **Print** • **Selection** • **OK** or press ↵ **(Enter)** to accept the other settings.	• Select the range you wish to print. • **Ctrl/P** • **Selection** • **OK** or press ↵ **(Enter)** to accept the other settings.
protect cells	• Highlight the cell or cell range which you want to remain unlocked. • **Format** • **Cells** • **Protection** • Click once on the **Locked** checkbox to remove the √ so that the locking is switched off. • **OK** • **Tools** • **Protection** • **Protect Sheet…** • Ignore the **Password optional** text box which is offered and click **OK** to apply the protection of the sheet without a password.		
record file storage details	Tip: Ensure that you always write down the step number and filename for each unique file that you are aksed to save.		
remove cell protection	• **Tools** • **Protection** • **Unprotect Sheet…** • Key in a password if one has been used.		

Objective	Menu Bar *select ...*	Tool Bar *click ...*	Keyboard Shortcut *press ...*
replicate entries	• Select the cell to be copied. • Click and drag the mouse across the range required to highlight it. • **E̲dit** • **Fi̲ll** and choose one of the following: • **D̲own** • **R̲ight** • **U̲p** • **L̲eft** *or* position the mouse at the edge of the active cell until it changes to a ✛ (cross) and then click and drag the mouse across the range required to copy the cell contents across.	 if the range is below if the range is to the right if the range is above if the range is to the left	 *or* press **Ctrl/D** *or* press **Ctrl/R**
save a file (under new name)	• **F̲ile** • **Save A̲s** • **Save i̲n** text box: if **3½ Floppy (A:)** is not already shown, click on ▼ at right side of text box and highlight this or the appropriate drive, where your file is to be saved. • **Save as t̲ype** text box: if **Microsoft Excel Workbook** is not already shown, clicking on ▼ at right side of text box and highlight this option to ensure that your file is saved as an Excel file. • **File n̲ame** text box: a default filename, such as Book1, will appear here. Select this name by placing the mouse pointer at the beginning and clicking and dragging to the end of the name. Key in your chosen filename, e.g. **TASK1C**. • **S̲ave** button: click this now to save your file (or press ↵ (Enter)).		
save (or replace) existing file	• **F̲ile** • **S̲ave** • Follow steps above for 'Save a file'.	🖫 **Save**	**Ctrl + S**
select relevant data	Tip: • Read the question carefully. • Highlight the key requirements. • Then extract the relevant data.		
use integer and decimal format	• Select cells to be formatted. • **F̲ormat** • **Ce̲lls** • **Number** • *display in integer format:* From **C̲ategory**, select **Number**; from **Decimal Places**, select **0** *display to two decimal places:* From **C̲ategory**, select **Number**; From **Decimal Places**, select **2**. • Click **OK**	• Select cells to be formatted. • Click required icon once to add or remove one decimal place from figure in selected cell. ⊞ **Increase Decimal** *or* ⊞ **Decrease Decimal**	
use SUM, COUNT and AVERAGE functions	• Select the **cell where you want the result** of your function to appear. • Type the = sign. • Type the appropriate function: **SUM** gives the sum of the range of cells; **COUNT** gives the number of numeric values in the range; **AVERAGE** gives the average of the values in the range. • Select the **beginning of the range** (by keying it in *or* pointing to it) and the **end of the range**, separated by a : sign and **enclosed in brackets**, e.g. AVERAGE(B5:B10). • Click ✓ **Enter** box or press ↵ (Enter).	To use the **SUM** function: • Select the **cell where you want the result** of your function to appear **Σ Autosum** • Click the ✓ **Enter** box in the Formula Bar.	